The Politics of Parliament

Parliamentary debate is a fundamental aspect of democratic lawmaking. Although lawmakers everywhere seek to express their views in parliament, there are large discrepancies in who has access to the floor across political systems. This book explains how parties and their members of parliament (MPs) structure parliamentary debate. Parties may actively seek to prevent some members from taking the floor while promoting opportunities for others. In doing so, they attempt to control the message that their partisans convey in parliament. The authors provide a theoretical model to explain the design of procedural rules in parliament, how the party leadership interacts with rebel backbenchers, and how MPs represent voters. The book explores political institutions, intraparty politics, electoral politics, and legislative behavior. It develops and tests a new theory of parliamentary debate, using data from the United Kingdom, Germany, New Zealand, and the European Parliament.

SVEN-OLIVER PROKSCH is Assistant Professor of Political Science at McGill University. His research focuses on comparative political institutions, party politics, legislative behavior, European politics, and political text analysis. He is the coauthor of *Reforming the European Union: Realizing the Impossible* (2012).

JONATHAN B. SLAPIN is Associate Professor of Political Science and Director of the Center for International and Comparative Studies at the University of Houston. His research focuses on comparative political institutions, legislative behavior, European politics, and European integration. He is the author of *Veto Power: Institutional Design in the European Union* (2011).

The Politics of Parliamentary Debate

Parties, Rebels, and Representation

SVEN-OLIVER PROKSCH
JONATHAN B. SLAPIN

CAMBRIDGE
UNIVERSITY PRESS

University Printing House, Cambridge CB2 8BS, United Kingdom

Cambridge University Press is part of the University of Cambridge.

It furthers the University's mission by disseminating knowledge in the pursuit of education, learning and research at the highest international levels of excellence.

www.cambridge.org
Information on this title: www.cambridge.org/9781107421073

© Sven-Oliver Proksch and Jonathan B. Slapin 2015

This publication is in copyright. Subject to statutory exception and to the provisions of relevant collective licensing agreements, no reproduction of any part may take place without the written permission of Cambridge University Press.

First published 2015
First paperback edition 2015

A catalogue record for this publication is available from the British Library

ISBN 978-1-107-07276-3 Hardback
ISBN 978-1-107-42107-3 Paperback

Cambridge University Press has no responsibility for the persistence or accuracy of URLs for external or third-party internet websites referred to in this publication, and does not guarantee that any content on such websites is, or will remain, accurate or appropriate.

To Rebecca and Liam
SOP

To Jann and Harold
JBS

Contents

List of figures — *page* ix
List of tables — xi
Preface — xiii
Introduction — 1

Part I Modeling parliamentary debate — 15

1 A theory of parliamentary debate — 17
1.1 Democracy and debate — 18
1.2 The nature of parliamentary speech — 20
1.3 Parties, rebels, and speech – a theory — 24
1.4 Two illustrations — 28
1.5 A delegation model of parliamentary speech — 34
1.6 Summary — 41

2 Empirical implications — 43
2.1 Country-level variables – electoral systems — 44
2.2 Within-country variables – electoral tiers and candidate selection — 49
2.3 Effects of electoral incentives on debate participation — 52
2.4 Summary — 55

3 Research design — 56
3.1 Empirical strategy: an overview — 56
3.2 Cross-national comparison and party survey — 58
3.3 Case selection: Germany, the United Kingdom, the European Union, and New Zealand — 61
3.4 Measurement of latent concepts — 70
3.5 Summary — 72

Part II Empirical studies of parliamentary debate — 75

4 Debates and institutions — 77
4.1 Parliamentary rules — 78

4.2 Party rules 83
4.3 Summary 99

5 Debate participation: Germany and the United Kingdom 100
5.1 Hypotheses 100
5.2 MP status: when party leaders get involved 101
5.3 Ideological disagreement 115
5.4 Summary 123

6 Dissent in parliament and the media: Germany and the United Kingdom 124
6.1 Political reaction to the financial crisis, 2008–2009 125
6.2 Fiscal stimulus debates in the United Kingdom 129
6.3 Fiscal stimulus debates in Germany 136
6.4 Summary 147

7 Candidate selection and debate participation: a European perspective 148
7.1 Party debate rules in the European Parliament 149
7.2 Votes, rebels, and speaking time 152
7.3 Summary 161

8 Changing institutions: New Zealand 163
8.1 Electoral system change 163
8.2 Rules change in parliament 164
8.3 Behavioral change: budget debate participation 166
8.4 Summary 173

Conclusion 174

Appendix 181

Bibliography 186

Index 199

List of figures

1.1 Parliamentary debates in German news *page* 23
1.2 Expected relationship between latent intraparty disagreement and observed intraparty dissent 26
1.3 Overview of the strategic delegation game of parliamentary speech 36
2.1 Comparison of institutional scenarios 53
4.1 Institutions of parliamentary debate and personal vote seeking 80
4.2 Party survey: MPs' level of demand for speaking time in parliamentary party groups 84
4.3 Party survey: final say over the party's speaker list 86
4.4 Party survey: leadership monitoring of MPs' speeches 87
4.5 Party survey: monitoring MPs' statements in the media 88
4.6 Speech monitoring scale ($N = 36$) 90
4.7 Distribution of perceived intraparty cohesion ($N = 36$) 92
4.8 Distribution of party seat shares and government status ($N = 36$) 94
4.9 Relationship among intraparty cohesion, personal vote incentives, and party leader monitoring 96
4.10 Government parties' expectation regarding their MPs' speeches ($N = 18$) 98
5.1 Debate participation: leader involvement in the United Kingdom, 1979–2005 105
5.2 Debate participation: leader involvement in Germany, 1976–1998 106
5.3 Debate participation: district versus list MPs in Germany, 1976–1998 108
5.4 Effects of ideological distance between MP and party leadership on legislative speech counts in Germany and the United Kingdom 121

6.1 Parliamentary speeches in the United Kingdom mentioning "fiscal stimulus," 2008–2010 127
6.2 Parliamentary speeches in Germany tagged with keyword "economic stimulus," 2008–2010 128
8.1 Importance of representational activities in New Zealand (responses from candidate surveys) 167
8.2 Predicted probability of budget debate participation in New Zealand 171
8.3 Comparison of debate participation of rebel backbenchers and party leaders in New Zealand 172

List of tables

1.1 Parliamentary activities of British MPs *page* 22
3.1 Empirical strategy of the book 57
3.2 Party survey: list of participating parliamentary parties ($N = 45$) 60
4.1 Personal vote-seeking incentives and electoral systems 82
4.2 Parliamentary rules and electoral incentives 83
4.3 Missing values in the seven monitoring questions 89
4.4 Measuring personal vote incentives 93
4.5 Linear regression models of party leadership monitoring 95
5.1 Overview of parliamentary speeches in the United Kingdom and Germany 102
5.2 Models of parliamentary speech in the United Kingdom, 1979–2004 (all MPs) 111
5.3 Models of parliamentary speech in the United Kingdom, 1979–2004 (only MPs switching between backbencher and leader status) 112
5.4 Models of parliamentary speech in Germany, 1976–1998 (all MPs) 113
5.5 Models of parliamentary speech in Germany, 1976–1998 (only MPs switching between backbencher and leader status) 114
5.6 Models of parliamentary speech in Germany, 1976–1998 (only MPs switching between electoral tiers) 115
5.7 Modeling the effect of ideological disagreement in the United Kingdom (2001–2005) 118
5.8 Modeling the effect of ideological disagreement in Germany (2005–2009) 119
5.9 Probit model of budget speeches in the United Kingdom (2011) and Germany (2010) 122
6.1 Overview of UK data on legislative action on stimulus package 129

6.2 United Kingdom: legislative behavior of Labour MPs in budget debates, 2008–2009 134
6.3 Ordered probit model of UK MPs' level of dissent 135
6.4 Marginal effects of party leadership status and margin of victory on the level of intraparty dissent in the United Kingdom 136
6.5 Overview of Germany data on legislative action on stimulus package 137
6.6 Germany: party behavior of government MPs (CDU/CSU and SPD) in fiscal stimulus debates, 2008–2009 140
6.7 Probit models of German MPs' level of floor activity and dissent 142
6.8 Germany: coalition behavior of government MPs (CDU/CSU and SPD) in fiscal stimulus debates, 2008–2009 144
6.9 Germany: relationship between intraparty and coalition dissent on activities of government MPs (CDU/CSU and SPD) in fiscal stimulus debates, 2008–2009 145
6.10 Germany: legislative behavior of government MPs (CDU/CSU and SPD) in fiscal stimulus debates, 2008–2009 (ministers and junior ministers excluded) 145
6.11 Probit models of German MPs' coalition dissent 146
7.1 European Parliament: process of allocating speaking time 150
7.2 European Parliament: political group priorities in allocating speaking time 151
7.3 Proportion of MEPs giving a speech as a function of voting and candidate selection mechanisms (vote-speech sample from Sixth European Parliament, 2004–2005) 156
7.4 Explaining parliamentary speeches in the European Parliament (1999–2004) 159
7.5 Predicted speech counts in the Fifth European Parliament (1999–2004): substantive effects of national rebel defection and candidate selection 161
8.1 Budget debate participation in New Zealand (logit) 170
A.1 Chapter 5 simulated predicted speech counts (with 95 percent confidence intervals) for different types of German MPs 185

Preface

While sitting together as students in a graduate seminar at the University of California, Los Angeles (UCLA) about 10 years ago, we began to wonder how political scientists might improve on existing measures of party ideology in European politics. Political texts, such as election manifestos and parliamentary speeches, provide a tremendous source of information on the position-taking strategies of politicians. Parliaments meanwhile store their records in easily searchable online databases, making content accessible to researchers for analysis. Over the past decade, our musings on how to use these data have led us down a variety of paths. Initially, we were most interested in using political texts, such as party manifestos, to estimate ideology. This interest resulted in the development of *Wordfish*, a text-scaling approach we initially applied to party manifestos. As we turned our attention to parliamentary speeches, however, we quickly realized that our theoretical understanding of the language politicians use in speech was far inferior to our theoretical understanding of other sources of information regarding ideology, such as election manifestos and roll-call vote records. Without stronger theoretical guidance as to what speeches can tell us about ideology, we felt we could not make any further headway in the field of ideal point estimation. Parliamentary speech provides a wealth of information on policy stances, but to use it effectively, we need to know more about the politics driving speech itself. While digging deeper into the issue, we discovered that political debate, as a subject of research, had received little attention from legislative scholars. There has been little comparative theorizing to link parliamentary debate to the role that parties play in political representation, or how other institutions, such as electoral rules, may affect these relationships. This book represents the culmination of our efforts to provide such a theory and to explore these relationships.

Writing this book has been a multiyear project and we have benefited from the feedback of many colleagues and friends along the way. Several people have read complete versions of the manuscript, including Thomas Bräuninger, Thomas Gschwend, Chris Kam, Orit Kedar, Kira Killermann, Thomas König, James Lo, Will Lowe, and Mike Thies. Others have read previous versions of individual chapters. This list includes Eduardo Aleman, Tanya Bagashka, Ken Benoit, Serra Boranbay, Simon Hix, Justin Kirkland, Ken Kollman, Michael Shackleton, Elisabeth Schulte, Georg Vanberg, and Jonathan Woon. We have presented results from this project at many institutions and conferences over the years. We are grateful to seminar participants at Texas A&M, Rice University, the University of Houston, Penn State, Trinity College Dublin, Washington University in St. Louis, Essex University, Empirical Implications of Theoretical Models Europe, Deutsche Vereinigung für Politische Wissenschaft Working Group on Behavioral Decision Making, University of Mannheim, McGill University, and Nuffield College at Oxford University. Kira Killermann, Linh Nguyen, and Sander Ensink assisted with data collection, and Jann Slapin, who has selflessly served as Jonathan's editor since elementary school, assiduously proofread the final version. We also thank John Haslam and Sarah Green, editors at Cambridge University Press, whose encouragement facilitated the revision and ultimate completion of the manuscript. Lastly, we owe a debt of gratitude to George Tsebelis, who served as our mentor and advisor while at UCLA. His intellectual impact can be found throughout our work, and this book is no exception.

We also thank several scholars for providing us with data and additional information about the cases under investigation. Jeff Karp, Jack Vowles, and Chris Kam have provided us with candidate surveys, and data on parliamentary voting and leadership positions in New Zealand. The research librarians Ruth Graham and Tony Reed from the New Zealand parliamentary information office graciously sent us additional information about parliamentary practice in New Zealand, as did David Bagnall (Senior Parliamentary Officer, Parliamentary Relations and Policy Group Office, Clerk of the House of Representatives). We thank Thomas Gschwend, Hermann Schmitt, Andreas Wüst, and Thomas Zittel for sharing the German candidate survey data. We also thank the many parliamentary party group representatives and administrators who participated in our survey.

Sven-Oliver Proksch acknowledges funding from the European Community's Seventh Framework Programme (FP7/2007–2013) under grant agreement number 239268 (Marie Curie International Reintegration Grant). We are also grateful to the Mannheim Centre for European Social Research and the Research Center SFB 884 on the Political Economy of Reforms for hosting a book manuscript workshop in June 2011. The University of Mannheim, McGill University, Trinity College Dublin, and the University of Houston have supported our research as we have undertaken this project. Portions of Chapters 1 and 5 were previously published as "Institutional Foundations of Legislative Speech," *American Journal of Political Science* 56(3): 520–537 (2012), and Chapter 7 is based on results previously published as "Look Who's Talking: Parliamentary Debate in the European Union," *European Union Politics* 11(3): 333–357 (2010).

Lastly, we offer our gratitude to our very supportive families. Our deepest thanks go to our wives, Rebecca and Aurelija, who tolerated our many Skype conversations and graciously hosted us whenever we visited each other in Mannheim, Dublin, Houston, or Montreal. Our project and our lives would have been much less rich without their intellectual support, love, and constant encouragement. And our wonderful children, Liam, Benjamin, and Olivia, allowed us to sleep and work most of the time, and kept us smiling when not engaged in either of the previous activities.

Introduction

Democracy thrives through debate. Democratic parliaments are open forums where elected representatives engage in arguments over policy. Parliamentary debate is, therefore, a fundamental part of democratic lawmaking – in all parliaments, members debate bills before they vote on them. Because debates are public, they provide members of parliament (MPs) an opportunity to represent the views of constituents on the floor and give voice to voters' concerns. But floor time is a scarce resource, and MPs are not always able to participate in debate when they would like. Parties may actively seek to prevent some members from taking the floor while promoting opportunities for others. In doing so they attempt to control the message that their partisans convey in parliament. This book takes a comparative institutional approach to explain participation in parliamentary debates and to explore its relevance for party politics and political representation. We uncover strategic interaction between parties and their members and provide insights into the relationship between party leaders and backbenchers, particularly party rebels who often disagree with official party policy.

We consider parliamentary debates as a forum for public communication that parties and their MPs exploit for electoral purposes. Rather than using floor speeches in an attempt to win political arguments, persuade opponents, or credibly signal voting intentions, we argue that MPs use floor speeches primarily to communicate policy positions to other members within their own party, to members of other parties, and, most important, to their voters. Political institutions, however, affect how parties and their MPs use parliamentary debate. We show that parties vary in the degree to which they monitor and control their MPs' speeches. When electoral institutions provide parties with incentives to present the voting public with a unified front, parties actively monitor their MPs to ensure that they communicate the party message. When electoral politics mean MPs must seek personal votes by creating a name for themselves, parties make fewer efforts to control their MPs' floor speeches. Thus, the incentives that electoral institutions create for partisan control have a fundamental impact on the nature of parliamentary speech and on how parties and MPs use it as a tool of representative democracy.

Our general argument that political institutions, and electoral institutions in particular, provide parties with an incentive to control what their members do is certainly not new. Rather, it has been developed by a long line of scholars (e.g. Downs, 1957; Cox and McCubbins, 1993; Aldrich, 1995). What is new is our attempt to apply this logic systematically to our understanding of parliamentary debate. This topic has been largely overlooked by political scientists interested in legislative institutions. But it has the potential to offer many new insights into party politics and representation. The book explores political institutions, intraparty politics, electoral politics, and legislative behavior by developing and testing a comparative institutional theory of parliamentary debate. We aim to give parliamentary debate the attention it deserves and, in doing so, contribute to a more nuanced understanding of how democratic institutions and political parties work.

Dimensions of parliamentary debate

Before moving to the core theoretical argument of the book, presented in detail in the next chapter, we briefly explore the various ways in which parliamentary debate matters for democratic politics and what we can learn about politics by studying debate. Broadly speaking, parliamentary debate is important for political representation because it creates a link between voters and their representatives and because its organization affects the lawmaking process. Our theory links these two aspects of speech in a single, coherent argument about how parliamentary debate matters for representative democracy.

Political representation and satisfaction with democracy

First and foremost, the actions of elected politicians in a representative democracy should be "responsive to the wishes of the people" (Powell, 2004, p. 273). Modern democracy can be thought of as a chain of delegation, with the transfer of power from citizens to elected representatives as the first link (Strøm, Müller, and Bergman, 2003). Regular elections ensure that citizens are able to hold politicians accountable for their actions. Political parties provide the crucial "democratic linkage" as they recruit candidates, organize election campaigns, mobilize voters, offer distinct policy alternatives, and participate in government policy-making (Dalton, Farrell, and McAllister, 2011, p. 7). But parliamentary parties are not unitary actors. Elected members of parliament make up parliamentary parties, and, for the most part, these MPs – not parties – engage in parliamentary activities. MPs handle constituency casework, work in parliamentary committees, prepare legislative initiatives, vote on bills, and – importantly for this book – participate in parliamentary debates. Unlike other aspects of the policy-making process, parliamentary speeches require an audience to be an effective tool for representation. Voting can take place behind closed doors and still fulfill its primary representative function – the aggregation of preferences to produce policy. If speeches, on the other hand, had no audience, MPs could not make known to their constituents that they stood up for their concerns in parliament. Only when media follow and report on debates, or when politicians themselves point to their own parliamentary speech record, do parliamentary speeches fulfill a representative function. The transparency of parliamentary debate is the necessary condition for rhetorical political representation. Citizens expect representatives to hear their concerns and give them voice, and MPs demonstrate that they listen and are responsive by participating in debates.

The extent to which citizens are aware that lawmakers espouse their views during the lawmaking process may affect their overall satisfaction with democracy. Imagine an elected parliament that decided to hold all of its plenary sessions behind closed doors. This decision would significantly weaken the link between voters and their representatives because the former could no longer hold the latter accountable. Although voters would view the outcome of the policy process, they would not be able to determine where specific parties or representatives stood on the issues. Democratic constitutions, therefore, have explicit provisions to ensure parliamentary sessions are public.[1] Even when individual votes are not recorded, speeches always are. Thus, when

[1] For example, both the German and French constitutions state that sittings of parliament shall be public (see article 42 of the German Basic Law and article 33 of the French constitution).

debates lead to effective representation of citizens' views, citizens may develop a more favorable attitude toward democracy. It is sometimes hypothesized, for example, that proportional representation (PR) electoral systems lead to better ideological congruence between citizens and elected representatives (e.g. Huber and Powell, 1994) and consequently to higher levels of citizen satisfaction (Lijphart, 1999, p. 286). In such systems, political parties receive a share of parliamentary seats that is proportional to the vote share received in the election. A proportional system may better represent a range of citizens' views by offering voters greater choice at the polls than a majoritarian system that favors fewer and larger parties. Thus, because proportional representation tends to produce multiparty systems, we might expect parliamentary speeches to accurately reflect the diverse views of the electorate, in turn leading to higher levels of citizens' satisfaction with democracy. Even if a voter's preferred party is not in government or directly affecting policy, at least that voter has representatives in parliament giving voice to his or her concerns.

The theory and evidence for the relationship between proportional representation, representation, and democratic satisfaction are mixed at best, however (Blais and Bodet, 2006). Early tests of this argument examined satisfaction with democracy by distinguishing between consensus and majoritarian systems (Anderson and Guillory, 1997). Using Eurobarometer survey data for 11 countries, Anderson and Guillory find that "losers," that is, voters who supported an opposition party in the previous election, have higher levels of satisfaction with democracy in consensual than in majoritarian systems. In contrast, "winners" are less satisfied with democracy as the system becomes more consensual. Along the same lines, using data from the *World Values Survey* (Klingemann, 1999), Lijphart (1999) finds that citizens in consensus democracies are, on average, more satisfied with democracy than citizens in majoritarian democracies.

But several scholars, paying closer attention to electoral institutions, have challenged these results. Relying on the *World Values Survey* data, Norris (1999) finds that – contrary to her expectation – confidence in democracy is greater in countries with majoritarian systems than in those with proportional representation. Overall, she states that the "findings indicate that institutional confidence is most likely to be highest in parliamentary democracies characterized by plurality electoral systems, two-party or moderate multi-party systems, and unitary states" (Norris, 1999, p. 234). Reassessing her earlier results with updated data, Norris (2011) shows that the average level of democratic satisfaction is highest in majoritarian systems, followed by proportional systems, and lowest in mixed electoral systems. These results echo those of Aarts and Thomassen (2008) who use data from the *Comparative Study of Electoral Systems* (CSES) covering 36 elections in 35 countries. Their study concludes that proportional systems do *not* enhance the perceived representativeness of the political system compared with majoritarian systems. Moreover, proportional representation systems are associated with *lower* levels of satisfaction with democracy than majoritarian systems.

These mixed findings present a puzzle to scholars of democracy. How do different models of representative democracy affect citizens' attitudes, and what role do parliamentary institutions and parties play? We address these questions by examining how electoral incentives shape intraparty politics, and specifically the allocation of speaking time in parliament. The diversity of viewpoints represented in parliamentary speech in proportional systems may not be as great as one might expect due to tight partisan control. Compared with parties in proportional systems, parties in majoritarian systems tend to exercise less control over parliamentary speeches, allowing their members to speak their mind. Thus, although PR may lead to more parties in parliament, it does not necessarily lead to greater diversity in the viewpoints actually expressed on the floor.

Institutions and the policy process

Members of parliament do not use parliamentary speeches solely to voice constituency concerns. Parliamentary speech can play a more direct role in the policy-making process as well. Because speechmaking takes up precious plenary time, MPs may use speeches to slow down the political process. Gary Cox has identified unregulated plenary time as the core problem in a so-called legislative state of nature (Cox, 2006, p. 141). When there are no rules to structure or limit debate, any MP may obstruct the legislative process simply by speaking ad nauseam. According to Cox, this makes the de facto decision rule "closer to unanimity than to majority," because any member can effectively block any bill by speaking. In reality, a legislative state of nature does not exist – all parliaments have adopted rules that structure and limit debate. Nevertheless, these rules vary significantly. Even when a member cannot block a bill through endless debate, extensive debate can slow down the legislative process and reduce the number of items the parliament may include on its agenda.

Perhaps the best known rule governing debate is the filibuster (and corresponding cloture rule) in the US Senate. Senators may speak indefinitely on a bill unless a three-fifths majority cuts off debate. Effectively, the supermajority requirement to limit debate leads to delays and obstruction of the political process (Tsebelis, 2002; Koger, 2010). Similarly, in New Zealand, the standing orders of the House of Representatives did not contain limits on debate until the 1930s. As a consequence, obstruction of parliamentary business could occur due to unlimited debate, so-called stonewalling (J. E. Martin, 2006, p. 126). In comparative context, scholars have shown that the extent to, and speed by, which governments can cut off debate have important implications for government control over the legislative agenda (Döring, 1995; Tsebelis, 2002; Rasch and Tsebelis, 2011).

The degree of government control over plenary time affects how opposition parties have an impact on policy and express policy positions. Opposition parties in parliamentary systems are largely excluded from policy-making, which is primarily the responsibility of the government. Instead, they use their representatives in parliament to scrutinize the actions of the cabinet and the parties in government and offer policy alternatives to voters. Plenary sessions provide opposition politicians an ideal forum in which to perform these functions. Members of the opposition can use speeches to highlight perceived flaws in government policy and to offer suggestions to improve a bill. Parliamentary debate also provides opportunities to members of coalition governments. Martin and Vanberg (2008) argue that coalition partners may use speeches to emphasize party policy over the coalition compromise, in particular for policy issues on which the coalition is divided. In such instances, they show that governing parties engage in lengthier debates on government bills. Moreover, they expect that this behavior is more pronounced as elections approach. Speech becomes an important tool for coalition partners to monitor each other and to signal to voters a distinct party platform. In short, both opposition and government parties can use parliamentary speech as a tool in the policy process.

The significance of parliamentary speech becomes even more evident when considering parties as collective, rather than unitary, actors.

Typically, scholars have examined intraparty politics by studying defections on roll-call votes (Cox and McCubbins, 1993; Hix, 2002; Carey, 2007; Kam, 2009). There are several reasons for this focus. Substantively, voting is the way that policy gets made – if a bill does not receive a sufficient number of votes, it does not become law. In parliamentary systems, the fusion of the executive and the legislature means that lost votes can lead to the termination of governments and early elections. From a practical point of view, voting data are readily available for a large number of parliaments. We argue, however, that if our goal is to understand how MPs stake out positions different from their party leadership, or other aspects of intraparty politics, then roll-call votes may not be the best place to look.

First, precisely because votes decide the fate of policy – not to mention the fate of governments – they are subject to a high degree of partisan control. Many MPs may cast a vote with their party leadership even though they do not want to, either because the consequences of dissent would often be too drastic (e.g. leading to the termination of a government) or the individual punishment for doing otherwise would be too great (e.g. loss of support from the party). Voting against one's party on a whipped vote is the ultimate act of defiance. There are many other acts of defiance that an MP who disagrees with his or her leadership can take that are less severe. Indeed, party discipline on voting is so high in many parliamentary systems that roll-call votes are actually taken rather infrequently, and voting is often done in party blocs or by unrecorded voice vote. Although defections occasionally occur, most often such votes simply reflect the division between government and opposition parties.

Second, even in the absence of strong partisan control, votes offer an unrefined instrument for expressing opinions. There are only three options: to support a bill, to reject it, or to abstain from voting. Members cannot explain what they wish they could have voted for simply by casting a vote. Moreover, the variety of "opinions" MPs can express in votes is severely hampered by the voting agenda, usually set by the government in parliamentary systems. Parliamentary debates, in contrast, offer MPs a forum for expressing a wide range of more nuanced viewpoints. Oftentimes, excerpts of these debates are broadcast on television or reprinted in the press. Even though the general public may pay little attention to specific parliamentary debates, MPs can point to transcripts of their floor speeches when discussing their positions with their constituents.

Deliberative democracy

Finally, parliamentary speech may have normative implications for politics. The philosopher John Stuart Mill has written that ideally a parliament is a "Congress of Opinions . . . where those whose opinion is over-ruled feel satisfied that it is heard, and set aside not by a mere act of will, but for what are thought superior reasons" (Mill, 1991, p. 116). Speeches, in this view, ought to lead to better policy and politics – after argumentation, the superior policy prevails and everyone is more satisfied as a result. Thus, scholars of deliberative politics often argue that convincing speeches lead to better democracy. These studies focus on how representatives engage in deliberation to justify legislation "by giving reasons for their political claims and responding to others' reasons in return" (Thompson, 2008, p. 498). As a consequence, some scholars put an explicit emphasis on the role of argumentation and respect during parliamentary deliberations and ask whether political dialogue is constructive or not (Steiner et al., 2004). The motivation of such approaches is inherently normative as deliberative theorists view the resulting policy decisions to be "more legitimate because they respect the moral agency of participants" (Thompson, 2008, p. 498). There are attempts to operationalize the concepts empirically. For instance, Steiner, Bächtiger, Spörndli, and Steenbergen (2004) construct a "discourse quality index" for parliaments in four countries. This index considers the context of the speech (free or interrupted), the level and the content of justification, the level of respect, and the presence of constructive politics. Theoretically, the authors are interested in examining the effect of consociational institutions on the quality of parliamentary discourse, but they find that "at least in legislative settings, it appears that it is very difficult to move actors away from positional politics in their speech acts and in the direction of consensus solutions" (Steiner et al., 2004, p. 136). It appears, then, that deliberative ideals are not well reflected in parliamentary discourse. Politicians put greater emphasis on position-taking than on deliberating and arguing. This is precisely the phenomenon our book explores.

Our take: representation and intraparty politics

The primary aim of this book is to explain how parties and their members of parliament structure legislative debate and, in doing so, to provide new insights into intraparty politics and democratic representation. Our theory, which we elaborate in Chapter 1, starts with the premise that floor speeches contain information about MPs' policy positions, which, directly or indirectly through the media, are transmitted to voters. To the extent that the party leadership wishes the party to send a unified message to the public – a function of political institutions – leaders will attempt to control what party members say on the floor. In short, in countries where the electoral system creates strong incentives for parties to cultivate and protect a single party image to present to voters, party leaders monitor and control their MPs' access to the floor. In systems where there are greater incentives for MPs to cultivate a personal vote (and for parties to allow them to do so), party leaders exercise less control over speaking time. The model has rich implications for how parties design rules regarding the allocation of speaking time to MPs and the amount of pressure they put on their membership to toe the party line during speechmaking. These strategic considerations affect what we, as observers of parliamentary debate, get to see and hear on the floor of parliament and, therefore, the inferences we can draw about party politics from debates.

Our study moves beyond current, largely normative, scholarship on parliamentary debate, as well as literature on parliamentary behavior that focuses primarily on roll-call voting. Rather than viewing legislative speech as a tool for altering policy outcomes, we see it as a tool for communication between MPs, parties, and the electorate. Our approach is decidedly positive. Political institutions affect parliamentary speech, but in unexpected ways. The theoretical model explains the design of procedural rules in parliament, how the party leadership interacts with backbenchers, and how MPs represent voters. It also highlights how using legislative speech as data can provide insights into intraparty politics within parliaments that other forms of data, such as roll-call analyses, cannot.

Plan for the book

This book is organized in two parts: the first part, consisting of Chapters 1, 2, and 3, presents the main theoretical argument, empirical implications, and the research design; the second, consisting of Chapters 4 through 8, provides evidence using cross-national data;

offers system-level tests of the theory in the United Kingdom, Germany, and the European Union; and discusses the effects of electoral system change on parliamentary debate in the case of New Zealand. Finally, we offer some conclusions.

Chapter 1 lays out our *delegation theory of parliamentary debate*, which builds on models of intraparty politics, political institutions, and the electoral incentives these institutions create. We argue that scholars' laments about the inconsequential nature of speech for policymaking, or about the insufficiently "deliberative" nature of parliamentary debate, are largely inconsistent with the fact that legislators tend to spend a great deal of time preparing, delivering, and listening to speeches, and the fact that these speeches receive a fair amount of coverage in the press. Clearly, politicians *think* they matter, although not necessarily for the reasons a canonical textbook account of parliamentary debate might assume. We present a formal model of intraparty politics in which speaking time allocation is the result of a delegation game between party leaders and their backbenchers. Backbenchers wish to speak, and party leaders want to delegate the task of speechmaking to them, but party leaders worry that backbenchers may stray from the party message during floor debates. Electoral institutions determine the degree to which party leaders are willing to allow rebel views to come to the floor and thus determine how much time leaders are willing to delegate to backbenchers.

Chapter 2 explores the implications of the theory for different democratic institutions. On the basis of our formal model, we present our theoretical expectations with regard to the control of speaking time for various electoral systems and candidate selection mechanisms. In addition to examining the implications for the canonical closed-list proportional representation and plurality systems, we also examine our expectations for mixed-member systems, open-list systems, and other electoral systems. All of these systems create slightly different incentives for MP personal vote seeking and therefore influence the interaction of individual MPs with their parties. Notably, we also discuss the model's implications for debate in hybrid regimes with variation in candidate selection mechanisms by exploring the European Parliament (EP), the directly elected parliament of the European Union, in more detail.

Chapter 3 lays out the research design and empirical strategy for the remainder of the book. It discusses the type of data we use to test our theory, provides the reader with an overview of the systems we choose to examine in greater depth – the United Kingdom, Germany, the European Union, and New Zealand – and explains what we hope to learn from each of our empirical analyses.

Chapter 4 presents a first test of our theory using cross-national data. We present new data on how parliamentary debate is organized in parliaments across advanced industrialized democracies. We begin by examining the formal rules governing parliamentary debate as laid down in parliamentary rules of procedure. In addition, we present results from a survey of parliamentary party groups, asking them how they organize debates within their parliamentary caucuses. Our analysis reveals that in systems that create strong electoral incentives for parties to protect the party brand, parliamentary rules of procedure provide party leaders with numerous tools to prevent rogue backbenchers from taking the floor. In contrast, in systems where there is a strong incentive to cultivate a personal vote, parliamentary rules of procedure allow backbenchers to take the floor without party approval. Our party survey results suggest that party leaders closely monitor and control what is said on the floor of parliament, but this varies across parties and countries, as well. In particular, party leaders appear to decrease their monitoring efforts in systems with strong personal vote incentives as intraparty disagreement increases.

Chapter 5 examines speaking time allocation in greater depth in two specific cases – the German Bundestag and the UK House of Commons. These cases provide us with variation on our key independent variables and allow us to test the theory at the individual MP level. It offers a quantitative study of MP behavior, examining the variation of speeches in each of these systems and tracing parliamentary debate participation over more than two decades. We examine how often backbenchers take the floor compared with party leaders and study the effect of ideology on backbenchers' participation in debate. We find that party leaders in Germany are more likely to give a speech than party leaders in the United Kingdom. Party rebels, on the other hand, are more likely to give a speech in the United Kingdom. These results are consistent with our theoretical expectations that speech behavior varies with electoral incentives. Within Germany, we also examine differences between the MPs elected from party lists versus those elected out of single-member districts. We find evidence that where party leaders have a stronger incentive to protect the party "label," backbenchers, in particular those most likely to dissent from the party position, have a harder time gaining access to the floor.

Chapter 6 embeds the theory into a broader framework of dissent, examining how MPs express dissenting views inside and outside of parliament. We study various types of backbencher dissent – in the media, in parliamentary speeches, and in legislative votes – with respect to the economic stimulus packages put forward by the British and German governments in response to the global financial crisis in 2008. The debates over stimulus spending reveal substantial intraparty disagreement. Despite this dissent, backbenchers were unwilling to vote against their parties. They did, however, express their disagreement with their party leadership in the media and in floor speeches. Consistent with our theory, the hurdle for dissenting in the media is lower than in floor debates. Moreover, although MPs in both countries expressed disagreement with their party in the media, British MPs were more willing to dissent in speeches, while German MPs were more likely to toe the party line. Thus, a joint look at legislative speech and media dissent reveals internal party disagreement that analyses of voting behavior mask. In addition, we find that, in line with our theory, British MPs have more opportunities to express their views on the floor of parliament than their German colleagues.

Chapter 7 shows that not only electoral rules matter for debate participation, but that partisan control over the candidate selection process does as well. The European Parliament provides us with a unique opportunity to isolate the effects of candidate selection rules while holding many other factors constant. All members of the European Parliament (MEPs) are elected under proportional rules (although the rules do differ across countries to some degree) in national campaigns and are members of both national parties and European political groups. The formal parliamentary rules governing debate participation are the same for all MEPs, and all debate takes place within the same strategic environment. The rules governing how candidates are nominated for their respective national party lists, however, differ across countries, with parties in some countries employing more centralized candidate selection mechanisms. This institutional variation across EU member states allows us to examine the effects of candidate selection on the debate participation of party leaders and MEPs while controlling for the parliamentary context. We find that, unlike in closed-list parliamentary systems, rebels in the European Parliament – those MEPs who vote against their party group – often take the floor to explain their dissent, usually in terms of their support for their national party. As the speech delegation perspective suggests, MEPs are even more likely to go on the floor if national parties have greater central control of the candidate selection process.

Finally, Chapter 8 examines how rules governing parliamentary debate can change as a function of electoral system change. Here, New Zealand provides an ideal opportunity to explore how electoral incentives affect parties' calculations when designing rules to structure debates and considering how best to communicate positions to voters. Prior to electoral reform, which first came into effect with the 1996 election, New Zealand was a pure Westminster system with a single-member district plurality electoral system. Moreover, its traditions and institutions regarding parliamentary debate were very similar to those of the UK House of Commons. The introduction of the mixed-member proportional electoral system had the effect of increasing the number of parties in parliament and thus increasing the electoral system's proportionality. It also meant an increase in the importance of the party label for electoral success and the existence of coalition and minority governments, neither of which had existed before 1996. In effect, the electoral system change transformed the New Zealand Parliament from majoritarian to consensual. We show that while the parliamentary traditions continue to resemble those of a Westminster parliament, both the institutional rules governing debate and parliamentary practice no longer do: the rules give party leaders significant control over who has access to the floor, meaning that parties do indeed care how parliamentary debate is organized and how positions are communicated.

Citizens in democracies expect their representatives not just to make policy but also to give voice to their views in parliament and to present them with convincing arguments about why policies should or should not be changed. Parliamentary debates are a central element of representative democracy where MPs do exactly that. In this book, we offer a rational explanation for MP debate participation, and we explain why ideological viewpoints are represented more accurately during parliamentary debates in some political systems than in others. In the Conclusion, we discuss how these results affect various aspects of our understanding of how democratic political institutions work.

PART I

Modeling parliamentary debate

1 *A theory of parliamentary debate*

On 12 June 1991, Wolfgang Schäuble (Christian Democratic Union), a member of the German Bundestag, gave a passionate speech on the floor of parliament that is widely recognized to have changed German MPs' minds about moving the German capital from Bonn to Berlin. Before the 12-hour debate, indicative votes held within each parliamentary party group suggested a majority of MPs supported retaining Bonn as the capital. In his speech, Schäuble fervently argued for a move, and after the debate was over, a majority of MPs voted to relocate the capital (see interview with Wolfgang Schäuble in *Die Welt*, 2011). The current literature on parliamentary debate focuses on the persuasive effects of speech, as highlighted by this example. But speech may also serve as a form of political communication and position-taking for MPs and their parties. Schäuble was not just an ordinary MP. He was a cabinet member and minister of the interior, and thus a leading MP in the Christian Democratic Union. Initially, he was not considered as a speaker for the debate. But as a fervent supporter of Berlin as the capital, he was annoyed with intraparty opponents to the capital's move. During the preparatory party group meeting before the debate, he approached the leader of the Christian Democratic MPs from Berlin and offered to deliver the parliamentary speech instead (ibid.). Thus, as a cabinet member, Schäuble essentially put himself on his party's speaker list. He intervened in the debate as a senior party member to communicate the party position.

As this story suggests, there are two potential reasons why legislatures devote time to debate. First, debate may affect policy outcomes as MPs try to persuade colleagues of the superiority of their position or present new policy alternatives; second, speech allows MPs to stake out a position and communicate it to their parties and to voters. Our model assumes the second motivation; parliamentary speech is primarily an act of position-taking. To the extent that the party leadership wishes the party to send a unified message to the public – a function of political institutions – leaders will attempt to control what party members say on the floor. Constraints from political institutions translate into a systematic selection of parliamentary speakers. The selection of speakers, in turn, leads to strategic position-taking and affects how political preferences are communicated in parliament. As a result, the model offers a rational explanation for why some MPs are more active than others and why ideological viewpoints are represented more accurately during parliamentary debates in some political systems than in others. In this chapter, we first examine the nature of parliamentary debate and discuss how political scientists before us have studied it. Using formal theory, we then develop our own institutional model of plenary speech. Finally, we discuss the implications of the model for comparative analyses of parliamentary politics.

1.1 Democracy and debate

As discussed in the Introduction, the study of political debate has probably received the most attention outside of the realm of positive political theory and quantitative social science in the field of normative political philosophy. Normative theorists like Jürgen Habermas have long been concerned with the quality of democratic debate, arguing that democracy thrives through deliberative processes in which individuals attempt to persuade others through better argument (Habermas, 1985). Recently, political scientists have attempted to uncover which parliamentary institutions lead to "higher quality" parliamentary debates (e.g. Steiner et al., 2004; Bächtiger and Hangartner, 2010). These scholars, however, have not tied the nature and content of speech to party politics. Moreover, empirically defining what constitutes "high-quality" debate is far from straightforward and is an inherently normative undertaking.[1]

As with the normative scholarship, the little positive theoretical work examining political speeches does not examine them in the context of party competition and political institutions. Current work generally treats speech as cheap talk with limited effects on decision-making processes (e.g. Austen-Smith, 1990; Austen-Smith and Feddersen, 2006)

[1] There is another growing literature on democratic deliberation in the political behavior and public opinion literature, examining if and when voters engage in deliberative processes (e.g. Page, 1996; Neblo et al., 2010). This literature does not focus on parliamentary speech and political institutions, however.

or as a form of intraparty communication largely outside of parliament (Dewan and Myatt, 2008). Assuming that legislators are asymmetrically informed about the consequences of legislation, Austen-Smith (1990) presents a model in which speech, viewed as cheap talk, may influence decision-making through information revelation. He finds, however, that the role of debate in this model is limited to timing. MPs can only share the same information that they would otherwise reveal later during voting; this may improve legislation, but only in some instances (ibid., p. 144). Because speech is unlikely to have any direct impact on legislation, on the basis of his model, we would not expect to find any systematic variation in the organization of legislative debate. However, as Austen-Smith notes, the model cannot address whether speeches serve other functions, such as communication of policy positions to voters or parties.

Once party competition is taken into account, other explanations for parliamentary speech arise. MPs may keep electoral considerations in mind when delivering speeches in parliament. A growing literature has suggested that politicians use parliamentary speeches to attract media attention and to sell their preferred policy position to the public. Until relatively recently, empirical scholarship on parliamentary speech has focused primarily on the US context. However, as we demonstrate in the chapters to come, in terms of parliamentary speech the United States is a somewhat unusual case. In practice, members of the US House and Senate have far more freedom to take the floor to express their personal beliefs than MPs in other political systems. There is significantly less partisan control in the US Congress compared with other parliaments. Thus, speech in the American literature is generally viewed as something that individuals do rather than an activity that parties coordinate, and even when parties do attempt coordination, members of Congress do not necessarily follow the party line. Studies have found that ideologically extreme members of the US House make more use of unconstrained floor time, that they are sensitive to their district interests in floor speeches, that members of the minority party speak more often, and that members more ideologically distant from their party leadership are less willing to give speeches supporting the party position (Maltzman and Sigelman, 1996; Hall, 1998; Morris, 2001; Harris, 2005). Nevertheless, these findings point to the relevance of parliamentary speech as a form of legislative behavior.

1.2 The nature of parliamentary speech

Before presenting our theory of how parties and their members use parliamentary speech, we first describe the various forms parliamentary speech can take. The civics textbook version of parliamentary speech tends to view it as a form of debate,[2] with MPs addressing one another in their speeches and participating in a highly organized conversation about policy-making. Steven Smith, in his discussion of reforms to floor procedures in the US Congress, defines debate as "a verbal contest between people of opposing views." He argues that "[d]ebate is inherently strategic, with each side of the argument anticipating the arguments of the other side, preparing to refute those arguments and avoiding arguments that weaken one's own case" (Smith, 1989, p. 238). Smith distinguishes between parliamentary speech as debate versus speech as deliberation, where the goals of speech include a careful consideration of all policy alternatives, broad participation, and careful reasoning to arrive at a consensus (ibid., p. 239).

In truth, parliamentary speech rarely looks looks like deliberation. Only now and then do speeches resemble a conversation of any kind. Rather than being an off-the-cuff conversation between members, speeches are often prepared well in advance and do not address or respond to speeches made by other members during a parliamentary session.[3] Politicians hope that their speeches change the minds of their colleagues – but with perhaps a few notable exceptions such as the speech by the German interior minister, they rarely do. Instead, they are often given before a half-empty (or even near-empty) chamber. Although Smith argues that the US House is more a debating chamber, whereas the Senate is more deliberative, he readily acknowledges that "[m]uch of the talk on the House and Senate floors has merely symbolic and theatrical purposes" and is directed at an external audience to "serve members' personal political goals" (ibid., p. 239). We do away with the civics textbook distinction between debate and deliberation and begin with the assumption that debate exists (almost) solely

[2] We often use the term "debate" to refer to parliamentary speech more generally. Here, we refer to a specific type of speech.

[3] Of course, some forms of debate are more conducive to back-and-forth exchange of views, such as oral questions during the Prime Minister's Questions in the United Kingdom.

for "theatrical" purposes, addressed to outside audiences for political – as opposed to policy – reasons. In other words, we examine parliamentary speech as a tool for position-taking for MPs and their parties.

Several empirical phenomena suggest that political parties use parliamentary speech to send policy signals when competing for votes. From a comparative perspective, parties in parliaments differ in the attention they devote to structuring legislative debates. Some parties write detailed rules to clarify which MPs receive priority in legislative debates, and others do not. Moreover, parliamentary rules of procedure provide different opportunities for backbenchers and party leaders to take the floor. In some parliaments, time is allocated directly to members; in others, it is allocated to parties, which are then responsible for delegating time to members. There are also many forums for speech-making within parliaments, each with different rules governing who may give a floor speech and how long they may talk. Depending on the parliament, there are debates on government bills, opposition bills, backbencher proposals, current events, and oral questions. Such wide variation in the rules regulating speech cannot be explained by cheap-talk models of private information transmission or by theories in which members attempt to persuade one another. Both of these existing approaches say little about institutional variation.

In addition, parties and their MPs clearly think that parliamentary debates matter (or at least potentially could matter) to voters. Legislators spend a substantial amount of time preparing for debates. If speechmaking were only about altering policy outcomes, given its ineffectiveness, we would not expect MPs to spend much time at all on writing speeches. However, surveys of MPs suggest otherwise. For example, British MPs report that attending House of Commons debates is one of their most important activities in terms of hours spent per week after constituency service. Table 1.1 shows average responses of legislators from the British Representation Studies conducted in 1992, 1997, 2001, and 2005 to the question of how many hours are devoted to particular activities in the average week when the House is sitting. The most time-intensive Westminster activity is dealing with constituency casework (13.7 hours per week). Excluding travel, parliamentary debates are the second most time-intensive activity. MPs spend almost the same amount of time on parliamentary debate as they do working in select and standing committees combined.

Table 1.1. *Parliamentary activities of British MPs*

Year	Parliam. debates	Select com.	Standing com.	Party com.	Constituency surgery	Travel	Constituency casework	Total
1992	7.85	2.17	3.94	2.60	3.10	6.71	14.56	66.13
1997	6.77	2.99	3.72	2.55	3.11	6.84	12.93	70.65
2001	6.94	4.53	4.04	2.82	3.47	6.93	13.48	73.39
2005	5.10	4.24	2.60	1.66	4.52	6.64	NA	61.87
Mean	6.66	3.48	3.57	2.41	3.55	6.78	13.66*	68.01

Note: Year indicates the British Representation Study. The question was phrased as follows: "Roughly how many hours do you usually devote to the following activities in the average week when the House is sitting?" Entries are average responses, some answer categories are omitted. The average for constituency casework (*) does not include 2005.

Given that legislators could spend their time on other activities, what is the benefit of investing time in debate? Because parliamentary speech occurs in a public forum, MPs must carefully choose their words. Even though voters almost never follow parliamentary debates as they happen, the content of parliamentary speeches can reach voters through the media. In Germany, a leading newspaper, the *Frankfurter Allgemeine Zeitung* (*FAZ*), has published 73 stories per year since 1950 specifically mentioning parliamentary debates, amounting on average to more than one story about each plenary session. Figure 1.1 shows the annual number of articles in the *FAZ* that mention parliamentary debates in the Bundestag.[4] The figure plots the average number of articles per year (dotted line), but also shows that there is variation over time. Most importantly, however, one of Germany's major newspapers regularly reports on debates. Although the numbers in the late 2000s had dropped to below average compared with the beginning of the decade, the annual number of articles does not seem to be lower than in previous instances (e.g. early 1960s and late 1980s). Note, however, that these numbers cannot tell us how parliamentary debate is reported in other media, in particular on television news and the Internet. Combined, the evidence suggests that the content of parliamentary speeches is indeed transmitted to the electorate. Being on the permanent

[4] We chose a restrictive full-text search criterion, meaning that the actual number of mentions may be higher.

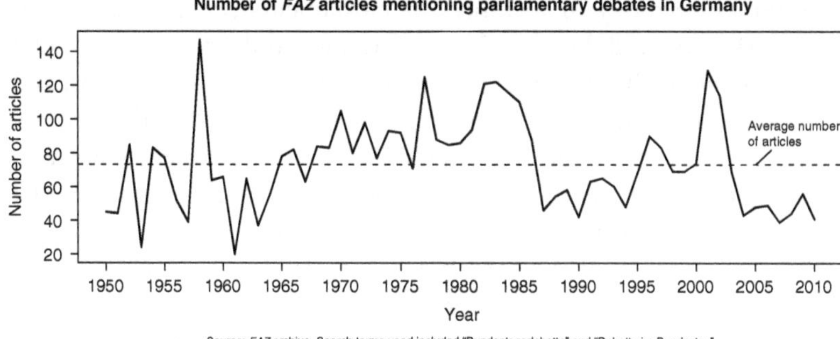

Figure 1.1 Parliamentary debates in German news

parliamentary record means that MPs always have the option to point to their speeches, but it also creates opportunities for others, in particular the media and members of other parties, to scrutinize what has been said on the floor. Legislators are aware that their speeches can potentially – if infrequently – reach voters, and therefore may have electoral consequences.[5]

Understanding the rationale behind parliamentary speeches has an additional benefit beyond expanding our knowledge about how legislative institutions and political parties work. In recent years, there has been a burgeoning literature using parliamentary speech as textual data. This literature has been the result of a technological revolution that has also arrived in democratic legislatures. Protocols of legislative debates are nowadays instantaneously accessible electronically. Many parliaments offer live feeds of legislative debates on their websites and make videos accessible to everyone. The availability of this massive data source has sparked increasing interest to attempt to extract systematic meaning from such speeches. New methods for estimating policy positions from political texts (e.g. Laver, Benoit, and Garry, 2003; Slapin and Proksch, 2008) or classifying political texts (Hopkins and King, 2010) have transformed the content analysis of parliamentary speech from a daunting task to a new and promising method for assessing ideal points and policy conflict. Speeches are used

[5] In fact, research suggests that parliamentary speeches can have consequences for citizens' political engagement. Salmond (2007), for instance, has shown that question time that allows for spontaneous questions in parliament can positively affect citizens' level of political information and electoral turnout.

to estimate ideology of members of parliaments (Laver and Benoit, 2002; Monroe and Maeda, 2004; Bernauer and Bräuninger, 2009; Diermeier et al., 2012), governments (Giannetti and Laver, 2005), and parties (Proksch and Slapin, 2010). Others have used parliamentary speeches to assess congressional support for bills (Thomas, Pang, and Lee, 2006), the dimensionality and the nature of rhetorical conflict in Congress (Monroe, Colaresi, and Quinn, 2008; Schonhardt-Bailey, 2008; Quinn et al., 2010), the nature of ideology surrounding specific policies such as national security (Schonhardt-Bailey, 2005), or as indicators that government parties in parliamentary systems try to distinguish themselves from each other (Martin and Vanberg, 2008). However, if the parliamentary speech is the result of strategic interaction between party leaders and backbenchers, these data may not accurately reflect the concepts they are meant to measure. If a politician's intended message in a speech reflects a strategic, rather than sincere, position, the researcher can, at best, recapture the intended message, not the sincere policy position (Benoit, Laver, and Mikhaylov, 2009).

The remainder of this book seeks to uncover the strategic nature of parliamentary speech. Using our comparative theory of parliamentary speech, readers will learn, for example, why parliamentary debate in the United States looks so different from parliamentary debate in Germany. Moreover, the theory provides expectations for when parliamentary speech is most likely to reflect the underlying ideological disagreements in the policy debate. The next section of this chapter presents the theoretical model.

1.3 Parties, rebels, and speech – a theory

We take as the starting point of our theoretical inquiry two generally accepted propositions in comparative and American politics. First, political institutions – such as electoral systems, regime type, and candidate selection mechanisms – affect legislative behavior, and therefore party unity (Gallagher and Marsh, 1988; Carey and Shugart, 1995; Huber, 1996; Diermeier and Feddersen, 1998; Bowler, 2000; Bawn and Thies, 2003; Crisp et al., 2004; Hix, 2004; Carey, 2007). And second, parties seek to develop a brand to signal their core policy platform to voters. Voters save time by taking a cue about a candidate's position from the candidate's party "label," rather than gathering detailed information about everyone listed on the ballot

(Downs, 1957; Kiewiet and McCubbins, 1991; Cox and McCubbins, 1993; Aldrich, 1995). These two propositions are intricately linked; political institutions affect legislative behavior because of the incentives they create for party leaders and backbenchers with regard to partisan dissent. Some political institutions (i.e. parliamentary government coupled with a closed-list PR electoral system) lead parties to fiercely protect party unity and backbenchers to toe the party line, whereas other institutions (i.e. presidential systems with majoritarian electoral systems) generate incentives for party leadership to give rebel backbenchers more free rein.

In closed-list proportional electoral systems in which voters cast ballots directly for parties rather than for individuals, party labels are of the utmost importance. To maintain the party's brand and to help the party win seats at election time, party leaders must control their elected members and prevent them from undertaking activities that contradict the party's primary message. In other systems, although the party as a whole benefits from unity, individual MPs may be hurt by toeing the line. Incentives to cultivate a personal vote mean that MPs will try to win votes through personal name recognition (Carey and Shugart, 1995). An MP may, for example, come from a district ideologically at odds with the official party stance. This creates a collective action problem: the party as a whole might be better off when members communicate party policy, but individual members are better off by defecting and presenting their own position while reaping the benefits from other members who toe the party line. The severity of this collective action problem is a function of political institutions, and solutions come in the form of party leadership and partisan institutions (Cox and McCubbins, 1993; Kam, 2009).

Comparative politics literature has focused primarily on how political institutions and electoral considerations affect party cohesion evident in roll-call voting (Londregan, 2002; Carey, 2007, 2009; Hix, Noury, and Roland, 2007; Kam, 2009). The assumption underpinning many of these studies is that divisiveness on roll-call votes signals party disunity and obfuscates the party message. Indeed, Kam (2009) has demonstrated that voting defections have negative electoral consequences for the party while providing the rebellious MPs with added name recognition. However, roll-call votes are not the only way parties display disunity: when a legislator delivers a speech on the floor of parliament that expresses a position at odds with the position of the

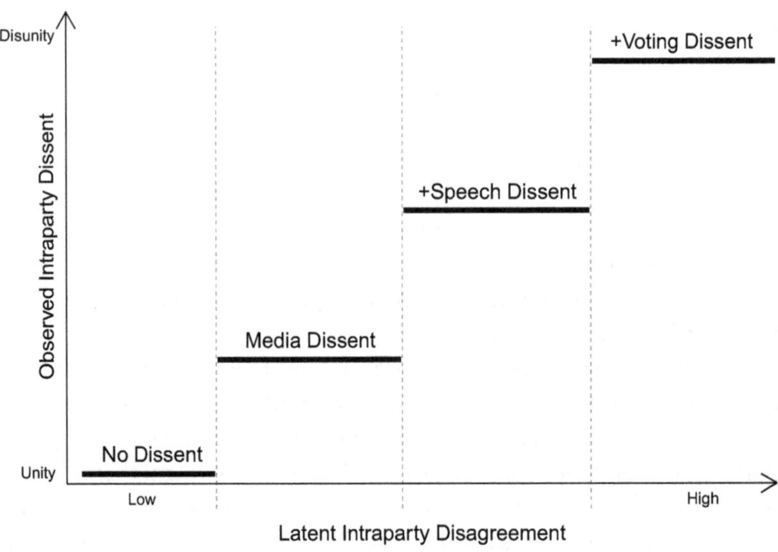

Figure 1.2 Expected relationship between latent intraparty disagreement and observed intraparty dissent

party leadership, that speech sends a mixed message to voters just as dissenting votes do. Moreover, roll-call analyses are not without their drawbacks. First, when not all votes are subject to a roll call but rather one may be requested by members of parliament or party groups, the decision to record a vote may be strategic. This can lead to a selection bias in the sample of votes researchers are able to observe, and this may distort inferences about the cohesion of parties (Carrubba et al., 2006; Roberts, 2007; Carrubba, Gabel, and Hug, 2008; Hug, 2010). Second, defecting from one's party leadership on a vote, especially on one that is both high profile and whipped, constitutes the ultimate act of defiance. Even rebel backbenchers who harbor significant doubts about their party's position with regard to a bill may toe the party line on a whipped vote. They may, however, engage in other acts of protest.

For different levels of latent, that is, fundamentally unobservable, intraparty disagreement, we hypothesize that backbenchers take different actions. Figure 1.2 shows our expectations with respect to the actions we observe as a function of the (unobserved) level of disagreement between a backbencher and the party leadership. For minor policy disagreements between a backbencher and the leadership, the backbencher will not engage in any rebellious action. As the level of disagreement grows, we may see the start of backbencher grumblings, beginning with relatively benign dissent and progressing to more serious acts of defiance. First, the MP may make statements contradicting the party leadership outside of the parliament, where the statements, although they may be picked up in the media, are not placed on the permanent parliamentary record and can always be refuted later. As latent disagreement continues to grow, the MP may next become willing to express his or her discontent on the floor of parliament. Finally, for the highest levels of disagreement, the MP may be willing to cast a vote against the party leadership. Most of the literature has focused only on this final stage, ignoring the variation that occurs before voting defections.

Electoral considerations thus create incentives for legislators to participate in debates. Legislative institutions, however, often constrain their ability to do so. Plenary time in legislatures is a limited resource. Formal rules are required to determine which bills come to the floor and the amount of floor time devoted to them. As mentioned in the Introduction, Gary Cox (2006) has referred to this scarcity as a "plenary bottleneck," arguing that institutional arrangements that provide some MPs with agenda-setting rights are necessary to prevent total legislative gridlock. Institutions not only dictate the nature of the legislation that comes to the floor but also determine who receives speaking time in debates on that legislation.

The plenary bottleneck in parliaments comprises two elements. The first is access to the *voting agenda* – the right of actors to make proposals to the legislature. The second is access to the *debate agenda* – the right of members to express opinions on the floor of parliament. The voting agenda has been the focus of much of the literature on legislative organization (e.g. Shepsle and Weingast, 1987; Cox and McCubbins, 1993; Döring, 1995; Rasch, 2000; Tsebelis, 2002; Cox and McCubbins, 2005). These studies all stress the importance of the voting agenda for the set of political outcomes that the political system can achieve. The second element of the bottleneck, however, remains surprisingly unexplored. We argue that where electoral rules provide parties with an incentive to cultivate a unified party label, party leaders have a greater incentive to control what their party members say during debates, and parties develop rules that provide leaders with the tools necessary to keep rebels off the floor. Where electoral rules create a weaker incentive for party leaders to protect a party label and a greater incentive for members to cultivate a personal vote, parties develop laxer rules regarding speaking time allocation, and rebels are allowed to speak on the floor.

1.4 Two illustrations

We illustrate this strategic perspective with two examples, one taken from the United Kingdom and the other from Germany, political systems with different electoral incentives that remain a focus throughout the book. Our goal is to demonstrate the importance of approaching parliamentary speech from a strategic, intraparty politics angle.

1.4.1 Heathrow expansion debate in the UK House of Commons

The first example comes from the UK House of Commons, members of which are elected in single-member districts by a "first-past-the-post" system. In 2009, the House held a debate on the most controversial public infrastructure project in recent British history: the expansion of Heathrow, the largest airport in the country. The expansion plans, which included the building of a third runway, caused a controversy among the members of the governing Labour Party. One outspoken critic, MP John McDonnell, represented the constituency (Hayes and Harlington) containing the airport. In a parliamentary speech on 15 January 2009, McDonnell expressed his strong disagreement with the airport expansion policy espoused by his own party leadership[6]:

> The decision today, for my constituents, is an absolute disgrace. The commitments that have been given on the conditions to be attached are spin. They are as worthless as the commitment that there would be no third runway. The decision is a betrayal of future generations, in terms of the environment, and a betrayal of my constituents, who will lose their homes, their schools, their cemeteries, their churches and their gurdwara. It is a betrayal of this House, and of democracy, not to have a vote in the House. We are not asking for a vote on every infrastructure project; we are asking for the most

[6] The speech records for this particular debate are available at the Hansard House of Commons Debates archive (UK Hansard, 2009).

significant project in a generation to be brought to this House for a vote. Will there be a vote, and why not? (*John McDonnell (Labour MP) during the parliamentary debate on 15 January 2009*)

As is evident from this speech excerpt, McDonnell was criticizing the government's decision to build a third runway not only on substantive grounds but also on procedural ones. The Labour government had decided to avoid a formal House vote on the issue. His fellow party member, Secretary of State for Transport, Geoffrey Hoon, responded to the criticism that there were indeed no plans for a vote but expressed some understanding for the MP's views:

I have made clear the position of the House in relation to such matters. It is a long-standing position that the House does not vote on quasi-judicial or planning matters. Nevertheless, I entirely understand that my hon. Friend puts his case with his customary passion on behalf of his constituents, but this is an issue for the country. Heathrow is a national airport serving the whole of the country. Necessarily, when judgments have to be made about the interests of the country, those decisions have to be made, however difficult they are – [Interruption.] (*Geoffrey Hoon (Labour, Secretary of State) during the parliamentary debate on 15 January 2009*)

The parliamentary debate then took an unexpected turn. Enraged by the answer, video footage shows how John McDonnell walked from the backbench down the aisle and tossed the ceremonial mace, the symbol of parliamentary authority in Britain that lies on the table in front of the Speaker of the House, onto an empty bench (BBC, 2009). This instance is documented in the parliamentary record: "John McDonnell, Member for Hayes and Harlington, having conducted himself in a grossly disorderly manner, was named by the Deputy Speaker," meaning that he was suspended for several days from the House (UK Hansard, 2009). Despite the suspension, McDonnell received support for his position from his fellow Labour MP and former junior minister, Kate Hoey:

On a point of order, Mr. Deputy Speaker. Will you clarify something? You say that my hon. Friend the Member for Hayes and Harlington (John McDonnell) is suspended, and many of us support not necessarily what he has done, but why he has done it – the fact that we are not going to have a vote in this House. Can you explain how long he will be suspended for? (*Kate Hoey (Labour MP) during the parliamentary debate on 15 January 2009*)

In his response, the Deputy Speaker acknowledged the importance of the matter and expressed sympathy that "voices should be heard" on the floor:

> The answer to the hon. Lady is five days. I counsel the House that I understand that the strength of feeling on this matter is very great, but many hon. Members are not only wishing to question the Secretary of State on the matter, but waiting for the other important business. I am sure that there will be other occasions when Members' voices will be heard on a matter of this importance. We should proceed. The hon. Member for Hayes and Harlington must now withdraw from the service of the House – [Interruption.] Without further comment. (*Deputy Speaker during the parliamentary debate on 15 January 2009*)

The message McDonnell was sending with his speech was targeted not just at his party but also at his constituency. After all, it was a way of showing that he was standing up for their interests, even though there was no formal vote on the matter in parliament. These interests were organized in a campaign group against the expansion, called Heathrow Association for the Control of Aircraft Noise. Its chair, John Stewart, later praised the MP as "a pivotal figure in [the] campaign; a giant of the movement" (Stewart, 2010, p. 16). The campaign explicitly hailed McDonnell's speech in parliament: "He [McDonnell] returned to his constituency to a standing ovation" (ibid., p. 41). Notably, McDonnell went on to keep his seat in the general election in May 2010 despite the overall vote loss for the Labour Party that resulted in a Conservative-Liberal Democrat coalition government under David Cameron. McDonnell comfortably won his constituency seat with 55 percent of the vote, compared with an overall average constituency vote share of 31 percent for the Labour Party.

Two facts are remarkable about this incidence. First, the MP criticized his own party leadership, and the leadership, in fact, acknowledged that the critique was justified on grounds of constituency representation. Second, the example demonstrates that the MP not only disagreed with the policy of the party but also that parliament did not vote on the policy. Thus, in this particular debate, intraparty dissent was observable *only* during debate, not in a recorded vote.[7]

[7] The government successfully insisted on not having a vote, but a few weeks later, the measure was brought to a vote by the opposition to split the government party. The expansion decision passed with a bare majority

1.4.2 *Euro crisis debate in the German Bundestag*

A very different kind of parliamentary speech and ensuing reaction occurred in the German Bundestag in September 2011 during a parliamentary debate on the extension of the European Financial Stability Facility (EFSF). In an effort to respond to the sovereign debt crisis in Europe, governments of Eurozone countries set up this facility to make loans to indebted member states up to an amount of € 440 billion. The objective was "to collect funds and provide loans in conjunction with the IMF to cover the financing needs of euro area Member States in difficulty, subject to strict policy conditionality" (Eurogroup, 2010). In 2011, euro countries furthermore agreed to increase the EFSF's scope of activity and guarantee commitments to € 780 billion. With Germany as Europe's largest economy bearing the brunt of the costs, MPs in the Bundestag had to approve an extension of German guarantee commitments from € 123 to € 211 billion. Amid domestic pressure to involve the parliament in fiscal decisions, the German government put the extension up for a vote in September.

During the days preceding the debate and final vote, the governing parties increased pressure on their MPs to support the extension. Indicative votes were held by the governing Christian Democratic Union/Christian Social Union (CDU/CSU) and Free Democratic Party (FDP) party groups two days before the debate. These suggested a bare absolute majority for the government, with 13 Christian Democratic MPs and six FDP MPs abstaining or voting against the extension (*Süddeutsche Zeitung*, 2011). The small margin led Chancellor Angela Merkel to personally call MPs to win their support. Remarkably, the passage of the vote was not in jeopardy because opposition parties, notably the Social Democrats (SPD) and the Greens, had announced their support for the measure. Nevertheless, the coalition aimed to secure an absolute majority solely with its own members – even though a simple majority among its MPs would have been sufficient to pass the measure – to avoid any suspicion of weakness of the governing coalition. In the end, the extension was approved by an absolute majority of the governing parties, supported by the SPD and Green Party

(*Guardian*, 2009). However, in May 2010, the plan to build a third runway at Heathrow was abandoned by the new Conservative-Liberal Democrat coalition government.

groups.[8] The government appeared to have secured a victory in the fight against the European debt crisis.

But the government's success was tarnished by media reports of an incident that occurred during the debate over the measure. In contrast to the UK House of Commons, where MPs stand up to "catch the Speaker's eye" to deliver a speech, parties in the German Bundestag control a fixed amount of plenary time and allocate this time to their members. Despite substantial internal opposition to the extension of the euro bailout mechanism, the governing parties initially decided *not* to grant dissenters any speaking time during the debate (Welt Online, 2011). In view of those latent disagreements, however, the president of the Bundestag, Norbert Lammert (a member of the CDU), decided to deviate from parliamentary procedure and grant two governing party MPs, with views contrary to the party leadership, *extra* speaking time outside of the party groups' allocated time – an unprecedented event in the Bundestag's history. The next day, the headlines read "Lammert causes scandal during Euro debate" (*Financial Times Deutschland*), "Euro dissenters enrage party grandees" (Spiegel Online), and "Dispute over speaking time for rebels" (*Stern*). Lammert's decision to grant Klaus-Peter Willsch (CDU) and Frank Schäffler (FDP) five minutes each to voice the reasons for their dissent on live television enraged the party leaders. Willsch used the opportunity to critique the EFSF, well aware that his position deviated from that of his party:[9]

> Today, unfortunately I do not speak for my party group, and I am thankful to the President of the Bundestag that I may nevertheless present my thoughts here. . . . We do not have the money in the form of guarantees amounting to 211 billion Euro – this is just for the EFSF; Greece is not yet included. I believe that the risk that we impose upon future generations is too large. We borrow this money that we are putting on display from our children and grandchildren; we do not have it. . . . We gave the people another promise. We said: no one is responsible for the debt of another country in this currency area. Every country needs to balance its own budget. This is exactly what we violate with this bailout policy. I think this is the absolute wrong way economically, and it contradicts my fundamental convictions. . . . I call upon

[8] On the roll-call vote, 523 MPs voted for the extension of the euro bailout mechanism, 85 voted no, 3 abstained, and 9 were not present. Among those MPs voting no, 10 were from the CDU/CSU, 3 from the FDP, 1 from the SPD, 1 from the Greens, and 70 from the Left Party (Deutscher Bundestag, 2011*a*).

[9] All speeches are available in Deutscher Bundestag (2011*b*).

everyone in the interest of future generations to end this policy as soon as possible instead of prolonging it with ever increasing volumes.... I am very thankful for the opportunity to speak here. Looking at my own party group, I say thank you for bearing it. (*Klaus-Peter Willsch (CDU/CSU) during the parliamentary debate on 29 September 2011*)

Frank Schäffler from the FDP used even harsher words in his critique of the governing parties:

On February 11th, 2010, the heads of state and government of the European Union agreed to a collective breach of law.... We were promised in the German Bundestag that help for Greece would be a one-time assistance, the absolute exception, and nothing else. The ink was still wet when a day later in Brussels the current debt shield, the EFSF, was established.... You use the fear of a collapse of the financial system to lead Europe into a new level of centralism. (*Frank Schäffler (FDP) during the parliamentary debate on 29 September 2011*)

The reaction of the party leaders followed promptly. Volker Kauder, the party group leader of the CDU/CSU, heavily criticized the decision of the Bundestag president to grant dissenters extra speaking time: "I consider this decision to be wrong. If all those speak who have a dissenting view from the party group, the system would collapse" (Spiegel Online, 2011). Fearing that the decision would set a precedent for future debates, leaders and whips from other parties joined the critique. Gregor Gysi from the Left Party – whose members collectively voted against the government's proposal – supported the CDU/CSU party group leader saying: "I am worried and scared. Either the party group has the guts and grants the opponents three minutes of its speaking time or it does not. But like this, these are new times!" (*Stern*, 2011). The Green Party group whip, Volker Beck, considered the speeches an "outrageous incident" (Welt Online, 2011). A week later, the president of the Bundestag clarified his actions in a newspaper interview, stating that he stood by his decision to grant extra speaking time but expressed some understanding for the reactions of the parties:

The party group leaders are, of course, right that the parliamentary sessions must remain calculable in their operations. In the future, we will certainly see no debates in which each member presents his personal opinion to the plenary of the Bundestag. (*Norbert Lammert, as quoted in the Stuttgarter Zeitung, 2011*)

The harsh reactions from the party leaders to this unusual scenario emphasize the control parties may exercise over what their MPs say on the floor of parliament, even when the outcome of a vote is not affected.

1.4.3 Summary

In sum, these anecdotes tell two different stories of the organization of parliamentary debate. Although in both instances MPs dissented from the party line, the circumstances, conditions, and reactions were quite different. In the United Kingdom, the rebel backbencher could count on a regular procedure under which the Speaker recognizes any MP to deliver a speech. After delivering his statement, a representative from the party leadership even acknowledged the critical views and the right of the MP to express them. In Germany, the dissenting speeches represent a rare exception to the rule. In fact, parties drew up speakers lists that had excluded the intraparty critics. It was the president of the Bundestag who had to do away with existing parliamentary practice to let the dissenting MPs speak, something that the parties had explicitly tried to rule out. The harsh reactions to this decision show that party leaders wish to retain strict control over what their members say on the floor of parliament. We now present a formal model to explain both why the rules allocating speaking time are so different in the United Kingdom and Germany and why the leadership's reaction to dissenting speech was so muted in the former and so harsh in the latter. Because of electoral considerations, UK party leaders have little problem delegating speaking time to rebels, whereas German electoral laws make it much more costly for party leaders to allow dissenting views on the floor. The rules governing debate are shaped to give the leadership the degree of control it needs.

1.5 A delegation model of parliamentary speech

In our model, floor speeches are the result of a delegation game played between the party leadership and backbenchers. In many democracies, as in the German example just discussed, both parliamentary and party rules allow party leaders to control access to the floor. Even in systems where *parliamentary rules* mean party leaders cannot formally prevent backbenchers from giving a floor speech, such as in the United Kingdom, party leaders can still design *party rules* to control who takes the floor. For example, party leaders could ask to preapprove backbencher speeches that potentially clash with the party line and punish backbenchers who speak without first seeking approval. Likewise, party whips could monitor the content of backbencher speech and seek to punish dissenting members. Over the long term, parties in parliament might come to an agreement to change the parliamentary rules because all parties face the same electoral incentives. In short, rules controlling access to floor time are endogenous; parties design them to give MPs, and therefore the party, the best chance at reelection (we provide evidence for this assertion in Chapters 4 and 8).

Although party leaders are expected to actively communicate party policy, they have an incentive to delegate floor time to members. Backbenchers likely have specialized knowledge about a bill and may, therefore, be in a better position to speak about it than the party leader. In addition, the leader may wish to provide MPs with the opportunity to build a reputation on the floor and within the party. Where the electoral system requires the MP to cultivate a personal vote for reelection, this may be particularly important. However, delegation involves costs. Whereas party leaders know exactly what they would say if they were to give a speech, they do not exercise such precise control over their backbenchers. An MP could publicly deviate from the party line. Dissent in speeches may serve as a pressure release valve for party members at odds with the party position, but there are costs. If a sufficient number of MPs give such speeches, they could dilute the value of the party label. The leader can limit these costs by making it more difficult for the MP to take the floor.

The basic elements of our model are presented in Figure 1.3. After an MP is recognized as a potential speaker on behalf of the party, a party leader decides whether to delegate floor time to this MP or whether to deliver a speech on behalf of the party. If delegated to, the MP must decide what ideological position to express in his or her speech. The member can either toe the party line, express his or her own sincere ideological position, or deliver a speech that lies somewhere in between these two positions. The leader's decision to delegate floor time, as well as the member's decision about the type of speech to give, are functions of ideology, parliamentary institutions, and electoral concerns.

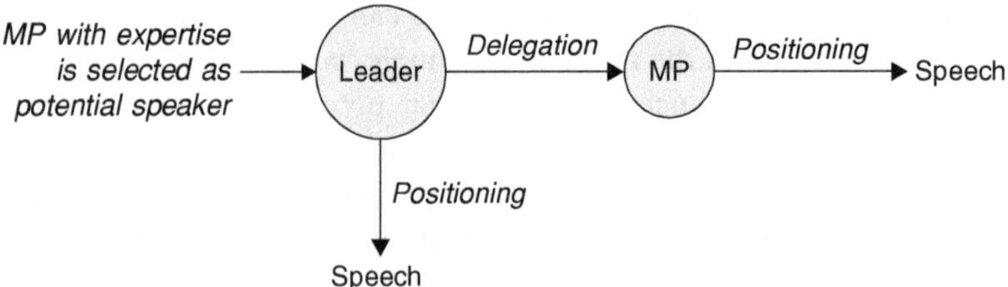

Figure 1.3 Overview of the strategic delegation game of parliamentary speech

Formally, the parliamentary party is composed of n backbenchers and one leader, each of whom has an ideal point in a one-dimensional policy space. Each backbencher M_i has an ideal point $x_i \in \Re^1$. The party leader L's ideal point x_L is set to 0 without loss of generality; it is assumed to represent the official party policy. The game starts when the party delegation is allocated speaking time according to the parliamentary rules of procedure. First, a potential speaker from within the party delegation is identified. The recognition rule is neutral and a member is selected at random – every member M_i is recognized with equal probability p. After having observed the chosen M's identity, the party leader L chooses either to deliver a speech on behalf of the party, x_S^L, or to delegate this task to the member M who delivers a speech x_S^M. We assume that party leaders will know with certainty the ideal point of the party member. If L chooses to deliver a speech, he or she will advocate the official party policy on the floor of parliament, his or her own position x_L. If L decides to delegate the task of speechmaking, party member M delivers a speech that contains a policy message located between M's and L's ideal points, $x_S^M \in [x_M, x_L]$. In other words, a party member will propagate his or her ideal point, the party leader's ideal point, or something in between.

1.5.1 *Utility functions of party leaders and backbenchers*

A member's position may differ from the leadership's position because of his or her personal preference or because of the preference of the electorate. Members seek to advocate their preferred policy alternatives, while, at the same time, they try to secure access to political office. Members' behavior on the floor of parliament also has an impact on their prospects of receiving support from the party leadership.

If a party member is a reliable defender of the official party line, the member can expect promotion or other benefits in the parliament or in the party and support from the leadership in the next election. However, members face a trade-off between these two goals. For some, the promotion of their favored policy alternative is clearly more important. These members will value expressing their preferred policy alternative over toeing the party line. For others, advancement in parliament or the party is a more desirable goal, in which case they will downplay their individual opinions and put greater weight on the party message in their speeches. We capture the trade-off between policy and office through an MP-specific weight parameter. The party member's utility function is as follows:

$$U_M = -\lambda_M(x_S^i - x_M)^2 - (1 - \lambda_M)(x_S^i - x_L)^2, \qquad (1.1)$$

where x_S^i is the position of the speech delivered by $i \in \{L, M\}$, $\lambda_M \in (0, 1]$ is the weight the member places on deviations from his or her own policy position in parliamentary speeches, and $1 - \lambda_M$ is the weight placed on deviations from the leader's position. When the leader delegates, the speech x_S is delivered by the member, who cares both about the degree to which a speech he or she delivers deviates from his or her own position, as well as the degree to which the speech deviates from the party leader's position. A member may value party unity to the extent that it helps with his or her reelection bid. The party leadership is likely to reward members who display behavior that fosters party unity. To receive benefits from the party, such as leadership positions within the parliament or the party, party support for a reelection bid, or a safe position on the party list in a closed-list electoral system, the member must show support for the party's official position. Party support for a member is likely to increase as a member's floor speeches display greater support for the party leadership's position. Finally, when the leader does not delegate, the position of the speech x_S will equal the leader's position $x_L = 0$. In this case, the member suffers a utility loss $-\lambda_M x_M^2$ because he or she is unable to advocate his or her position at all.

Leaders trade off the goal of maintaining a clear party message with the goal of public visibility.[10] Intraparty disagreement can damage the

[10] Parties may maintain the party message and still allow members to express some diversity of preferences on the floor. In fact, party leaders may wish

party by weakening the leadership, pitting one party faction against another, and causing confusion about the party message in the media and the electorate, all of which can cost the party votes at election time. Moreover, if members continuously speak out against the official party line, the leadership of the party may be destabilized or challenged. However, the party leadership also has an incentive to allow party members to take the floor as policy experts. They help the party build and maintain a public profile independent of the actual party platform. A party can only build a public profile if its members are visible, have developed a recognizable profile, and can campaign on a proven track record of accomplishments and activity. The goals of party unity and public exposure are difficult to achieve simultaneously. If leaders deliver parliamentary speeches themselves, they ensure party unity but they reduce the public exposure of their backbencher MPs and thus the party profile. If leaders delegate all speechmaking to their MPs, they raise the profile of the party's MPs but put party unity at risk. In fact, both goals are achievable simultaneously only if one of two conditions is met. First, leaders and MPs have exactly the same preferences, an unlikely event given that parties are heterogeneous collective actors. Second, even when MPs disagree with the party leadership, they defend the party policy exactly as leaders would want them to. The latter possibility will be explored by our model. We represent the leader's trade-off between party unity and party profile as a leader-specific weight parameter. The party leader's utility function is as follows:

$$U_L = -\pi_L(x_S^i - x_L)^2 - c_L + I_{L=D}(c_L + (1 - \pi_L)e_L), \qquad (1.2)$$

where x_S^i is the position of the speech delivered by $i \in \{L, M\}$, $\pi_L \in (0, 1]$ is the weight the party leader places on party unity, $1 - \pi_L$ is the weight the leader places on the public exposure of the party, $e_L > 0$ is the public profile benefit received by the leader if the leader

members to express some diversity of views to appeal to a wider set of voters. This interpretation is also in line with our model. For large, catch-all parties, the party "label" may need to be sufficiently flexible to appeal to a relatively diverse set of voters. However, in systems in which party "labels" are important, we expect party leaders to carefully monitor and control any expression of diversity to make sure it does not contradict the party's core message. Party leaders will manage the party message to ensure that it is sufficiently flexible and yet coherent.

delegates to a member ($I_{L=D} = 1$), and $c_L > 0$ is the cost that the leader pays if he or she decides to deliver the speech. If the leader gives a speech, $x_S = x_L = 0$, there is no loss to party unity. However, there is a loss if the leader delegates and the member propagates a position other than x_L. All else equal, the leader prefers to delegate the task of speechmaking to the member. The public exposure benefit e_L is positive. Members gain experience on the floor of parliament, honing their skills for future party leadership roles. The cost to the leadership of giving a speech c_L is also positive. Preparing a speech requires time and effort that could be better spent on other activities. Leaders are unlikely to be experts on all topics, so speech preparation means acquiring the necessary information, something specialist MPs are already likely to possess.

1.5.2 Equilibria

The game is sequential. First, a member, chosen at random, is recognized as a potential speaker.[11] The party leader then learns the policy preference of the selected MP, x_M, as well as the weight, λ_M, he or she places on expressing his policy position. The leader decides whether to delegate the task of speechmaking, and, if delegated to, the member selects the position of his or her speech and gives the speech on the floor. We examine the conditions under which the leader will delegate the task of speechmaking to the member. The equilibrium concept is subgame perfection.

Proposition: *If the party leader delegates, the member gives a speech* $x_S^* = \lambda_M x_M$. *Delegation occurs if and only if:*

$$x_M \leq \sqrt{\frac{e_L(1-\pi_L)+c_L}{\lambda_M^2 \pi_L}}. \tag{1.3}$$

The proof is in the Appendix. If delegated, the member selects x_S to maximize his or her utility. A member who solely values his or her

[11] In reality, some MPs are more likely to be experts on some issues than others. For simplicity, we assume that expertise within policy areas is distributed across the entire ideological spectrum of the party, but we later control for it in the empirical analysis.

own position ($\lambda_M = 1$) will give a speech at his or her own ideal point. A member who highly values the position of the party (λ_M close to 0) will give a speech very close to 0, the leader's ideal point x_L. A member who values his or her own and the party's position will give a moderate speech. The leader, knowing the location of the speech that the member will give if delegated time, must decide whether to delegate time. He or she does so only when the condition in equation 1.3 holds. When the ideological distance between the member and the leader crosses the threshold, the leader does not delegate to prevent the member from delivering a speech that differs substantially from the official party policy. In this case, the leader's utility is simply $-c_L$, and the member's is $-\lambda_M x_M^2$.

1.5.3 Comparative statics

These equilibria inform us about the type of party member to whom a party leader is likely to delegate floor time and the position of the speech the member is likely to give. When a member holds an ideological position sufficiently distant from the position of the party leadership, the leader will not delegate floor time to avoid a public intraparty disagreement and will instead give the speech him- or herself. This result, however, is mitigated by the weight that party leaders and members place on party unity. In political systems in which party unity is valued less, the party leader will delegate to a more ideologically diverse set of members. The model furthermore suggests that unless a member shares the exact same position as the leader or does not care about expressing his or her own policy position at all, a member's speech will never perfectly match the position of the speech the leader would choose to give him- or herself. Nevertheless, the leader is willing to sustain some policy loss to give members public exposure and to avoid the costs of preparing the speeches him- or herself.

In instances when members place great weight on signaling an individual position over the position of the party (λ_M approaches 1), delegation becomes less likely. The same is true when a party leader places greater emphasis on party unity rather than public exposure of MPs (π_L approaches 1). Party leaders are more likely to delegate speaking time to members as the benefits to the party from providing members with public exposure increases (e_L becomes larger). This means that political systems that favor personal vote-seeking behavior of legislators should exhibit higher participation rates of MPs on the floor. As it becomes more costly for the leadership to prepare the speech (c_L becomes larger), delegation is also more likely. This can happen when the MP has specific policy expertise required to convey the party position effectively.

The model thus explains the vastly different party responses to rebel speech in the previous illustrations from the UK House of Commons and the German Bundestag. In the United Kingdom, where the electoral system generates incentives for members to build up name recognition and cultivate a personal vote, members place greater weight on signaling a personal, rather than party, position, and party leaders place less weight on party unity. Backbenchers have the opportunity to take the floor, and it is not a particularly remarkable event when a backbencher speaks against the party position. In Germany, electoral politics means parties place much more emphasis on unity and backbenchers are expected to toe the party line. The benefits to the party from backbenchers gaining public exposure is minimal. Backbenchers with dissenting views are generally kept off the floor. In the instance described earlier, rebels came to the floor only when the president of the Bundestag changed these rules. The parties' angry reactions to the dissident speech demonstrate the degree to which parties feel they must maintain control over their speaker lists.

1.6 Summary

This chapter has put forward a theory of parliamentary debate that focuses on intraparty politics and electoral incentives. In doing so, we move beyond current, largely normative, literature on parliamentary debate, as well as literature on parliamentary behavior that focuses primarily on roll-call voting. Rather than viewing parliamentary speech as a tool for altering policy outcomes, we see it as a tool for communication between MPs, parties, and the electorate. Unless we view parliamentary debate as part of strategic party competition, it is impossible to explain the wide variety of forms that debates take on cross-nationally, or even why MPs spend time on debates at all. Our model generates testable implications for the levels of partisan control over debate participation, who participates, and what they say. The next chapter further examines the empirical implications of our model for various political systems, and Part II of this book offers tests of this model, first by focusing on cross-national comparisons of parliamentary rules and then by examining debate participation in a variety of parliaments.

2 *Empirical implications*

The theoretical model presented in the previous chapter generates empirical implications for the nature of parliamentary speech. The model makes predictions regarding the status of the speaker – backbencher or leader – the position expressed in speeches, and the degree to which backbenchers ought to make concessions to the official party position in their speeches. The parameters of the model vary according to electoral incentives and party pressures created by the political system. In addition, parameters may vary across members within a single parliament as members face different incentives resulting from variation in candidate selection mechanisms and – in mixed-member electoral systems – different types of electoral mandates. In this chapter, we explore the implications of our formal model by varying the parameter values to match the incentives created by different electoral environments. We examine both country-level variables, such as electoral institutions, and variables that may vary across members within a single country, such as candidate selection methods and varying electoral mandates.

In a nutshell, our theory suggests that behavior in parliament varies with incentives for personal vote seeking and the demands the political system creates for party unity. In systems in which members and parties benefit when backbenchers develop name recognition among voters, backbenchers ought to take the floor more often, and they ought to be more willing to buck party leadership in their speeches. In systems in which incentives to generate personal name recognition are lower, party leaders ought to dominate parliamentary debate, and backbenchers ought to toe the party line when granted speaking time. We now explore various aspects of political systems according to the incentives they create for members to seek a personal vote and generate name recognition and then discuss how these incentives affect parliamentary debate.

2.1 Country-level variables – electoral systems

2.1.1 Majoritarian electoral systems – strong personal vote seeking

Ballot structure is an important variable determining a member's need to develop name recognition. When the candidate's name, rather than the party name, is the most salient feature on the ballot paper, the candidate must ensure that voters know who he or she is (Norris, 2004, chap. 10). Majoritarian electoral systems of all stripes tend to place individual candidates' names before parties on the ballot papers, making candidate name recognition particularly important for reelection. Ballot papers in the single-member district (SMD) plurality elections in the United States, the United Kingdom, Canada, and France all list candidate names before party names. The same also holds for the alternative vote system used in Australia. Therefore, both backbenchers and their party leadership in these systems have an incentive to ensure that voters know who their representatives are and that these voters know their representatives are standing up for their views in the legislature. Nevertheless, there are differences across major majoritarian systems, depending on regime type.

The electoral independence between the legislature and executive in presidential systems means that party leaders do not place as much weight on party unity as they do in parliamentary systems. Parties do not need to be cohesive to secure the confidence of the government, and party labels are less important because each MP runs his or her own reelection campaign. The strong electoral connection in the US Congress (Mayhew, 1974) means that party leaders do not have a strong incentive to interfere with the speeches of legislators, even if they are ideologically at odds with the party position. There is ample empirical evidence that floor participation is unregulated. For instance, Hall has shown that members of the House of Representatives participate more actively on the floor "the stronger the interest of a district subconstituency in the legislation" (Hall, 1998, p.198). This suggests that members of Congress explicitly take into account the interests of their constituencies in speeches. Hall shows that this effect is particularly strong for agricultural issues: "when it comes to representing cows, if not constituents, House members can hardly be called unresponsive" in floor debates (Hall, 1998, p. 199). Maltzman and Sigelman (1996) find that rank-and-file members of the House give significantly more one- and five-minute speeches than ranking committee members and that ideologically more extreme legislators do the same. Maltzman and Sigelman argue that rank-and-file members typically have fewer opportunities to affect the legislative agenda and that legislative speeches offer them the opportunity to do so. This finding is in line with what we would expect in our comparative theory of parliamentary speech. Similarly, ideological extremists use speeches to promote their views in a majoritarian system.[1] Yet some research suggests that the party leadership nevertheless attempts to orchestrate unified speech campaigns in the House (Harris, 2005). Focusing on a single party – the Democrats – Harris argues that the position chosen by members of Congress in speeches are driven largely by individualistic incentives, even when party leaders make strong efforts to coordinate the party message. In instances of coordination, party members with safe seats and with ideologically more extreme positions are unwilling to support the party message. In short, although party leaders may be able to exert some control over the party message in floor speeches, they do not prevent rebels from taking the floor. Others have shown that legislators' awareness of the electoral impact of speech is also evident in speeches delivered by US senators. Quinn and coauthors have demonstrated that senators put more emphasis on symbolic and social issues in their speeches when elections approach, whereas retiring senators give fewer such speeches (Quinn et al., 2010, p. 224). We are unlikely to find similar results, however, in parliamentary systems in which parties are able to exert greater control over their members and governments have significant influence over the parliamentary agenda. In the context of the speech delegation model, a presidential system with majoritarian electoral institutions is reflected in actors' utility functions in the following manner: MPs place a high value on their own policy position (high λ), whereas party leaders moderately value their MPs' exposure (moderate e) and place low weight on party unity (low π).

[1] In their multivariate analysis, Maltzman and Sigelman also find evidence that party leaders give more speeches, a result that appears to be at odds with our prediction. But they suggest that this result was driven primarily by two highly active party leaders, Gingrich and Bonior, who demonstrated "heavy use" of one-minute speeches and special orders (Maltzman and Sigelman, 1996, p. 826).

The mutual dependence between the legislature and the executive in parliamentary systems creates somewhat different motivations for legislators. This is true even when one considers majoritarian electoral systems, thus holding the effects of electoral institutions constant. Legislative parties in parliamentary systems need to support a government, and governing parties will generally place more value on unity than parties in a presidential system do. The same should be true for opposition parties whose MPs are in "standby mode" for government and constantly present alternatives to the government's program. Nevertheless, these stronger incentives for party unity should be moderated by electoral institutions that emphasize legislators' incentives to seek personal votes. In parliamentary systems with electoral politics that emphasize personal vote seeking and name recognition over party unity, parties are likely to value public exposure of backbenchers more, and place less weight on maintaining party unity. Such effects are strongest in electoral systems with single-member districts, such as the United Kingdom's first-past-the-post system, Australia's alternative vote system, or France's majoritarian runoff system. Members also need to place more emphasis on their own positions and less on the position of the party. Although the party can help get a member elected, the member must pander to his or her electoral district rather than the party. The party has comparatively less to offer members in these candidate-centered systems, but the control of parliamentary offices can create advancement incentives for legislators that make parties in these systems appear more disciplined (Kam, 2009). Although the party leadership may try to retain more control than they would in a presidential system, we still expect that leaders delegate speaking time to their membership to allow them to make a name for themselves and to express the opinions of their district. In the context of the speech delegation model, a parliamentary system with majoritarian electoral rules is reflected in actors' utility functions in the following manner: MPs place a moderate to high value on their own policy position (moderate–high λ), whereas party leaders moderately value their MPs' exposure (moderate e) and place a moderate weight on party unity (moderate π).

2.1.2 *Open-list PR – moderate personal vote seeking*

Open-list proportional systems, under certain conditions, can also create incentives for personal vote-seeking activities to generate candidate name recognition. Party reputation is often important in open-list systems, and party names may feature prominently on the ballot. However, these systems allow voters to indicate a preference for individual candidates, rather than simply voting for a party list, as is the case in closed-list PR systems (discussed later). Nevertheless, institutional variation across open-list systems leads to a range of different predictions about how these systems affect legislative behavior. Carey and Shugart (1995) have argued that intraparty competition on open lists – and, therefore, the incentive to seek a personal vote – increases with district magnitude (see also Shugart, Valdini, and Suominen, 2005; Chang and Golden, 2007). Legislators compete for preference votes, making them more likely to engage in activities that cater to targeted groups of voters in the electoral district. Similar intraparty competition occurs when voters only cast a single vote in multiseat districts, such as in Japan before 1993 under the single nontransferrable vote (SNTV) system (Cox and Thies, 1998) and as remains the case in Ireland under the single transferable vote (Marsh, 2000; S. Martin, 2010). To distinguish themselves from their partisan colleagues and to develop personal reputations, legislators in systems that encourage intraparty competition may make use of different parliamentary activities, including various forms of legislative speech (S. Martin, 2011).

Yet within open-list systems, there is variation with regard to the ability of voters to express preferences. In some systems, preference votes are required; in others, they are optional (Katz, 1986). Sometimes preference votes affect the order of the candidates on the list, sometimes they do not. Thus, in practice, we should observe different incentives for speechmaking depending on the exact institutional nature of the open-list system. Open-list systems should create incentives similar to single-member district majoritarian rules when district magnitude is high and voters are required to indicate preferences (moderate to high λ and e, and lower π). On the other hand, we would expect incentives regarding legislative behavior to resemble closed-list systems when the district magnitude is lower, voters have an option to vote for the party list as presented to them, and parties have centralized procedures of generating these lists, rendering preference votes relatively meaningless (low λ and e, high π).

Lastly, just as with SMD electoral systems, incentives for partisan control within open-list PR countries also vary across regime type.

Several Latin American countries, including Brazil, Chile, and Peru, combine open-list PR electoral systems with presidential regimes (other countries including Argentina, Costa Rica, and Ecuador, combine presidentialism with closed lists discussed later). These presidential open-list PR systems are particularly personalistic, and congressional parties are often relatively undisciplined, especially compared with European parliamentary parties (Ames, 1995, 2001; Carey, 2009), although they do tend to display higher unity on roll calls than US parties (Morgenstern, 2004, p. 46). Moreover, presidentialism has an independent effect on party discipline above and beyond the effect of intraparty competition generated by open-list electoral systems (Carey, 2009, pp. 150–153). Thus, in presidential open-list systems, we would expect parties to exercise relatively little control over speaking time – perhaps more than is exercised in the US system but less than is exercised in most parliamentary systems, with the possible exception of the Westminster-style parliaments.

2.1.3 Closed-list PR – weak personal vote seeking

Parties in closed-list PR electoral systems, such as Israel and Italy, place high value on party unity as voters rely heavily on party "labels" to make up their mind come election time. Party names feature prominently on the ballot, oftentimes followed by the names of a few top party leaders. Voters rarely know the names of the party backbenchers representing them. A legislator's personal reputation and public exposure do not bring parties many benefits because electoral politics is less about the personalities of individual parliamentarians than about voters' perception of parties in these systems. This tends to be true both in presidential and parliamentary systems. Parties in closed-list PR presidential regimes, such as Argentina, have tended to display higher degrees of unity than parties in open-list PR presidential systems, approaching levels found in parliamentary systems (Morgenstern, 2004).

In terms of our model, party leaders in closed-list PR systems are likely to place a high weight on party unity (high π) and have an exposure reward close to zero (very low e). Likewise, members of parliament are likely to place greater weight on the party position than on their own position (low λ). The party controls access to most things that members value. Without the support of the party, reelection is impossible. It is also nearly impossible to make a name for oneself in politics without climbing the party ranks. All this entails placing the party position over one's own. The leadership will be selective in who they allow onto the floor.

2.2 Within-country variables – electoral tiers and candidate selection

Of course, country-level variables affect parliamentary behavior, but in many countries, members serving in the same parliament may face very different incentives. In countries using mixed-member electoral systems, some members of parliament are elected one way (e.g. SMD plurality), whereas other members of the same parliament are elected in a different manner (e.g. a closed party list). Likewise, parties within the same system may use very different candidate selection mechanisms, giving party leaders more or less control over their members. We now investigate the implications of our model for within-country variation in members' behavior.

2.2.1 Electoral tiers in mixed-member electoral systems

We begin our exploration of within-country variation by looking more closely at the incentives created by the mixed-member electoral systems. In these systems, some MPs are elected off closed-party lists using a proportional electoral formula; in others, they are elected from single-member districts. Many consider these systems to have considerable advantages – they provide "the best of both worlds" (Shugart and Wattenberg, 2003) by generating "(1) constituent ties to voters in their localities via nominal representation in single-seat districts, and (2) relatively strong and cohesive nationally focused parties promoted by the election of many members from the party lists" (Shugart, 2003, p. 26). Others, however, point out that party and MP incentives in SMDs within a mixed system are not the same as those in a pure SMD plurality system (Cox and Schoppa, 2002; Ferrara and Herron, 2005; Karp, 2009).

Moreover, there are two types of mixed systems – mixed-member proportional (MMP) and mixed-member majoritarian (MMM) – which create different incentives for parties and members. In both MMP and MMM, parties draw up candidate lists that cannot be altered by voters, and they also run candidates in single-member districts. Voters vote twice. First, they cast a ballot for a closed-party list, and then they vote for a candidate in their single-member electoral district. In MMP systems, such as Germany and New Zealand, although the winners of the SMDs are guaranteed a seat in the new parliament, the SMD votes do not determine a party's overall seat share. Instead, parties' seat shares are proportional to the number of votes they receive on the list vote. Party leaders' incentives are, therefore, similar to those in a pure closed-list system; they wish to maximize the number of ballots cast for their party list (Bawn and Thies, 2003). To do so, they place significant weight on party unity.

Backbenchers in MMP systems face different incentives depending on whether they are elected off the list or from a district, and, as a result, parties may exert more control over some members than others. Members elected off the list face incentives similar to backbenchers in any other closed-list PR system, and they are likely to weigh the party's position quite highly. Their reelection chances increase when the party wins a higher percentage of list votes. Members elected out of a single-member district, on the other hand, have a seat regardless of how many votes are cast for their party's list. They simply need to retain voters' support in their district. These members are likely to place greater weight on their own preferences than on the preference of the party. Because the party places high value on unity, party leaders may seek to exercise more control over MPs elected from single-member districts, who have a greater incentive to contradict the party message to attract voters, than those elected off the list.[2] Thus, by looking at these two types of candidates for election in MMP systems, we can generate predictions by altering only one of the parameters of the model, λ. Members elected from SMDs should place greater value on their own policy position (have a higher λ) than those members elected off the list, and party leaders should seek to exercise greater control over these SMD MPs.

This contrasts with MMM systems, in which a fixed portion of the parliament is elected out of single-member districts, and the remainder

[2] Of course, even candidates elected out of SMDs care about the overall number of seats their party wins. They wish to see their party have more influence over policy and would like their party to join the government. However, their personal fate is less tied to the party's overall electoral outcome. Moreover, they are generally dependent on their party to run them in their district.

of MPs are elected from closed party lists. This system is currently used in Japan, Hungary, and Lithuania and was used in Italy from 1993 to 2005 and in Russia from 1993 to 2007. As under MMP, voters in MMM systems cast two votes – a party list vote and a district vote. However, the list votes do not compensate for any disproportionality created by the district votes. Thus, the incentives MMM systems create for party leaders are different from the incentives created by MMP systems (Bawn and Thies, 2003; Thames and Edwards, 2006). In these systems, members elected out of SMDs ought to be subject to fewer partisan constraints, and thus ought to behave more like members elected in pure SMD systems.[3] Here, we would expect to see SMD MPs take the floor somewhat more often and be more willing to speak their mind than list MPs, who are completely dependent on the party for reelection.

2.2.2 Candidate selection mechanism

Lastly, we examine the expectations of our model with respect to candidate selection mechanisms. Within a single regime, even members elected using the exact same electoral rules in the exact same district may face differing incentives if their parties employ different means for selecting candidates to run for office. In some parties, candidate selection is highly centralized and remains the purview of high-ranking party leaders, whereas in others, it may be more decentralized. It may be handled by local party branches or through within-party elections (e.g. primaries). In more centralized systems, members are beholden to the central party leadership for their seats, whereas in decentralized systems, members may have to seek the support of local leaders or voters rather than the central party leadership.

Although some literature has explored the nature of candidate selection mechanisms and their effects on member behavior and democratic representation (e.g. Gallagher and Marsh, 1988; Rahat and Hazan, 2001; Hazan and Rahat, 2006; Rahat, Hazan, and Katz, 2008), intra-party selection mechanisms remain difficult to study in comparative perspective. Selection mechanisms are often determined by party rules

[3] However, the degree to which behavior among the types of MPs actually differs may depend on other variables as well, including whether they ran both in a district and on the list, the relative safety of their district seat, and their career path (Herron, 2002).

rather than election law, making them difficult to track and document. They can change from party to party and from election to election. Thus, although they are no doubt an important electoral variable in influencing member behavior, selection mechanisms are often poorly measured. We examine the effects of candidate selection by looking at parliamentary behavior in the European Parliament, the directly elected legislative body of the European Union. The European Parliament provides a good case for looking at the effects of candidate selection because all members are elected using relatively similar rules – some form of proportional representation – but variation exists in the degree to which parties exercise central control over their members, and this variation has already been shown to affect member behavior (Hix, 2004).

2.3 Effects of electoral incentives on debate participation

Figure 2.1 plots the simulated positions expressed in parliamentary speeches and the type of speaker (MP or party leader) as a function of the selected member's distance from the party leadership and the incentives created by the electoral rules described earlier. In all systems, as the member's position deviates from the leader's position, the MP's speech also deviates from the speech the leader would give. However, the MP's position expressed in the speech also deviates from his or her own position (because $\lambda < 1$). If a member were to completely disregard his or her own position and only give speeches expressing the leader's position, the speech position line would be horizontal at zero. On the other hand, if a member were to completely disregard the party position, the speech position line would be a 45-degree line (depicted in the figure by the gray line). For a given ideological distance between the MP and the leader (shown on the horizontal axis), the deviation of this speech from the 45-degree line represents the member's concession to the leadership. Once a particular ideological threshold is crossed, depicted in the figure by the dashed vertical line, the leader stops delegating to the member and gives the speech him- or herself. The scenarios differ, first, in how much the MP moderates his or her speech (denoted by the deviation of the black from the gray diagonal line) and, second, in the point at which the party leader intervenes (denoted by the location of the dashed vertical line).

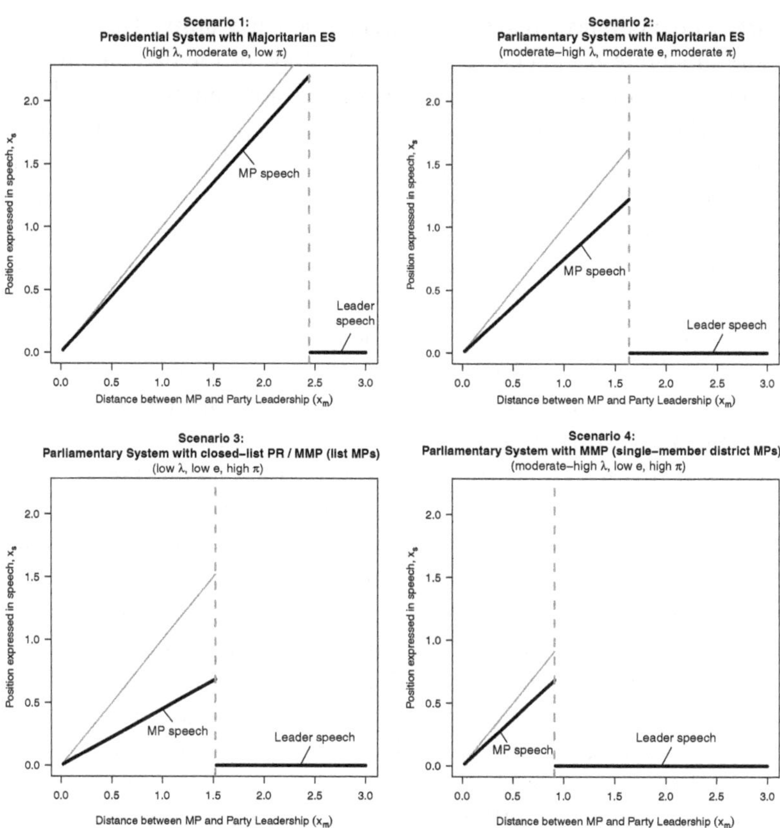

Figure 2.1 Comparison of institutional scenarios

In the first scenario, representing a system with high personal vote-seeking incentives such as the United States, the party leadership has few incentives to intervene because there is little weight placed on party unity. A member's speech will correspond closely to his or her true ideology,[4] meaning he or she barely needs to moderate the content of the speech to get the leader to delegate to him or her. In scenario 2, representing moderately high personal vote-seeking systems such as Westminster parliamentary democracy, the MP places slightly reduced weight on his or her own position compared with scenario 1, and the

4 Or at least the ideology of the constituents with whom they are attempting to communicate.

party leadership now places more weight on party unity. This yields a more moderate backbencher speech (the slope of the diagonal line is flatter) and a threshold value that leads the leadership to cease delegation earlier relative to scenario 1. Scenario 3 represents low personal vote-seeking systems, such as parliamentary closed-list PR (and those MPs elected off the list in MMP electoral systems). Here the leader allows the member to express an even smaller range of positions on the floor, and the member moderates his or her speech even more compared with scenario 2. Leaders are less likely to delegate to potential rebels. Open-list systems would fall somewhere in between scenarios 2 and 3, depending on the incentives to build personal reputations. Scenario 4 represents those MPs elected in single-member districts in parliamentary MMP systems. Comparing this scenario with those MPs elected off the list (scenario 3), party leaders are less willing to delegate speeches to district MPs. Members elected out of SMDs are less willing to moderate their speeches as their ideology deviates from that of the leadership. Independent of whether the MP was elected off the list or from a SMD, leaders are only willing to accept an MP's speech that deviates so far from the party line. When faced with two backbenchers, one elected from an SMD and the other elected off the list, with the exact same ideological distance from the leadership, there is a range of ideological positions in which the leadership is willing to delegate to the list member but not to the SMD member. Consequently, single-member district MPs in a MMP system will display parliamentary speech patterns very different from single-member district MPs in a majoritarian system, but they will also differ from the list candidates in their own system. A nonstrategic perspective would predict that single-member district MPs should deliver *more* speeches than their list counterparts because of their stronger electoral connection, but our model suggests otherwise.

Returning to the examples of dissenting speech in the United Kingdom and Germany from the previous chapter, John McDonnell, in his "Heathrow" speech, would have faced constraints similar to those depicted in scenario 2. Given his disagreement with the leadership, he took a position in his speech as close to his ideal point line as possible (the gray diagonal) and, despite his rebellious views, he managed to avoid party punishment (he was punished by the Speaker for removing the mace but not by his party for his rebellion). In fact, he profited electorally by gaining the support from an activist group that campaigned against the Heathrow expansion. The German example falls in scenarios 3 and 4. Party leaders intervened in the speaker lists of their party and included only MPs who were willing to support the official party line – in fact, the leaders of both the Christian Democratic Union/Christian Social Union (CDU/CSU) and the Free Democratic Party (FDP) parliamentary groups were among those who spoke. The dissenting speeches by German MPs Willsch and Schäffler, however, are not on the equilibrium path according to our model and should never have happened. Klaus-Peter Willsch, the CDU rebel, was elected to the Bundestag in 2009 out of a single-member district rather than off the party list. He faced the constraints depicted in scenario 4 – he had a high incentive to speak his mind, but the party had a particularly strong incentive to keep him off the floor. Schäffler was elected off the party list and faced the constraints depicted in scenario 3. These MPs' views were clearly beyond the threshold at which the parties cut off delegation of speaking time. They never would have been aired publicly in parliament if the president of the Bundestag had not gone against standard parliamentary procedure by granting the MPs extra time. Thus, our model explains the party leaders' allocation of speaking time, as well as their angry reaction to President Lammert's actions.

2.4 Summary

This chapter has laid out the expectations of our model for a variety of political systems that create different incentives for parties to control the behavior of their MPs. In systems in which party leaders and their MPs share an incentive to allow MPs to create a name for themselves and connect with voters, party leaders will exercise less control over MPs' access to speaking time in parliament. In systems in which presenting a coherent party "brand" is more important for winning seats than individual name recognition, our model predicts that party leaders will try to exercise significantly more control over the allocation of floor time and the message that MPs convey in speeches. We have, therefore, provided a theoretical link among political institutions, electoral incentives, and the structure of parliamentary debate. The following chapter lays out the data and empirical strategy we use for testing these theoretical claims.

3 *Research design*

Our theory has implications for how parliaments organize debates, to what extent party leaders monitor and control the allocation of speaking time within the party, the level of participation of backbenchers and leaders, and the level of dissent of MPs. To test these implications, we employ a research design that encompasses a wide variety of data sources from different political systems at different levels of analysis. Our study combines cross-national analyses of parliamentary institutions and party rules, party-level analyses of speech patterns across legislative terms, and MP-level analysis of participation in parliamentary debates. This chapter provides a detailed explanation of the various cases, data, and methods we use to test our theory.

3.1 Empirical strategy: an overview

We begin with an overview of our empirical strategy, presented in Table 3.1. The table also shows how each chapter and case allows us to identify the effect of the weight party leaders and backbenchers place on party unity (π and λ in our theoretical model). We start in Chapter 4 with a cross-national investigation comparing the procedures for allocating speaking time in the parliaments of advanced industrialized democracies. We complement our analysis of parliamentary rules of procedure with data on party rules gathered from experts within each party in 2011. The goal of this party survey is to learn more about the internal rules of parties regarding the monitoring of backbenchers' legislative speeches, as well as to glean information about the ideological cohesion of parliamentary party delegations.

In Chapter 5, we examine the variation in debate participation in two parliaments – the UK House of Commons and the German Bundestag. We take the United Kingdom as an example for a Westminster system and Germany as an example of a multiparty parliament with proportional representation electoral rules. Within both

Table 3.1. ***Empirical strategy of the book***

Chapter	Level of analysis	Primary data	Political system	Time period	Identification
(4)	Country & Party	Parliamentary procedures	Cross-national	2011	Coding of rules
		Party survey			Common questionnaire
(5)	Party & MP	Debate participation	Germany	1976–1998, 2005–2009	MMP, MP panel, candidate survey
			UK	1979–2010	Plurality, MP panel, candidate survey
(6)	MP	Debate on fiscal crisis	Germany & UK	2008–2009	Identical policy context
(7)	Party & MP	Debate participation	European Parliament	1999–2004	Candidate selection rules, voting defection
(8)	MP	Budget debates	New Zealand	1991–1999	Electoral system change, voting defection, MP panel

countries, we first conduct party-level analyses, looking at the ratio of leader to backbencher speeches under the assumption that at least some level of latent intraparty conflict exists. Next, we implement a panel design to examine whether members change their speaking patterns when their leadership status changes. Finally, we identify the level in conflict between individual MPs and backbenchers through candidate survey data and estimate the effect of disagreement on speechmaking. Moreover, in Germany we are able to examine the effects of different electoral incentives by comparing MPs elected in the different electoral tiers of the MMP system.

In Chapter 6, we examine MP dissent both inside and outside parliament on the fiscal stimulus packages negotiated in Germany and the United Kingdom during the financial crisis of 2008 and 2009, providing us with a similar context in terms of both policy and timing. On these highly salient bills, we are able to examine how backbenchers dissent on votes, in parliamentary speeches, and in the media. Chapter 7 turns attention to the European Parliament, a case that allows us to explore how different candidate selection mechanisms affect behavior within a single parliament. We also examine the relationship between voting defection and speechmaking. Finally, Chapter 8 presents data on speech participation on budget debates in New Zealand during the 1990s, a period in which New Zealand underwent significant electoral change, switching from a Westminster first-past-the-post system to a proportional system similar to Germany's. By tracing behavioral changes in the set of MPs who served in parliament both pre- and postreform, we demonstrate the almost immediate impact of electoral laws on behavioral patterns of rebel MPs, identified through roll-call vote defections during the prereform period. Taken together, the results across the subsequent chapters show not only that parliamentary debates are structured differently across political systems but that parties and MPs participate in legislative debate according to our speech delegation model introduced in the first two chapters of this book.

3.2 Cross-national comparison and party survey

As a first test of our theory, we examine rules regarding speaking time in the parliaments of a wide variety of advanced industrialized democracies. According to our theory, rules governing access to the floor of parliament are endogenous to the personal vote-seeking incentives generated by a country's electoral system. We expect countries with electoral systems that generate greater incentives for personal vote seeking to have parliamentary rules that make it easier for backbenchers to take the floor without formally seeking the approval of their party leaders. Thus, we examine parliamentary rules regarding the allocation of speaking time and code the degree of control they give to party leaders. We also code the incentives for personal vote seeking generated by the electoral system.

In addition to parliamentary rules that dictate how parties and their members gain access to the floor, parties develop their own internal rules, both formal and informal, about how floor time is delegated to their membership and how they deal with members who deviate from a party position in a speech. Parties rarely publish these rules, making them difficult to analyze. To learn more about such intraparty rules and practices regarding parliamentary debates, we sent a questionnaire to parliamentary group administrators and party leaders between March and November 2011 in 25 advanced democracies. Of the 152 parliamentary parties contacted, 45 returned the questionnaire. These parties are listed in Table 3.2. The resulting response rate of 29% is similar to response rates found in elite surveys (Stone and Simas, 2010). In total, at least one parliamentary party from 19 of the 25 countries responded to our request to fill out the survey.[1] We first identified MPs with parliamentary leadership roles or senior parliamentary party administrators on publicly accessible parliamentary websites. We then sent invitation e-mails to those contacts asking them to fill out the questionnaire through an online survey facility. The questionnaire was made available in English, French, and German. E-mail and letter reminders with a paper copy of the questionnaire were sent out several weeks after the initial contact. In cases of nonresponse, we also called the parliamentary parties to determine a qualified contact within the group and resent the questionnaire by e-mail.

In the next chapter, we examine these survey responses to understand how parties organize parliamentary debates and allocate

[1] Despite multiple reminders and possibilities to fill out the survey online or on paper, we unfortunately did not receive responses from parliamentary parties in the following countries: Finland, Luxembourg, Poland, Portugal, Spain, and the United States.

Table 3.2. *Party survey: list of participating parliamentary parties (N = 45)*

Country	Party
Australia	Liberal Party of Australia
Austria	BZÖ
	Grüne
	ÖVP
	SPÖ
Belgium	CD&V
	CDH
	N-VA
	PS
	SP.A
Canada	Bloc Québécois
	New Democratic Party
Czech Republic	Tradice Odpovědnost Prosperita 09 (TOP09)
Denmark	Dansk Folkeparti (Danish People's Party) (DF)
	Socialdemokratiet (Social Democratic Party) (S)
	Socialistisk Folkeparti (Socialist People's Party) (SF)
France	Groupe Socialiste, Radical, Citoyen et divers gauche
Germany	Bündnis90/Die Grünen
	Die Linke
	FDP
	SPD
Hungary	Fidesz – Magyar Polgári Szövetség
Ireland	Fine Gael (FG)
	Páirtí Lucht Oibre (Labour)
Israel	Ha'avoda
	Haatzma'ut
	Habayit Hayehudi (Jewish Home)
	Ra'am-Ta'al
Italy	Lega Nord Padania
Netherlands	VVD
New Zealand	Greens
	NP
Norway	Arbeiderpartiet
	Senterpartiet
	Sosialistisk Venstreparti
Slovenia	SNS
	ZL-SD
Sweden	KD
	MP
Switzerland	CVP/EVP/glp
	Fraktion der Schweizerischen Volkspartei
	Grüne Fraktion
	Sozialdemokratische Fraktion
United Kingdom	Liberal Democrats
	Plaid Cymru

speaking time among their members and to what extent party leaders monitor what MPs say on the floor of parliament. We furthermore report responses of senior party members about their perceived level of ideological heterogeneity within the party and augment the data set by including the type of personal vote incentives in each country. Taken together with information on parliamentary rules, this data set enables a unique cross-national look at the institutions of parliamentary debate.

3.3 Case selection: Germany, the United Kingdom, the European Union, and New Zealand

Although our survey allows us to compare parliamentary and party rules across a wide variety of countries, our theory operates within countries at the level of party and MP. Thus, to adequately test our theory, we must look at the interaction between parties and their MPs *within* specific parliaments. We select parliaments that provide variation on our key independent variables – incentives for party leader control and personal vote seeking – and allow us to test our theory against alternative explanations. Thus, we examine four parliaments in depth: the German Bundestag, the UK House of Commons, the EU's European Parliament, and the New Zealand House of Representatives.

The United Kingdom, Germany, and New Zealand are parliamentary systems, whereas the EU is a hybrid system, most accurately described as a separation-of-powers system, rather than a pure parliamentary or presidential democracy. With regard to electoral incentives, the EP more closely resembles the United Kingdom than Germany; parliamentary parties have a stronger incentive to protect the party label in Germany than in either the United Kingdom or the EP. Thus, on the basis of our theory, we expect German party leaders to strictly control backbenchers, whereas we expect British and EP backbenchers to take the floor more often. The EP furthermore allows us to study how MPs behave when candidate selection mechanisms vary across members.

Moreover, these cases allow us to test our theory against traditional explanations for how parliaments structure debate. Textbooks often separate parliaments into two categories – majoritarian "debate" parliaments and consensus "working" parliaments (Gallagher, Laver, and Mair, 2006, pp. 63–65). The nature of debate in parliament is considered a function of the type of government and political culture.

In majoritarian parliaments, including Westminster systems, a single party tends to control a majority of seats, meaning the government generally does not need to account for the views of the opposition in policy-making. The opposition, therefore, is relegated to speech-making. Alivizatos (1990), for example, describes the Greek parliament – typically controlled by a single-party majority government – as a "forum for 'vague, repetitive and usually outdated monologues"' and debate as "endless lists of speakers who make repetitive speeches which add nothing to what has already been said" (as cited in Gallagher, Laver, and Mair, 2006, p. 63). Likewise, the UK House of Commons is often criticized "as a place of theater rather than a serious working body" where rhetorical abilities may be valued over real substance or policy knowledge (Gallagher, Laver, and Mair, 2006, p. 63).

Political culture is a second plausible explanation. Whereas British political culture is often raucous and confrontational, Scandinavian culture, for example, "emphasizes modesty and conscientious work rather than theatrical self-advertisement" (Gallagher, Laver, and Mair, 2006, p. 65). Parliaments in the Anglo-Saxon world generally tend to witness more lively debate, with applause and jeers from opposing sides of the aisle not uncommon. Continental working parliaments, on the other hand, generally hear more staid, prepared statements. Needless to say, parliamentary web streams from the United Kingdom, Ireland, Canada, and New Zealand make for more entertaining viewing than those from northern Europe (Salmond, 2007).

Parliamentary rules may reinforce these cultural and institutional effects. In Westminster systems, MPs tend to view the ability to state their positions on the floor as a fundamental right. Rather than parties controlling access to the floor, the non-partisan Speaker of the House is responsible for controlling the flow of debate. In "working" parliaments, party leaders dominate debate, and backbenchers are content to participate in the policy process through committee work. Our argument suggests an institutional explanation for the differences in the nature of debate that we see in these parliaments, although it is slightly different from a simple "majoritarian–consensus" or "debate–working" parliament divide. Regardless of the general nature of debate – confrontational versus subdued, raucous versus respectful, flowery rhetoric versus policy wonkery – electoral incentives determine the degree to which party leaders control the speaker lists and the content of speakers' messages. The debate–working parliament distinction tends to correlate with partisan control, but theoretically this need not be the case. Even if parliamentary debate culture is the same across countries, the level of partisan control may vary. If one were to consider traditional debate–working parliament distinctions, we might expect the Bundestag and the EP to look similar, with the United Kingdom and New Zealand looking somewhat different. In terms of partisan control, however, the EP should function similarly to the United Kingdom, and New Zealand should be more similar to the United Kingdom prior to electoral change and more like Germany after. Thus, because these parliaments vary on these key variables, we are able to test our theory against other competing explanations. We now introduce the four parliaments and provide a brief overview of parliamentary debate in each.

3.3.1 German Bundestag

Germany provides an example of a parliamentary democracy in which the electoral system creates strong incentives for the party leadership to protect the party label. In the German MMP electoral system, the electoral success of the party in the closed-list vote determines the overall allocation of seats in the Bundestag. Rules regulating access to the floor reflect this fact. Party leaders play a significant role in the allocation of speaking time to MPs. Each parliamentary party receives speaking time according to a formula that accounts for both proportionality and parity between government and opposition parties (Schreiner, 2005). This formula, formally known as the *Berliner Stunde*, or Berlin Hour, is the result of an agreement among the parliamentary parties at the start of each parliamentary term. It literally refers to how time in an hour-long debate is divided among the parties. For example, in the 17th Bundestag, for every hour of debate the governing parties were granted 32 minutes while the opposition received 28 minutes. Specifically, the CDU/CSU received 23 minutes, the FDP 9 minutes, the SPD 14 minutes, the Left Party 7 minutes, and the Greens 7 minutes.

Once allocated time, the parties then decide on their own speaker lists. The relevant institutions governing the *intraparty* allocation of speaking time can be found in the rules of procedure for each party group (*Fraktion*). These rules provide the party leaders with procedural means to prevent dissident speakers from taking the floor, or at least monitor them when they do. The Christian Democrats have working groups composed of the relevant parliamentary committee members from the group who propose a list of speakers. The selected speakers are supposed to speak on behalf of the group in the parliament and support the party leadership (CDU/CSU, 2005, articles 8(4) & 18). Deviant declarations on the floor need to be preapproved by the leadership. The Green Party's rules regarding speakers mirror those of the Christian Democrats. Working groups within the party delegation can compose lists of speakers, and these speakers are expected to present the party leadership's position. Moreover, the task of deciding speaker lists can be handled solely by the party group leadership (Greens, 2007, articles 5(a) & 6(2)). The Social Democrats have even more stringent procedures to control the speaker list. The party group determines the speaker list and designated speakers must represent the official party line in parliament (SPD, 2004, p. 466). Other speeches must be a rare exception. Before giving a speech contradicting the party line, MPs must notify the party group and discuss the content of their speech with the group leadership. The intention to issue a declaration in parliament needs to be announced to the leadership in advance as well. Lastly, the FDP's rules of procedure also stipulate that public declarations on behalf of the party group can only be given by the party group leadership or a member of the group that has been assigned this task (FDP, 2005, article 14).

In short, the party leaders in the German Bundestag are able to exercise strict control over who takes the floor to give a speech on behalf of the party. Both parliamentary and partisan rules emphasize the role of the leadership over backbenchers.

3.3.2 UK House of Commons

The British Westminster system creates stronger incentives for personal vote seeking than the German system. As a result, we expect backbenchers to take the floor much more often in the UK House of Commons. In contrast to the Bundestag, the UK House of Commons rules of procedure make no mention of parties in the allocation of speaking time, but they do set out in detail the rules structuring parliamentary debate. The rules stress the rights of individuals to make speeches, and they also reflect the parliament's history and culture as a debating chamber. Members, for example, are not allowed to read their speeches, and they are expected to remain in their place following their speech. The Select Committee on Modernization of the House of Commons has suggested, "that members wishing to take part in a debate should be in the chamber to hear the opening speeches.... If called, they should make reference to the previous speech or speeches before developing their own ideas and remain in the chamber for at least the next two speeches so that they can hear the reactions to their own contribution" (McKay, 2004, p. 425). These guidelines highlight the importance of debate in the House of Commons. Nevertheless, the fact that a committee had to make these recommendations highlights how debate even in the United Kingdom falls short of the ideal of deliberation. Despite time constraints, a limited back-and-forth discussion between two or more MPs is possible, as long as a speaking MP is willing to "give way."

Backbenchers do not require the formal support of their party leadership to give a speech, and there are several ways for backbenchers to take the floor. Rather than parties controlling the House of Commons' speaker list, this task is delegated to the nonpartisan Speaker of the House. During a debate, it is the Speaker's job to control the flow of speakers. MPs from any party who wish to speak may submit their name to the Speaker in advance. This does not ensure that an MP will be called, however. Instead, those who wish to speak must catch the Speaker's eye by rising from their seat. The Speaker will then attempt to organize a balanced discussion by alternating between speakers on each side of the floor. Although the Speaker may give frontbenchers precedence over backbenchers, the frontbenchers cannot prevent the Speaker from calling on any particular backbencher. In fact, the newest members are given the highest precedence. A new MP who has not yet made a speech is generally called before other MPs rising at the same time, and the member is allowed to make his or her maiden speech (McKay, 2004, chap. 18).

Other mechanisms exist for a backbencher to take the floor, as well. For example, a backbencher may submit a 10-minute rule bill under Standing Order 23. On Tuesdays and Wednesdays, one member is allowed to present a motion and give a ten-minute speech in support of the measure. Because these bills rarely become law, they tend to provide members with a means to get floor time to go on the record about an issue that is important to them or their constituents. Although parties remain highly cohesive on votes, the parliamentary rules provide any number of ways for backbenchers to seek floor time to give speeches.

3.3.3 European Parliament

The European Parliament is different from national parliaments in several ways and thus requires a little more explanation. The political system of the EU combines elements of parliamentary democracy with elements of a separation-of-powers systems. The EU functions like a parliamentary system with interdependent legislative-executive relations because the EP must approve the Commission, the EU's executive body, and has the sole right to censure it. But unlike a parliamentary system, the Commission cannot dissolve the EP, and the censure vote requires a super-majority in the EP, making it difficult for the EP to censure the Commission on ideological grounds alone. As a consequence, and unlike government coalition formation in parliamentary systems, there is no "inbuilt government majority in the European Parliament" (Hix, Noury, and Roland, 2007, p. 21). With regard to electoral incentives, all members of the EP are elected using some variant of a proportional representation electoral system, but the parliamentary groups have little incentive to protect a party label. Because electoral systems vary to some degree across member states, using the EP as a case allows us to gain traction on some independent variables, such as candidate selection mechanisms, which we would not otherwise be able to analyze by looking at national parliaments alone.

First, electoral system variables that affect the importance of the party label, such as the use of open versus closed lists, district magnitude, and candidate selection mechanisms, vary across member states within the EU. Second, unlike elections to national parliaments, EP elections are generally considered second-order, national contests (Reif and Schmitt, 1980; Reif, 1984; Marsh, 1998; Hix and Marsh, 2007). Held once every five years at the same time across all EU member states, the elections are generally marked by voter apathy and low turnout. Moreover, national (rather than pan-European) parties run the elections and tend to fight them on national issues. Oftentimes, voters simply view the elections as a referendum on the performance of the national government, and governing parties tend to lose votes compared with the previous national election.[2] This lack of contestation

[2] This has the effect of populating the EP with national opposition parties, which creates some interesting patterns of parliamentary behavior, especially with

for political leadership in European election campaigns has led scholars to lament the continued existence of a "democratic deficit" in the European Union (Follesdal and Hix, 2006). The electoral disconnection between European political groups and citizens raises questions about the extent to which the parliamentary behavior of members of the EP (MEPs) matters for their reelection.

Because national parties run EP election campaigns, MEPs must serve two different principals: the *national party* and the *European political group* (Hix, 2002, 2004; Hix, Noury, and Roland, 2007). Elected members enter the EP as members of national parties, but once inside, these national party "delegations" join European political groups. This causes a dilemma because both of these principals control resources that MEPs value. National parties control candidate selection and run election campaigns. In addition, national parties control access to offices in the national arena, which is of importance if MEPs intend to return to domestic politics (Scarrow, 1997). European political groups, however, control office allocation within the EP, including the election of EP president, the allocation of committee chairs, and committee reports. These groups have installed specific mechanisms to monitor the actions of their members. Group whips monitor whether MEPs follow voting instructions from the group leadership, and group coordinators maintain regular surveillance of members' activities in committees (Kreppel, 2002; Hix, Noury, and Roland, 2007, pp. 134–135). National parties and European political groups are therefore able to reward and punish MEPs, who face the challenge of appeasing both principals. Numerous studies have found that this tension affects voting behavior (Hix, 2004; Hix, Noury, and Roland, 2007; Lindstädt, Slapin, and Vander Wielen, 2011), but we do not know whether this tension affects parliamentary speech making in the same way.

Given the importance of national parties in European election campaigns, European political groups have little incentive to protect, or even develop, a party brand. The political groups wish to exercise control over their membership on votes to pass their legislative agenda, but they have little need to control what backbenchers say on the floor. Even if the media were to report on internal dissent in speeches,

regard to opposition party oversight of EU affairs (Proksch and Slapin, 2011; Jensen, Proksch, and Slapin, 2013).

there is little chance that it would affect electoral outcomes because the political groups do not run the election campaigns. At the same time that the groups have little incentive to control speech, MEPs have a strong incentive to use it. MEPs who need to vote against the majority of their European political group for national reasons have the greatest incentive to take the floor to give a speech. They can use their speaking time to explain their vote to the leaders and members of their European political group in hopes of mitigating possible punishment. In addition, they can use the opportunity to garner favor with their national party for reelection purposes by publicly reiterating their national stance.

The institutions regarding the allocation of speaking time in the EP grant European political groups an important role. They have the power to allocate speaking time to their members during plenary debate, similar to parties in many continental European parliaments (Corbett, Jacobs, and Shackleton, 2007, p. 145). Although several MEPs have reserved speaking time, including rapporteurs, draftsmen of opinions, and authors of motions for resolution, the largest proportion of speaking time is allocated to the political groups of the EP. According to the rules of the EP, a first fraction of speaking time is allocated equally among all political groups, and then additional time is allocated in proportion to the total number of their members. Then, each group allocates its speaking time among the national delegations and individual MEPs, who themselves can request speaking time.

The EP, however, has also set aside floor time for explanations of votes. Following a vote, every MEP is entitled to give an oral or written explanation of his or her voting decision. They may speak for one minute or provide a 200-word written statement to be included in the parliamentary record.[3] In addition, if a member is unable to speak during regular plenary debate due to time constraints, he or she may provide a written statement to be appended to the official report of the debate.[4] Thus, although it is theoretically possible for political groups to keep dissident views off the floor during regular debate, they cannot

[3] European Parliament Rules of Procedure, 7th Parliamentary Term, March 2011, Rule 170.

[4] European Parliament Rules of Procedure, 7th Parliamentary Term, March 2011, Rule 149 para. 12.

keep these views off the debate record or prevent them from being aired during explanations of votes.

3.3.4 New Zealand House of Representatives

For our final case, we turn to the New Zealand House of Representatives. Before the electoral reform referendum of 1993, New Zealand could be considered the quintessential example of a Westminster system. As a unitary, unicameral, parliamentary democracy employing a SMD plurality electoral system, it provided a canonical example of a majoritarian democracy (Lijphart, 1999, p. 21). Following two referendums on electoral reform, the 1996 election was the first held under a mixed-member proportional (MMP) system.[5] The MMP system is the same as the system used in Germany, in which voters are granted two votes – one for a party list and one for a member running in a SMD. The party list vote totals determine the overall seat share parties receive in parliament, but SMD winners are guaranteed a seat in the chamber. If a party wins more SMDs than seats it is entitled to on the basis of the list vote, "overhang" seats are created to ensure a proportional result. The introduction of the MMP system has had the effect of increasing the number of parties in parliament and thus reducing the electoral system's disproportionality. It has also meant coalition and minority governments, both of which had not existed before 1996. In effect, the electoral system change transformed the New Zealand parliament from majoritarian to consensual (Lijphart, 1999, pp. 25–27).

New Zealand's traditions and institutions regarding parliamentary debate were (and remain) similar to those of the UK House of Commons. For example, the non-partisan Speaker of the House is responsible for controlling the flow of debate, members stand to "catch the Speaker's eye," and new members are given the right to make a maiden speech. With electoral system change, and the multi-party parliament it would create, the parties anticipated the tremendous effects on the business of the House. In the year before the 1996 election, the parties took steps to modify parliamentary rules. The overall goal was to

[5] For a history of electoral reform in New Zealand and an explanation of its effects, see, among others, Vowles et al. (1995), Boston et al. (1996), and Nagel (2004).

transform parliament from one that was strongly majoritarian to one based on the principle of proportionality. One of the most important changes was the strengthening of the committee system, and, in particular, the creation of a Business Committee. Each parliamentary party is entitled to a representative on the Business Committee, typically the party's chief whip, and the Committee is chaired by the Speaker. It strives for unanimity or near-unanimity in its decision-making, and it is charged with the tasks of drafting the parliamentary agenda, as well as determining the size and membership of parliamentary select committees. The advent of the Business Committee meant changes in the way the parliament organized debate and the tools party leaders had to control their members. The effects of these changes are discussed in much greater detail in Chapter 8.

3.4 Measurement of latent concepts

Having discussed the cases we use to test our theory, we turn our attention to the data we require for each of our cases. In an ideal world, we would be able to measure the true conflict between backbenchers and their party leadership on each issue, the weight each places on party unity, as well as the policy position of each speech given on the floor of parliament. If we had this information, we would be able to gauge how far a backbencher's speech deviated from the official party position and empirically plot the theoretical relationships posited in Figure 2.1.

Of course, it is not possible to directly measure any of these variables. To measure the distance between party leaders and backbenchers would require us to know the true position of both the party leadership and every backbencher on the policy under consideration. We are never able to observe these positions; instead we only observe actions taken by these members that provide information about what their latent, or unobservable, ideology might be. Spatial models of voting, for example, attempt to estimate the ideology of members of parliaments on the basis of observed behavior on roll-call votes (e.g. Clinton, Jackman, and Rivers, 2004). Comparativists have tended to estimate party ideology on the basis of what party leaders write in their manifestos (e.g. Klingemann et al., 2006; Slapin and Proksch, 2008). However, these approaches suffer from the problem that observed behavior is the result of both ideology and strategic behavior. We do not know the degree to which the position expressed in the behavior is the result of strategic considerations or untainted ideology.

Again, we cannot know the precise weight that each MP and leader places on party unity for a given policy issue. Instead, the theory suggests that these weights vary systematically with institutions – namely, electoral rules that generate personal vote-seeking incentives: proportional representation versus plurality systems, closed versus open lists, electoral tiers, and candidate selection mechanisms. It is precisely for this reason that we examine the cases introduced earlier in this chapter.

It is equally difficult to estimate individual positions taken in speeches. There is no well-established method by which a human or machine can read or listen to a speech and unequivocally state the ideology being expressed on one or multiple policy dimensions. We cannot precisely state how the content of any particular speech maps onto a latent issue scale without making some strong assumptions. In content analysis, these assumptions include the validity of a dictionary or codebook meant to capture ideological content or the expectation that the number of times individual words appear in a speech is a function of a latent ideological position. However, given the diversity in topics, content within topics, and the ways in which rebels can express dissent, no existing measure can ascertain comparative individual parliamentary speech positions at the issue level.

Rather than measuring the positions members take in speeches, we instead focus on the observable implications of our model for the frequency of speechmaking. Although we may not be able to estimate individual ideology, weights placed on party unity, and positions expressed in speeches with certainty, we can examine how often backbenchers take the floor compared with party leaders across various institutions and over time. Our theoretical model predicts that party leaders are more likely to reserve floor time for themselves in systems where the party label matters more – this empirical implication is directly observable. Therefore, throughout much of the remainder of the book, our dependent variable will be speech participation – quite simply, did a member take the floor to give a speech (and how often)?

We also take advantage of the measures of individual ideology that we do have available to us to operationalize our other independent variables. To measure ideological distances between backbenchers and party leaders, we rely on candidate surveys in Germany and the United Kingdom, and we look at voting behavior in the EP and New Zealand.

Although response rates are not always great, candidate surveys offer a reasonably good means to estimate the ideology between individual members of parliament and their leadership. At election times, candidates in Germany and the United Kingdom were asked a battery of questions, including questions about where they place themselves and their parties on an ideological dimension. Although we cannot place the positions of floor speeches on this dimension, we use this measure of ideological disagreement between backbenchers and their leaders as a predictor of the number of speeches an MP makes. In the EP, where roll-call votes are somewhat more common than in European national parliaments (roll calls account for approximately one-third of votes taken in the EP), we examine how often a member casts a vote against the majority of his or her political group. Here, we take voting defection as an indicator of high latent disagreement between a member and the political group. In New Zealand, we similarly examine individual voting defection scores in the 1990–1993 parliament as an indicator of disagreement across the whole period under examination. We are unable to look at roll-call votes in later periods as the parties moved to bloc voting with the new electoral rules. We discuss all of these variables in more detail in the next chapters.

3.5 Summary

This chapter has laid out our research strategy; we have explained our cross-national survey, case selection, and the measurement of our key concepts. The institutions of the four parliaments we study in the remainder of the book reflect the incentives created by the political and electoral system. In Germany, parliamentary party leaders have the means to check party members and to reduce the informational asymmetries regarding the type of speech delivered. The rules also ensure that the party leadership remains central in deciding who may deliver the party message in parliament. In contrast, parties in the United Kingdom have not developed formal means to prevent rebels from taking the floor. The institutions reflect the fact that creating a name for oneself on the floor of parliament is potentially important for an MP's reelection and the party's success. The institutions of the EP allow those members who disagree with the political group the opportunity to express their disagreement on the floor. Finally, in New Zealand, the rules regarding speaking time changed following the electoral system change in 1996 in ways predicted by our model. We have described the observable implications of our theory with regard to debate participation. Even though measuring latent ideology in speeches is not straightforward, we can directly observe who participates in debates. In the next chapter, we examine the institutions and partisan rules of debate across political systems.

PART II

Empirical studies of parliamentary debate

4 *Debates and institutions*

We begin our empirical analysis with a broad overview of the institutions governing debate across a range of democratic countries. We demonstrate that countries with institutions that create incentives for MPs to cultivate a personal vote also have rules that provide MPs with greater opportunities to speak freely on the floor of parliament. Moreover, we test the hypothesis that both parliamentary and partisan rules are endogenous to the incentives a system provides for personal vote seeking. In systems that generate a greater incentive to protect the party label, we expect parties to make it difficult for rebels to express their views on the floor. Parliamentary rules provide a first line of defense for party leaders. Given the electoral incentives, all parties in parliament may agree to draft parliamentary rules governing debate that give leaders a say over who is allowed floor time. Then, within parties, leaders may develop party-specific rules about how to allocate time to backbenchers and how to handle members who make speeches that do not express the position of the party.

We first classify countries' parliamentary rules of procedure according to the degree of control they give parties over their members' floor access. We are able to place parliaments into three categories – those whose rules give individual members a right to floor access and provide parties with little control, those where the rules favor party leader control but still provide an avenue for individuals to take the floor without party consent, and those where getting on the party's speaker list is effectively the only way to participate in debate. Second, we turn our attention to parties, and, using our new elite survey of parliamentary parties, we examine whether parties seek to exert more control over their backbenchers' speeches in systems with less personal vote seeking. We find that it is indeed the case that parties exercise more control over their MPs' access to the floor in countries where the electoral institutions incentivize parties to protect the party label.

4.1 Parliamentary rules

All parliaments have rules regulating access to the floor. Without constraints on debate, a single MP could endlessly tie up parliamentary affairs by refusing to yield the floor. However, there are numerous ways to write these rules, and some rules give members more leeway to express their own opinion than others. For instance, in systems in which all members are guaranteed access to speaking time, backbenchers are not required to announce their intention to speak before doing so, they are granted equal time as party leaders, and parties have fewer tools to control rebellious backbenchers. In contrast, where the rules severely restrict the number of speakers, parties have the ability to draft speaker lists, and leaders are granted significantly more time, the party leadership is much better able to control the party message.

Before exploring rules in specific parliaments, it is useful to discuss the large variety of rules that exist. Because we view rules governing speech as endogenous, we treat the universe of rules as a menu from which politicians – or more specifically, party leaders – can hypothetically choose. They choose rules that provide them with the optimal level of control over their membership, given the political system within which they operate.[1] Parliamentary rules generally regulate speech in three ways: they determine who is allowed to take the floor, the process by which members come to the floor, and how long they may speak.

We start by examining who is allowed to take the floor. In most, if not all, parliaments, there is a set of members who are guaranteed floor time. These members often include committee members and chairpersons from relevant committees, rapporteurs, and government ministers. Access to the floor for other members varies. In practice, however, time constraints often mean not all members who want to

[1] We treat the choice of party leaders as exogenous throughout the analysis. Of course, party leaders are chosen by the party membership, however. We believe the assumption of exogenous party leadership is justified as members have an incentive to select party leaders who will pursue policies and develop rules that are best for the party. In other words, backbenchers will support party leaders who create rules to restrict backbencher speaking time because they know that doing so is the best strategy for the party. In essence, they are using the choice of party leader to create a credible commitment. They choose a party leader who prevents them from taking the floor to tie their own hands so they cannot pursue a strategy that may be good for them but bad for the party as a whole.

speak are able to take the floor on every bill. This leads us to the next consideration with regard to rules regulating speech – the process through which members take the floor.

Parliaments generally regulate access to the floor in one of two ways. Either parties draw up their own speaker lists – and thereby control which members of their party take the floor – or a nonpartisan figure, usually the Speaker of the House or president of parliament, recognizes the right of individual members to speak. Clearly, the first method offers parties significantly more control. Continental European parliaments tend to give parties control over speaker lists, while Westminster systems generally require that members seek floor time by "catching the Speaker's eye." In the latter system, members wishing to give a speech must stand to indicate their desire to talk. The Speaker must then recognize them. In some instances, the Speaker may give precedence to some members, such as party leaders, over others, but this decision is often at the discretion of the Speaker.

Lastly, rules govern the length of time a member may speak. If these rules generally allow party leaders more time than backbenchers, the rules tend to favor partisan control. The US Senate exists at one extreme, placing no limits on speaking time. This creates the possibility of a filibuster. Debate can only be cut off when 60 senators vote for cloture. Most chambers put specific time limits on members' speeches. These limits can be as short as one minute (one-minute speeches in the US House of Representatives, for example) or they can be significantly longer. Speeches in the UK House of Commons, for example, average around 10 to 12 minutes. Some parliaments explicitly give party leaders extra time compared with backbenchers, and other parliaments do not. This can vary across types of bills as well.

On the basis of these rules, we can classify countries by the degree to which party leadership is favored over backbenchers in terms of floor access. We code the parliamentary rules of procedure for lower chambers in 22 advanced industrialized democracies, focusing on one particular variable – the degree to which speaker lists drawn up by the party leadership are favored over individual access to the floor. At one extreme, party lists do not exist and all floor time is reserved for individuals. At the other, the only way to get to the floor is through the party. In addition, there is an intermediate category in which, according to the rules, there is some opportunity for individual access, but party lists tend to be favored.

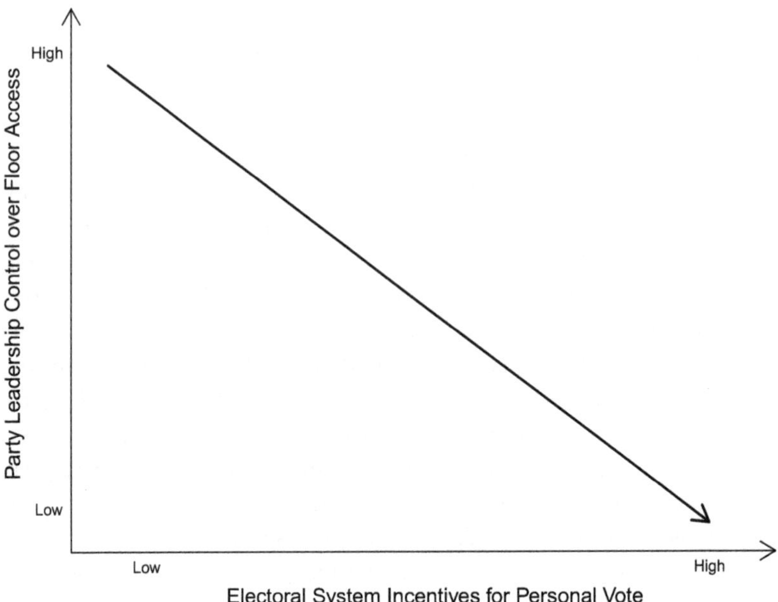

Figure 4.1 Institutions of parliamentary debate and personal vote seeking

Our theoretical expectation, depicted graphically in Figure 4.1, is that when electoral systems create greater incentives for members to seek a personal vote, parliamentary rules limit the ways in which leaders exercise control over their members' access to the floor. These rules are designed so that party leaders are able to credibly commit to provide backbenchers the floor time they need to seek a personal vote. Or, in the case of party-centric systems, the rules provide leaders with tools to ensure that backbenchers who may deviate from the party line cannot come to the floor.

In addition to coding parliamentary rules with regard to party leadership's control over the speaker list, we also classify countries' electoral systems according to the incentives they create for personal vote seeking.[2] We classify systems in which voters cast ballots for individual candidates as systems with a strong incentive for personal vote seeking. These systems include single-member district plurality, alternative vote, single transferable vote, and open-list systems in which

[2] We do so on the basis of information in Carey and Shugart (1995), Gallagher and Mitchell (2005), and Farrell (2011).

voters are required to vote for an individual rather than a party (e.g. Finland). Systems in our middle category include mixed-member systems and open-list systems in which voters are presented with a list and may either vote for the list or cast a ballot for an individual.[3] The low-incentive category includes countries with closed-list systems. Table 4.1 presents our classification of countries by the personal vote-seeking incentives created by electoral systems.

We also present cross-tabulations for the incentive to seek a personal vote and the degree to which parties are favored in the parliamentary rules allocating speaking time. The results of this three-by-three classification are presented in Table 4.2. Our theory predicts that most observations should lie on the diagonal – countries with a strong incentive for personal vote seeking should have rules that allow easy access to the floor, countries with moderate personal vote seeking should prioritize party speeches but provide backbenchers with opportunities for floor access, and countries with weak personal vote seeking should strictly limit individual floor access. This is precisely the pattern we observe. Of the 23 observations for which we have been able to get parliamentary rules of procedure, 15 (65 percent) lie on the diagonal.[4] There are no instances of countries with strong personal vote-seeking incentive blocking individuals access to the floor, and no instances of low personal vote-seeking countries allowing individuals unfettered access. A chi-squared test reveals a strongly statistically significant relationship between these two variables ($\chi^2 = 14.54$, $df = 4$, $p = 0.006$).

Except for the Czech Republic, all of the countries in the "individual access" column are Westminster-style democracies or former British colonies that may have retained aspects of British parliamentary culture. This raises the question of whether we are simply finding a

[3] Some could reasonably take issue with how we classify countries, especially in this middle category. There is a rather high degree of variance in how much preference votes matter across systems in which they are possible but not required. In some countries, they rarely affect the candidates' ranking (e.g. the Netherlands and Austria), whereas they are more important elsewhere (e.g. Belgium). Our classification simply suggests that the incentive to seek a personal vote is higher whenever the possibility for casting a vote for a candidate exists, compared with systems in which it does not exist.

[4] We only have 22 countries, but we count New Zealand twice – once before the electoral system change of 1996 and again after the change. As we discuss later in the book, parliamentary procedure regarding the allocation of speaking time changed drastically after the electoral system switch.

Table 4.1. *Personal vote-seeking incentives and electoral systems*

Country	Electoral system	Ballot structure	Personal vote incentive
Australia	Alternative vote	Ordinal rank	Strong
Canada	SMD plurality	–	Strong
Ireland	STV-PR	Ordinal rank	Strong
Finland	List	Preference mandatory	Strong
France	SMD runoff	–	Strong
New Zealand (pre-1996)	SMD plurality	–	Strong
United Kingdom	SMD plurality	–	Strong
United States	SMD plurality	–	Strong
Austria	List	Preference possible	Moderate
Belgium	List	Preference possible	Moderate
Czech Republic	List	Preference possible	Moderate
Denmark	List	Preference possible	Moderate
Germany	MMP	–	Moderate
Hungary	MMM	–	Moderate
Netherlands	List	Preference possible	Moderate
New Zealand (post-1996)	MMP	–	Moderate
Norway	List	Preference possible	Moderate
Slovenia	List	Preference possible	Moderate
Sweden	List	Preference possible	Moderate
Israel	List	Closed	Weak
Italy	List	Closed	Weak
Portugal	List	Closed	Weak
Spain	List	Closed	Weak

Note: The degree to which preference votes matter for determining a candidate's placement on the list varies across country. We opt to place all countries in which preference voting is an option in the intermediate category.

"Westminster," or British political culture, effect. Is parliamentary tradition based on British norms driving the choice of rules regarding plenary time rather than calculations about providing backbenchers with exposure on the floor? To alleviate the concerns of a Westminster effect, it is useful to examine countries that have changed their electoral laws in greater depth. In such instances, we can examine whether they also change their rules regarding the delegation of speaking time

Table 4.2. ***Parliamentary rules and electoral incentives***

		Parliamentary rules for floor access		
		Individual access, no party lists	Party lists favored, individual access	Party lists, no individual access
Incentive for a personal vote	Strong	AUS, CAN, IRL, USA, GBR, NZL (pre-96)	FRA, FIN	
	Moderate	CZE	AUT, HUN, NZL (post-96), DEU, SWE, NLD	BEL, DNK, NOR, SVN
	Weak		ITA	ISR, ESP PRT

Note: Gray cells correspond to the theoretical expectations.

following the electoral rules change. Hence, we examine New Zealand in more detail in Chapter 8.

4.2 Party rules

The previous analysis has shown that parliamentary rules of procedure often grant parties a set amount of speaking time, which they can then allocate to their MPs. Even when the rules do not give parties the explicit right to allocate time to their members, parties may design internal rules and norms to keep dissidents at bay. Thus, looking at parliamentary rules may only partially explain the organization of debate. In Westminster systems, for example, the parliamentary rules generally allow backbenchers to take the floor without obtaining party approval first. But even in these systems, the parties must retain some control over their message. In Canada, for instance, a number of Conservative government backbenchers publicly complained in 2013 that the party leadership infringed their rights by not allowing them to speak on certain topics in one-minute member statements (Ryckewaert, 2013). Thus, parties can, in fact, design rules to silence dissidents even when the parliamentary rules would otherwise allow them to speak. Technically, in Canada, the Speaker should use speaker lists by whips

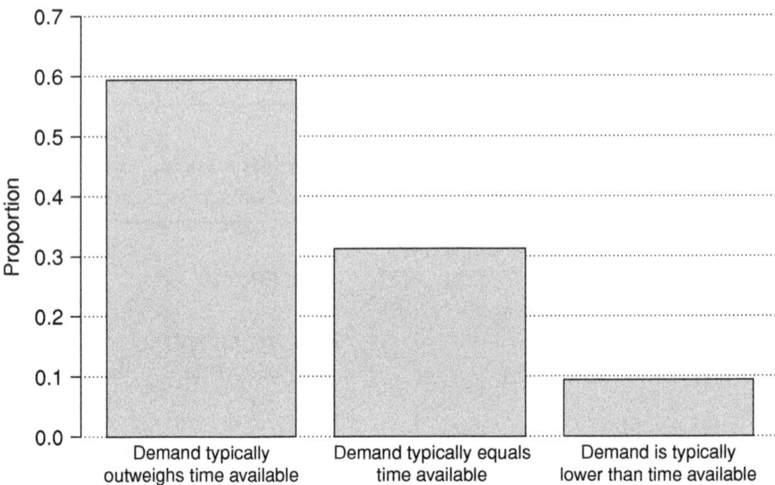

Figure 4.2 Party survey: MPs' level of demand for speaking time in parliamentary party groups
Note: $N = 32$ valid party responses. The question reads: "What is the level of demand among your group's MPs for the plenary speaking time reserved for the group?"

only as a guide. The fact that the backbenchers protested, however, demonstrates that the Conservative Party's attempt to silence them did not fully work; they felt they had the right to speak their mind in these one-minute statements, perhaps an indication of a more general lack of party control in these systems. Regardless, it is important to understand the process of control over speaking time and speech content within parties. To do so, we examine the results of our cross-national elite survey of 45 parliamentary parties. These experts were either MPs in party leadership roles or senior administrative members of the parliamentary party's secretariat.

We asked parties whether their MPs demand more speaking time than is available in parliament. If there is no conflict over access to the floor, rules should not matter. In other words, if party members can efficiently divide up the available time for debate ex ante, then there should never be a situation in which decisions over the final speaker list are necessary. But this is not the case. Figure 4.2 shows the responses to the question about the average level of demand expressed by their members for speaking time.[5] Speaking time is highly in demand. By far the most common response was that demand typically *outweighs* the time available (almost 60 percent of responses). The second most common response was that demand and supply are in balance (just above 30 percent of responses). This means that for only 10 percent of the parties in the survey, demand is insufficient to fill the time available. Thus, in most cases, MPs want to actively participate in parliamentary debate. Parties do have a need to decide on internal rules to provide some MPs with privileged access to the floor.

4.2.1 Party leadership monitoring of legislative speeches

The speech delegation model in Chapter 1 makes clear predictions about the conditions under which parties have an incentive to design internal rules that strengthen leaders' control over the party message delivered on the floor. The design of these rules is conditional on the personal vote incentives created by the electoral system and the ideological diversity within the party. We first measure the internal rules of the party by asking parties a battery of questions that touch on different aspects of leadership control in debates. Second, we use these answers to estimate a latent *party leadership monitoring* scale. We begin by describing the results from the party survey. The first question regarding rules granting party leader control asked who has the final say over the party's speaker list. Figure 4.3 shows that almost 75 percent of parties in the survey either collectively decide on the speaker list or grant the leadership the final say. In the first instance, MPs may decide in a weekly preparatory meeting on which colleagues to put on the speaker list. But leaders play an elevated role during such meetings by virtue of their office (and as chairs). This means that leaders may be influential even if parties indicate that the group takes a collective decision on the speaker list, and the numbers presented may underestimate the true influence of leaders. For the remaining 25 percent of responses, parties use a different mechanism. In these instances, parties responded that the party group is either too small to have a formal procedure or that the party spokespersons or committee members take the floor. Again, because party spokespersons are

[5] The question was only posed to parties that do have a set amount of speaking time available according to the rules of procedure or an interparty agreement.

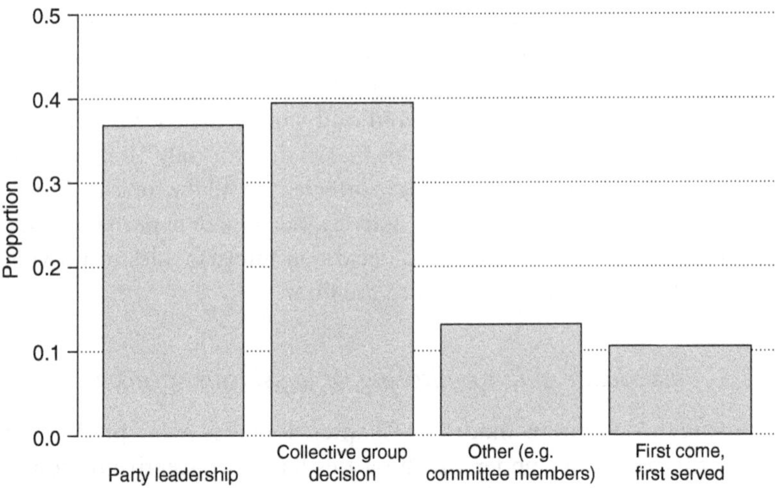

Figure 4.3 Party survey: final say over the party's speaker list
Note: $N = 38$ valid party responses. The question reads: "When your party allocates its reserved speaking time among MPs, who has the final say in your party group over the speaker list?"

often involved in defining party policy, one could count these instances toward an extended definition of party leadership. Finally, a neutral rule, according to which MPs, expression of demand determines the speaker list ("first come, first served"), is rarely used. This means that parties are likely to make deliberate choices with regard to the speaker and topic in question.

Vetoing the party's speaker list is a rather drastic sanctioning mechanism for a party leader to take. It may also not truly reflect the value parties attribute to the content of their MPs' legislative speeches. We therefore asked parties to report the extent to which the leadership monitors floor speeches by presenting them with five additional actions party leaders can take. These range from simple, passive monitoring of the speeches to active intervention and consequences for promotions within the party. Figure 4.4 shows the proportion of party responses that affirmed that the respective monitoring mechanism may be applied by the party leadership.[6]

[6] We excluded "don't know" responses. Thus, proportions are calculated only for responses indicating either "yes" or "no."

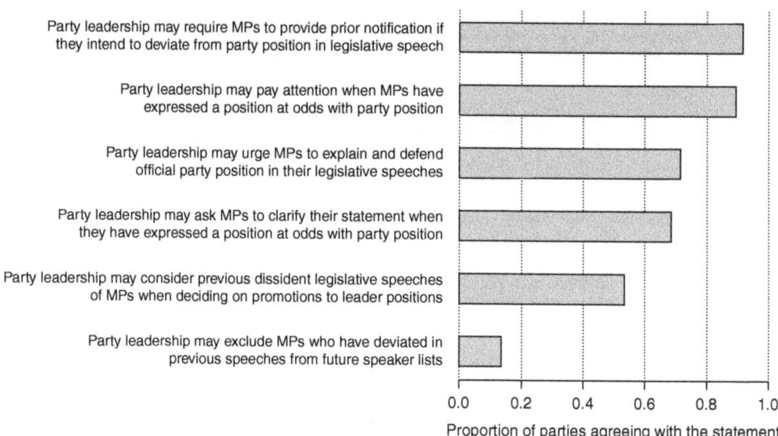

Figure 4.4 Party survey: leadership monitoring of MPs' speeches
Note: Number of valid responses ("yes" or "no") for each question from top to bottom: 36, 38, 35, 35, 30, 37.

Party leaders clearly listen for dissent. In approximately 90 percent of the parties surveyed, the party leadership may actually require MPs to provide prior notification if they intend to deviate from the party position in a legislative speech. Equally important, the party leadership pays attention when MPs have expressed a position at odds with the party position on the floor. This means that party leaders care a great deal about what is being communicated on the floor of parliament. In line with this finding, more than 70 percent of parties indicated that the party leadership may urge MPs to explain and defend the official party position in their legislative speeches. Given how parties structure debates internally, it is possible that legislative speeches reflect more cohesion within a party than actually exists because leaders apply gentle pressure and are alert. Dissent, however, does occur, and when MPs deviate in their speeches from the party line, party leaders often require an explanation afterward (almost 70 percent of cases). Thus, parties apply both an ex ante selection and screening mechanism with regard to content and speaker choice, and also an ex post control mechanism with regard to what has been said. The last question is whether party leaders consider sanctions for dissent in legislative speech. In approximately 50 percent of responses, the leadership may consider previous dissident speech when deciding on promotions to leadership positions.

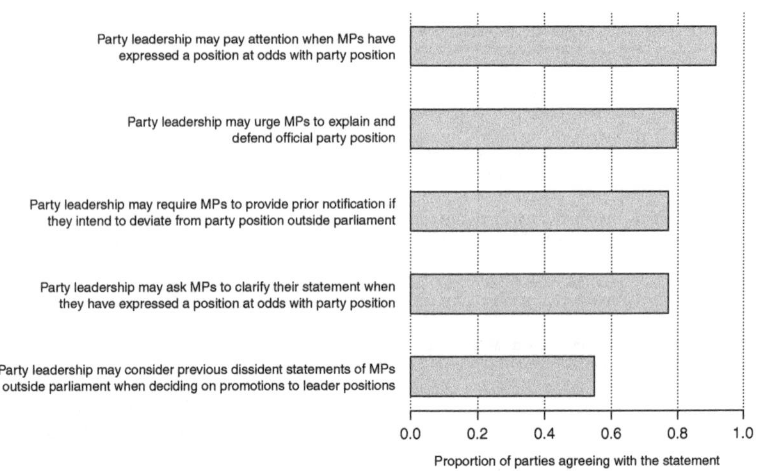

Figure 4.5 Party survey: Monitoring MPs' statements in the media
Note: Number of valid responses ("yes" or "no") for each question from top to bottom: 35, 34, 35, 35, 31.

Thus, in half of the parties, rebellious speeches can have a direct impact on MPs' career prospects inside the party. MPs themselves, however, do not need to fear exclusion from future speaker lists. This drastic form of sanctioning is rarely practiced.

Party leaders do not stop monitoring when MPs leave the floor. In the first chapter, we argued that speech delegation can be easily embedded into a general model of intraparty dissent. In the survey, we asked parties to what extent party leaders apply monitoring mechanisms to the statements MPs made *outside* of the parliamentary arena. Such statements include newspaper or television interviews, as well as posts on blogs. The pattern shown in Figure 4.5 is similar, with some interesting exceptions. Monitoring of verbal dissent is high, no matter where those statements are made. Approximately 90 percent of parties indicated that leaders may pay attention to dissent in media outlets. However, prior notification when intending to deviate is not necessarily as frequent for statements given in the media (77 percent) compared with statements on the floor of parliament (92 percent). Thus, parties appear to constrain MPs to a greater extent in legislative debates than in media statements, just as our theory would expect. On the other hand, party leaders would like a clarifying statement slightly more often when dissent goes through media outlets (77 percent) compared with parliamentary speeches (69 percent). A likely reason is that media

Table 4.3. *Missing values in the seven monitoring questions*

	Parties	Percent
Complete responses	25	56
1 missing response	8	18
2 missing responses	3	7
3 missing responses	1	2
4 missing responses	1	2
5 missing responses	0	0
6 missing responses	4	9
All responses missing	3	7

statements are given on an individual basis, without the leadership listening at the time statements are made. Although a speech during a debate may provide clear reasons for dissent, statements in the media may be short and possibly misrepresented or simply taken out of context. In any case, party leaders ask MPs to defend the party message slightly more often in the media than in debates (79 percent and 71 percent, respectively). Promotion decisions are affected equally by statements made during legislative debates (53 percent) and by statements in the media (55 percent). Clearly, speeches both inside and outside parliament fulfill an important role for intraparty career decisions.

The responses to the six questions regarding the extent of monitoring of legislative speeches (Figure 4.4) and the question about the final say over the party's speaker list (Figure 4.3) are indicators of the involvement of party leaders in parliamentary speeches. We use these data to estimate a latent *party leadership monitoring scale*. Our approach is as follows. We first construct a matrix with $N = 45$ parties in rows and the seven question items in columns. As is common with surveys, this matrix includes missing values because parties did not respond to all of the questions. Table 4.3 presents an overview of the extent of missing responses. Most parties responded to all questions in the survey. To calculate valid scores for the latent monitoring scale, we remove parties with more than two missing responses from the analysis, bringing down the total number of parties to $N = 36$.[7]

[7] The removed parties are the Israeli Jewish Home and Haatzma'ut, the Danish Social Democratic Party and Socialist People's Party, the Canadian Bloc Québécois, the Norwegian Labour Party, the Czech TOP09, and the German Greens and the Social Democrats.

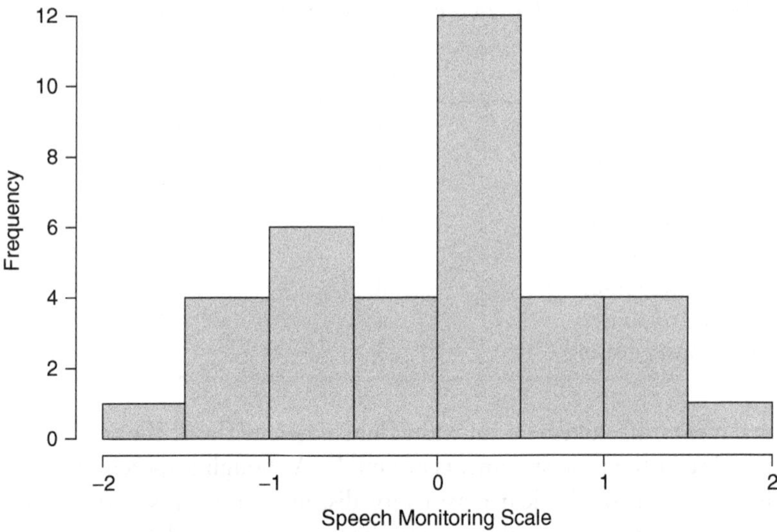

Figure 4.6 Speech monitoring scale ($N = 36$)

We estimate a one-dimensional item response theory model to extract the latent monitoring preference of parties.[8] Relying on a Bayesian approach to estimate the latent variable enables us to keep parties with nonresponses in the data set, as the missing values are imputed along the way. A possible concern is that the items actually do not measure the same underlying concept. To check the internal consistency of the question items, we calculate Cronbach's alpha for the 25 parties that have complete answers (Cronbach, 1951). The value of 0.75 indicates a good internal consistency. Figure 4.6 presents the distribution of posterior means of the draws for the latent monitoring preference (θ_i).[9] The estimates are constrained so that *higher* values

[8] The estimation is performed using the MCMCpack package for R (Martin and Quinn, 2006; Martin, Quinn, and Park, 2011). Assume that each party i has a latent preference for monitoring, denoted as θ_i and that each item has a difficulty parameter α_j and discrimination parameter β_j. We observe the response by party i on item j and assume the following unobserved utility:

$$Response_{ij} = -\alpha_j + \beta_j * \theta_i + \epsilon_{ij}$$

Errors are assumed to be distributed standard Normal, and we use uninformative default priors on the parameters.

[9] The number of burn-in iterations is 10,000, the number of Gibbs iterations for the sample is 100,000, and the thinning interval used in the simulation is 50.

mean *more* monitoring. This scale constitutes the dependent variable for the subsequent analysis of the effect of electoral rules and intraparty cohesion.

4.2.2 Explaining party leadership monitoring

We use the final component of the party survey to explore a central aspect of our theory: the relationship between intraparty cohesion, electoral institutions, and the extent of party leader involvement. If parties are ideologically more divided, controlling the message in parliamentary speeches should be more important for party leaders. However, this should only be the case for parties in political systems with few incentives to cultivate personal votes, as party labels matter for electoral success. In contrast, in systems that do create personal vote-seeking incentives, we would expect party leaders to loosen their grip on MPs as ideological diversity increases, because MPs can use speeches to make a name for themselves. This leads to the following hypotheses:

Hypothesis 1: *In systems with weak personal vote incentives, party leadership monitoring increases as parties become less cohesive.*

Hypothesis 2: *In systems with strong personal vote incentives, party leadership monitoring decreases as parties become less cohesive.*

Latent intraparty cohesion is a difficult concept to measure as we lack natural end points defining what "cohesion" means. Moreover, we are interested in latent cohesion rather than observed behavior. We want to explain the latter with the former. This is an important distinction, but difficult to convey in surveys. For instance, election studies or expert surveys often ask respondents to what extent they *perceive parties as being divided or united.* Such a question, however, alludes to perceptions of behavior. If we were to use such data, we would essentially capture the strategic component of our model (how party positions are communicated) but not the sincere component (how preferences are distributed inside the party). Even more problematic is that these questions induce nonresponse or bias due to their sensitive nature. Parties do *not* want to be perceived as divided, and if asked they may just as well underreport the level of disagreement. To cope with these methodological challenges, we opt for a different

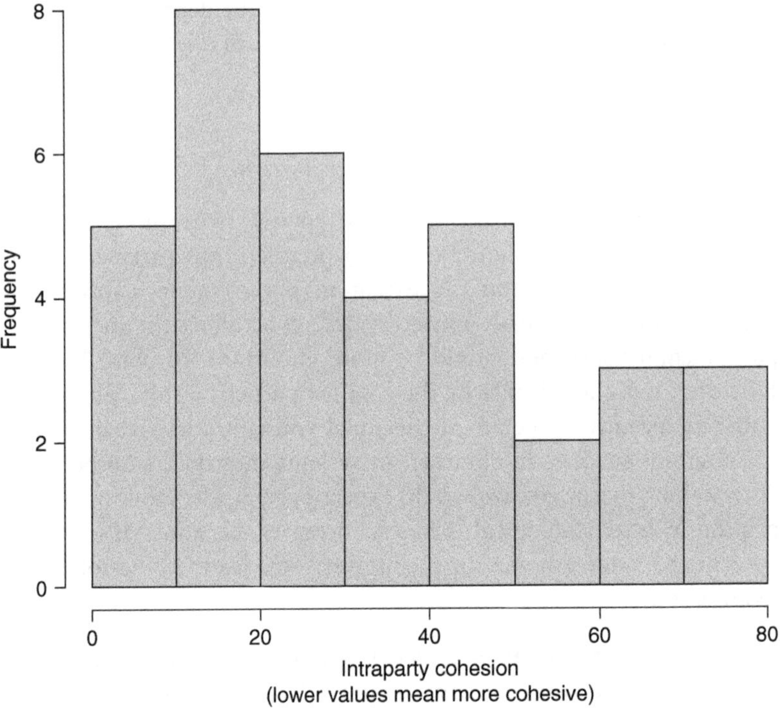

Figure 4.7 Distribution of perceived intraparty cohesion ($N = 36$)

kind of question wording, which we think encourages a neutral reporting of the distribution of preferences within party groups. In our survey, we asked senior party group administrators or party group leaders the following question: "When thinking back to the first day of the legislative term, how would you describe the representation of viewpoints inside your legislative party group?"

Respondents were then presented with a scale in which end points were defined as "All MPs of the group share the exact same ideological viewpoints on all issues" (0) and "The party group represents a diverse range of ideological viewpoints from the entire ideological spectrum" (100).[10] These responses are shown in Figure 4.7 and constitute our main independent variable. The plot shows that almost the entire available range was used to indicate intraparty cohesion, which

[10] The value was determined using a 100-point slider in the online survey.

Table 4.4. *Measuring personal vote incentives*

	(1) De jure categorical	(2) De facto categorical	(3) De facto dummy
Weak incentives	3	16	16
Moderate incentives	26	13	–
Strong incentives	7	7	20

Note: Entries are number of parties ($N = 36$).

reassures us that the question measures latent ideological views rather than observed behavior and also avoids bias toward overreporting of ideological congruence.

For each party, we code the personal vote incentives generated by the electoral system. We follow our initial categorization based on the formal electoral rules from Table 4.2. We create an ordinal variable and assign parties either a weak (0), moderate (1), or strong (2) incentive value. This coding follows the de jure understanding of electoral rules. Yet frequently the de facto effects of these rules are different. In some countries with open lists, party lists are in practice rarely changed by voters. Mixed-member proportional systems create complex effects for MPs, but for party leaders the overall vote share of the party matters, thus lowering the perceived personal vote incentives. We therefore create an alternative variable in which we recode parties from Austria, Germany, Netherlands, New Zealand, Norway, and Sweden from the moderate to the weak personal vote category. Finally, we also create a dummy variable in which parties from systems with moderate and strong incentives from the de facto trichotomous variable are coded as 1, and parties from systems with weak incentives as 0. Table 4.4 shows the distribution of parties in the categories for the three alternative codings. Rather than rely on just one, we perform our subsequent analysis for all three to verify that our analysis is not sensitive to the choice of the classification of parties.

We include two control variables in the final models. First, we control for the size of the parties, measured as the seat share in parliament. This allows us to control for the possibility that larger parties are ideologically more diverse, leading party leaders to put in place more checks than in smaller parties. Second, we include the government

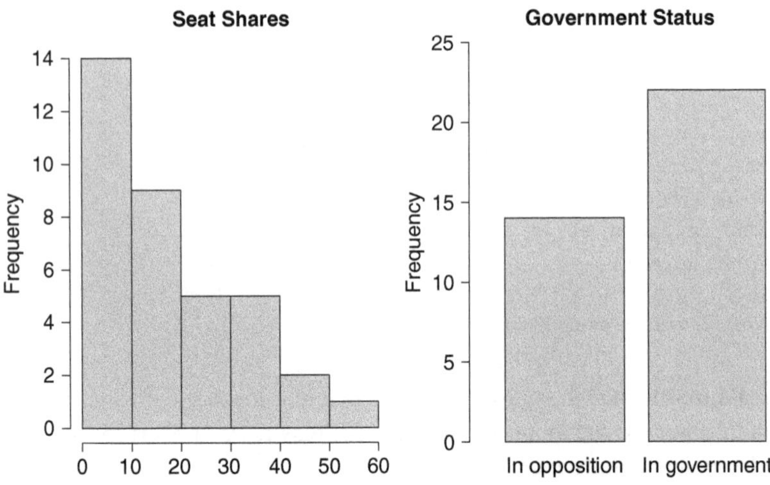

Figure 4.8 Distribution of party seat shares and government status ($N = 36$)

status of parties through a binary variable indicating whether parties are in government. Because of the necessity to secure parliamentary majorities, government parties may be under more pressure to keep their MPs in line than opposition parties. Figure 4.8 shows the distribution of parties for these variables. The plots show that the data set includes small and large parties and a balanced set of government and opposition parties.

Table 4.5 presents the results from the six ordinary least squares estimations. Party leadership monitoring is regressed on party cohesion, personal vote incentives, and the interaction between the two. For each of the three measures of personal vote incentives (de jure, de facto, de facto dummy), we first estimate the model without and then including the control variables. The coefficient for intraparty cohesion is positive when personal vote incentives are weak, although it is not statistically discernible from zero. This corresponds to the theoretical expectation in the first hypothesis: as a party becomes more divisive and more heterogeneous, monitoring by leaders appears to increase in party-centered systems (or at least does not decrease). The coefficient for the interaction between cohesion and personal vote, in contrast, is consistently and (in all but the first model) significantly negative. Most important, the net effect of cohesion on monitoring is negative for systems with personal vote incentives. This corroborates

Table 4.5. *Linear regression models of party leadership monitoring*

	(1)	(2)	(3)	(4)	(5)	(6)
Intraparty cohesion	0.002	0.015	−0.001	0.007	0.004	0.010
	(0.013)	(0.015)	(0.008)	(0.009)	(0.008)	(0.008)
Personal vote category (de jure)	0.384	0.754				
	(0.516)	(0.580)				
Cohesion × personal vote (de jure)	−0.017	−0.026*				
	(0.013)	(0.014)				
Personal vote category (de facto)			0.683*	0.953**		
			(0.345)	(0.364)		
Cohesion × personal vote (de facto)			−0.018*	−0.025**		
			(0.010)	(0.010)		
Personal vote dummy (de facto)					1.436***	1.646***
					(0.487)	(0.490)
Cohesion × personal vote dummy (de facto)					−0.032***	−0.038***
					(0.012)	(0.012)
Party size (seat share)		0.006		0.003		0.003
		(0.011)		(0.010)		(0.010)
Party in government (dummy)		0.493		0.572*		0.497*
		(0.329)		(0.302)		(0.269)
(Intercept)	0.161	−0.783	0.009	−0.736	−0.288	−0.888*
	(0.643)	(0.830)	(0.360)	(0.509)	(0.359)	(0.471)
R^2	0.156	0.239	0.199	0.299	0.294	0.378
Adjusted R^2	0.077	0.112	0.124	0.183	0.228	0.274
N	36	36	36	36	36	36

Note: Higher cohesion values mean less intraparty cohesion. $^{***}p \leq 0.01$; $^{**}p \leq 0.05$; $^{*}p \leq 0.1$.

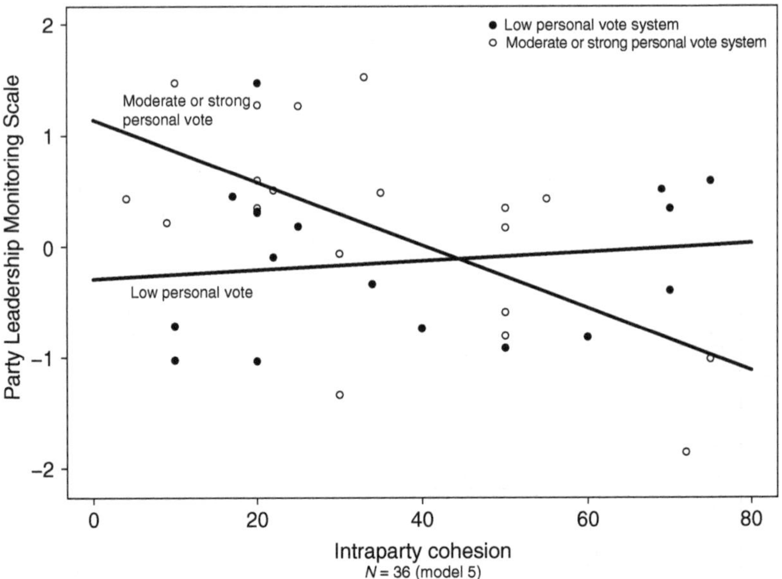

Figure 4.9 Relationship among intraparty cohesion, personal vote incentives, and party leader monitoring

the second hypothesis, namely that party leaders in candidate-centered systems refrain from monitoring when the party's MPs represent more diverse ideological viewpoints. These results hold when we control for the size and the government status of parties. There is some evidence that parties in governments do monitor their MPs more than opposition parties do, whereas party size does not appear to affect monitoring (although the sign has the expected positive sign).

For a more intuitive interpretation of the results of the interaction, Figure 4.9 plots leadership monitoring and party cohesion levels for weak and moderate to strong personal vote systems, including fitted lines for weak and for moderate or strong personal vote systems from Model 5. Although the fitted line for weak personal vote systems is positive – meaning that party leaders slightly increase their monitoring activity when polarization increases – the relationship is negative for systems with higher personal vote incentives. Intraparty cohesion appears to affect leader monitoring differently given the institutional context. Moreover, leaders in systems with strong personal vote incentives appear to give their MPs more flexibility than leaders in party-centered systems when it matters and the views inside the party are diverse. This is particularly true when intraparty disagreement reaches high levels (i.e. cohesion levels greater than 45), just as the theory predicts.[11]

Although these results appear to provide evidence for our theory, we note that there are limits to this kind of cross-national analysis. First, due to the low response rate that is common in all elite surveys, we have relatively few observations. Despite multiple contact attempts, only 36 parties could be included in the final analysis. Second, the measurements are noisy. By this we mean that intraparty cohesion is a difficult concept to compress onto a unidimensional scale. Even though respondents were given a scale with well-defined end points, the concept ignores other aspects, such as the strength of conflicts, the types of issues involved, personal scandals, or local interests. In this sense, we interpret the results not as hard evidence in favor of our theory but as initial confirmatory (but still only exploratory) evidence. The results, by and large, confirm the theoretical expectations from a cross-national perspective, but as is the case with all cross-national analyses of this style, the micro foundations of the theory necessarily remained unexplored. Therefore, subsequent chapters focus exclusively on selected parliaments to examine debate participation in much more detail than the cross-national analysis allows us to do.

4.2.3 Coalition government and legislative speeches

Our final analysis using the party survey relates to the role of political parties in government. We have argued that intraparty politics drives decisions about who will speak for the party. But do government parties change course when they need to endorse coalition compromises? When parties join coalition governments, considerations may shift toward a mode of compromise. In fact, the official party line may no longer represent the party position. Instead, parties may adhere to the coalition compromise and defend the policies of the coalition as a whole in parliament, in particular vis-à-vis a critical opposition.

[11] We also note that when the party is estimated to be homogeneous (cohesion levels smaller than 45), leaders appear to be more involved in moderate or strong personal vote incentive systems. Important for our analysis, however, is the negative slope for strong personal vote systems, which contrasts to the positive slope for weak personal vote systems.

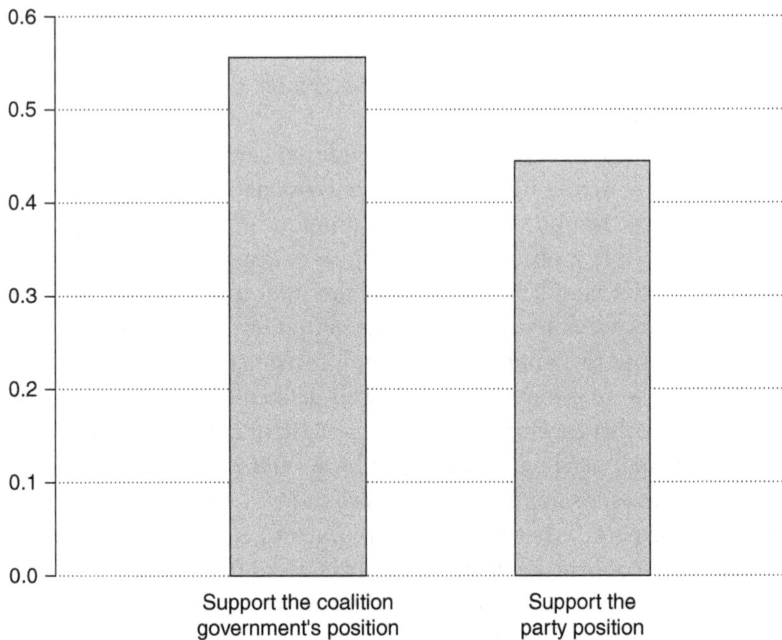

Figure 4.10 Government parties' expectation regarding their MPs' speeches ($N = 18$)

Alternatively, party leaders care about communicating positions to voters that can be distinguished from a coalition compromise (Martin and Vanberg, 2008), so as to keep a distinct profile among the electorate. We asked parties that were in a coalition government at the time of the survey to indicate what speeches the party expects from its MPs when the government and the party positions differ: "Suppose the coalition government's position differs on an issue from the position your party campaigned on. What does your party expect from your MPs' legislative speeches?"

As shown in Figure 4.10, in the majority of instances, government parties responded that the MPs are expected to support the coalition government's position, but a sizable number of responses indicated that they expect their MPs to defend the *party position* in their speeches. This means that legislative speeches can indeed serve as a tool for a party to publicly distinguish itself from the coalition partner. This finding is in line with the results of Martin and Vanberg (2008), who argue that legislative speeches provide a mechanism for coalition partners to communicate party, rather than coalition, positions to their constituents. What matters in the end is how party leaders interpret what constitutes the party line. Is it the coalition compromise or the platform of the party? Depending on the conflict within the coalition, these considerations may change throughout the course of governments. The data suggest that defending the pure party position is a substantial factor even after parties have joined coalition governments.

4.3 Summary

This chapter has offered cross-national data on how parliaments, and the parties within them, organize legislative debate. In addition to providing summary data on parliamentary and party rules, we have examined some key aspects of our theory. First, parliamentary rules tend to give parties more control over speaker lists in countries where the electoral system creates incentives for a personal vote. Second, our survey of parliamentary parties reveals that they both care about the content of legislative speech and tend to control their members in the manner predicted by our theory. The next chapters go on to test our theory in individual parliaments at the MP level.

5 Debate participation: Germany and the United Kingdom

At its core, our theory is about parliamentary behavior – which members of parliament take the floor and what do they say? In this chapter, we offer an empirical test of one component of this behavioral question. We examine the variation in parliamentary debate participation in Germany and the United Kingdom. The dependent variable is speech counts – how many times did each member of parliament give a speech? We test the empirical implications from Chapter 2 using several independent variables, including the status of the MP – backbencher versus party leader – and a measure of the level of latent disagreement between the MP and his or her party leadership based on candidate surveys. We demonstrate that the patterns of speech participation are quite different in these two parliaments but vary in accordance with our theory – party leaders play a more active role in Germany, whereas rebels are more likely to take the floor in the United Kingdom.

5.1 Hypotheses

We begin by deriving several hypotheses from the speech delegation model for debate participation in these two parliaments. First, Germany's mixed-member proportional (MMP) closed-list electoral institutions generate little incentive for MPs to cultivate a personal vote compared with the United Kingdom's single-member district (SMD) plurality system. As a result of the electoral system, German party leaders are also more concerned with protecting the party brand than British party leaders. Thus, we expect German party leaders to exercise greater control over the party message on the floor than British party leaders do. In terms of debate participation, we expect party leaders to take the floor relatively more often in Germany compared with the United Kingdom, and backbenchers to take the floor relatively less often.

Hypothesis 1: *Party leaders in Germany speak more frequently compared with backbenchers, whereas party leaders in the United Kingdom speak less often compared with backbenchers.*

With regard to ideology, we expect German party leaders to make a concerted effort to keep party rebels off the floor, as dissent in speech may potentially harm the party brand. Rebels in the United Kingdom, on the other hand, are more likely to take the floor. British party leaders have (purposefully) developed fewer mechanisms for controlling these rebels, and leaders realize that expressing dissent may help backbenchers make a name for themselves, fostering their reelection bids.

Hypothesis 2: *In the United Kingdom, MPs who are ideologically more distant from their party leadership are able to take the floor; in Germany, MPs who are ideologically distant from their party leadership are less likely to take the floor.*

Moreover, we can develop specific hypotheses for German MPs elected off the party list and MPs elected out of SMDs. Because backbenchers from SMDs have a greater electoral incentive to deviate from the party line to connect with their constituents, but party leaders have an incentive to protect the party brand, we expect party leaders to be particularly cautious about letting members elected from SMDs take the floor.

Hypothesis 3: *Members of the German Bundestag elected from SMDs take the floor less often than members elected off the party lists.*

Using data on speech participation, we now set out to test these hypotheses.

5.2 MP status: when party leaders get involved

We examine parliamentary speeches for each legislative term of the German Bundestag between 1976 and 1998 and of the UK House of Commons between 1979 and 2004. The data were collected from the online archives of both parliaments, and details about the data collection are provided in the Appendix. In both countries, left- and right-wing parties were in government during these periods. For each month and MP we counted the number of speeches delivered on the

Table 5.1. *Overview of parliamentary speeches in the United Kingdom and Germany*

	UK	Germany
Average monthly speeches		
... in parliament	4,213	181
... per MP	6.5	0.3
Share of MPs speaking at least once during their tenure	91.7%	99.9%

Note: Coverage for United Kingdom 1979–2004 and for Germany 1976–1998. Months with no speeches are excluded from calculations.

floor of parliament. Furthermore, we coded the MP's status within his or her party during each month (backbencher or party leader), and, for Germany, whether the speaker was elected off the party list or out of an SMD.

Without paying attention to leader or backbencher status, on the face of it, MPs in the United Kingdom are significantly more active in debate than their German counterparts. On average, more than 4,200 speeches are delivered each month in the House of Commons but just over 180 in the German Bundestag (Table 5.1). Yet this drastic difference is partially due to what constitutes a speech in the two parliaments. In the United Kingdom, business in the House includes ministerial statements, debates, adjournment debates, and debates on early day motions. Short interventions and exchanges between MPs are not only common but also significantly easier to engage in than in Germany because the flow of debate is regulated by the Speaker. As a result, a lively back-and-forth between government and opposition MPs is common. Moreover, central to debates in the House of Commons is question time, when opposition MPs can pose questions to members of the government.[1] In contrast, as discussed earlier, debates in Germany tend to be prepared in advance, speaking roles are predetermined by the parties, the speeches are longer, and, although possible, spontaneous exchanges between MPs remain rare. As a consequence, MPs in the House of Commons deliver many more speeches on average than their German counterparts. This appears to confirm the view of

[1] Written questions and answers are excluded from our analysis.

the United Kingdom as a debating parliament and Germany as a working parliament. Yet when comparing the share of MPs who participate in debates during their tenure, we see that the two parliaments are not that different. In both parliaments, almost all MPs deliver a speech at one point during their parliamentary tenure. The share is even higher in Germany than in the United Kingdom. Therefore, MPs in both countries participate in debates, albeit the definition of what constitutes a speech differs across the countries. We explore the variation in participation to test the predictions of the speech delegation model.

5.2.1 Party-level analysis

To look for broad patterns, we start by examining the data at the party level. Our model predicts that the speech participation rate of party leaders should be substantively different in the two systems. A direct comparison of the participation rates for parties, however, is not feasible because the definition of party leaders differs across systems. In Germany, party leaders include party group chairs (Fraktionsvorsitzender), party whips (Parlamentarischer Geschäftsführer), party working group chairs (Arbeitsgruppenvorsitzender), and party chairs (Parteivorsitzender). We exclude speeches given by MPs who were government members, including chancellor, ministers, and junior ministers. Leaders of governing parties in the United Kingdom include whips, parliamentary undersecretaries, and ministers of state. For the opposition, we define leaders as the shadow cabinet members and party leaders. We exclude speeches given by members of the cabinet. Government and cabinet members are excluded from the analysis because we cannot disentangle whether an MP gave a speech in the role of party leader or government member. This is especially problematic in the United Kingdom, where, even after excluding cabinet members, most party leaders from the governing party hold government roles (e.g. minister of state or parliamentary undersecretary). Thus it is difficult to determine whether leaders of the UK governing party are speaking in a parliamentary party leadership role or as a member of government. Because of this confounding between government and parliamentary leadership positions, parties in opposition offer the better test of our theory. In the party-level analysis, we only include MPs in our analysis whom we could uniquely assign as party leaders and backbenchers throughout the respective legislative term. We later relax this assumption when examining the data at the MP level.

When the proportion of leaders within parliamentary parties varies, either due to the nature of the political system or the size of parties, we cannot directly compare the proportion of speeches that leaders in different parties give. Instead, we need to establish a baseline expectation for the activity of party leaders. An institution-free expectation is that each MP has the same probability of receiving floor time. Thus, our null hypothesis is that the proportion of leader speeches within a party is proportional to leaders' seat share inside the party. We expect party leaders in Germany to give significantly more speeches than their seat share would suggest. In the United Kingdom, we expect party leaders' speech share to match or be lower than the baseline expectation. For each party and legislative term, we identify party leaders and backbenchers and calculate the proportion of leader speeches. To test whether the differences between speech and seat share are significantly different from each other, we generate 95 percent confidence intervals for the leader speech proportions through a nonparametric bootstrap. We simulate 1,000 speech scenarios by sampling from the leader speech vector and the backbencher speech vector with replacement. For each of these samples, the number of leader and backbencher speeches is counted and the proportion of leader speeches calculated. The confidence intervals cover the 2.5th and 97.5th percentile of the resulting distributions of leader speech proportions. These confidence intervals allow us to test whether the proportion of speeches is significantly different from the baseline expectation that speeches correspond to the seat share of the leadership relative to backbenchers.

Figure 5.1 plots the share of leader speeches relative to leaders' seat share for each legislative term and for the two major parties in the United Kingdom. For an easier visual interpretation, the plots are centered at the leaders' seat share. The dotted vertical line represents the null hypothesis. If the leader involvement is higher than predicted by the seat share, the points indicating the speech share would be to the right of this line, and if involvement is lower than predicted by seat share, the points would be to the left. The plots for the Labour and Conservative parties show that we cannot reject the null hypothesis that party leaders simply give speeches in accordance with what we would expect given their seat share whenever the parties are in opposition. The confidence intervals cover zero in four of the six opposition

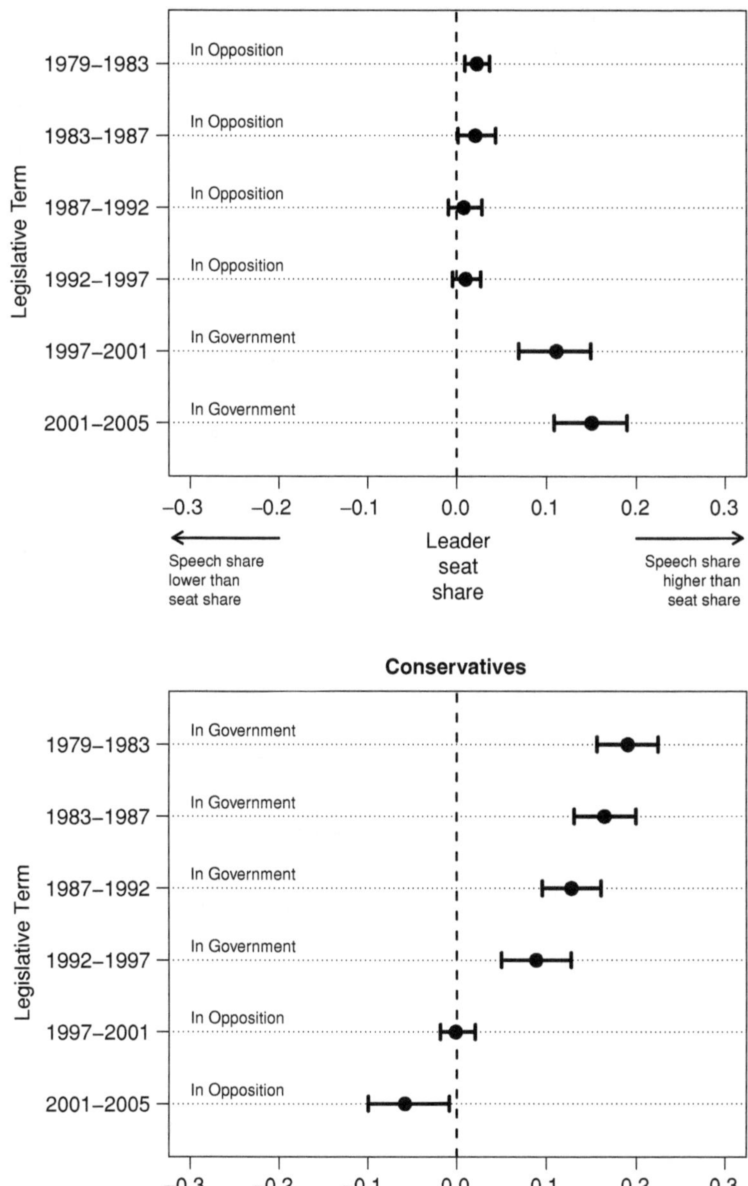

Figure 5.1 Debate participation: leader involvement in the United Kingdom, 1979–2005

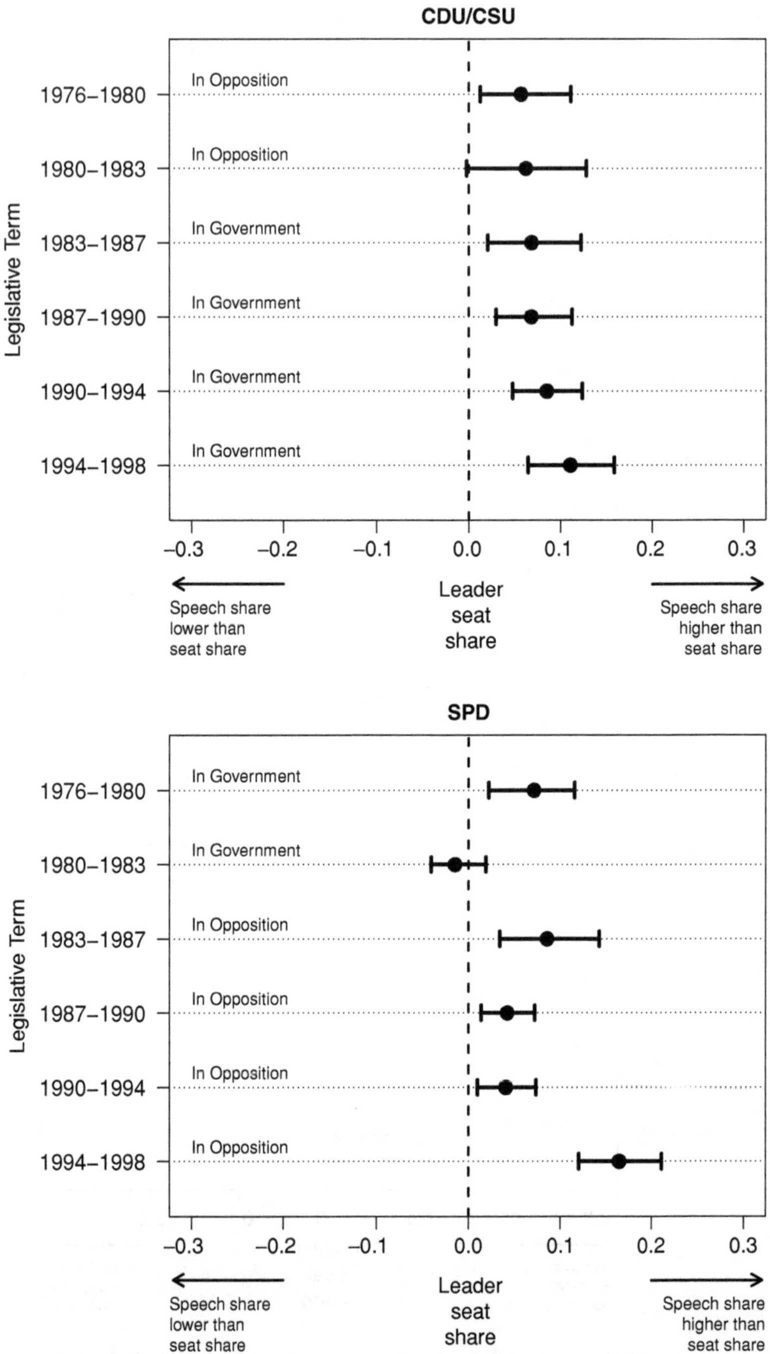

Figure 5.2 Debate participation: leader involvement in Germany, 1976–1998

scenarios. In contrast, leaders of governing parties give more speeches than expected under the null hypothesis.[2] Yet it is difficult to know whether leaders speak in their capacity as government members or as a party leader due to the difficulty in disentangling parliamentary roles from the governmental ones. The evidence from opposition parties thus supports the notion that British party leaders do allow more floor time for backbenchers.

The picture is drastically different in Germany. Figure 5.2 shows that party leaders of the major parties gave consistently *more* speeches than would be expected on the basis of their intraparty seat share. Across all legislative terms, the proportion of party leader speeches is higher. The results are consistently significant; in all but one term, the confidence intervals exclude the seat share.

In addition to examining the extent to which party leaders dominate legislative debates, the German system allows us to make a controlled comparison with regard to the weight MPs place on their position (λ_M). Our institutional model suggests that although MPs elected from SMDs would potentially prefer to give more speeches to bolster their personal image, party leaders have an incentive to keep them off the floor because SMD MPs have a weaker incentive to support the party line than list MPs. Leaders prioritize the goal of preserving the party label to maximize the list vote because this determines overall seat share. Therefore, the leadership ought to favor floor time for the party-oriented list MPs over the SMD MPs. Figure 5.3 plots the proportion of speeches given by backbenchers elected out of SMDs relative to their share of seats in the Bundestag for both major parties. As in the previous plots, the vertical line indicates the null hypothesis that district MPs give speeches relative to their strength inside the party. The results either suggest that we cannot reject the null hypothesis that MPs elected out of SMDs give speeches according to their intraparty seat share or indicate that SMD MPs do in fact give *fewer* speeches than expected. In no legislative term is the proportion significantly higher for SMD MPs.

[2] These results, especially those for the Conservatives, differ slightly from those presented in Proksch and Slapin (2012). Here, we use a different source for our speech data – the historic Hansard rather than the regular Hansard – which allows us to get a longer time-series. Unfortunately, the historic Hansard only has the speech record through 2004. Thus we are missing the last few months of the 2001–2005 term. In addition, while similar, the precise speech counts may vary slightly between the two sources as search engines and databases are not identical.

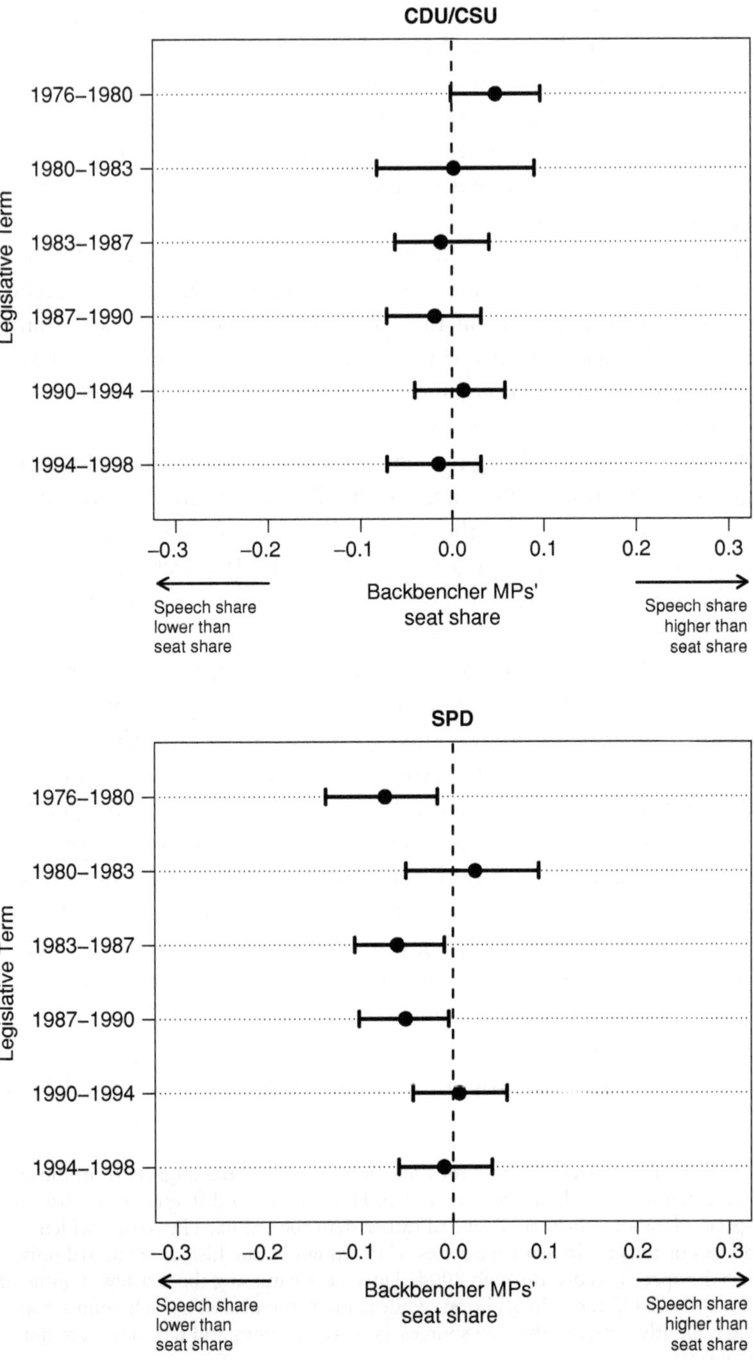

Figure 5.3 Debate participation: district versus list MPs in Germany, 1976–1998

We interpret this as strong evidence for our model. An alternative explanation for our result would be that district MPs actually demand less floor time because they are busier with other activities, such as connecting with constituents back in the district. To examine this possibility we have gathered the Bundestag's "list of excused members," the closest available data to a daily attendance roster (which is not recorded). If district MPs are less active in parliament because they are dealing with other constituency matters, we would expect them to excuse themselves from the plenary sessions more often. They do not; if anything, they excuse themselves slightly less often than list MPs.[3] This suggests that our results are not due to self-selection of district MPs.

Although it provides a good way to visualize backbencher and leader participation, one drawback to analyzing the data at the party level is that we need to make several simplifying assumptions. We can neither examine changes in speech participation of MPs who move up the ranks of the party during a term or across terms, nor can we control for idiosyncratic effects that make MPs prone to participation in debates. We therefore estimate a statistical model that allows us to do exactly this.

5.2.2 *MP-level analysis*

The historical archives provide us with a longitudinal count of MPs' monthly parliamentary speeches. We model these data using a mixed effects Poisson model. The systematic component models speeches as a function of the MP's party leader or backbencher status, government participation, and the interaction between status and government participation. The interaction is motivated by the previous aggregate analysis, suggesting that leaders of governing parties are substantially more active on the floor. Because we can isolate the effect of government status during the estimation, we choose a wider definition of leaders. In the United Kingdom, we assign MPs as leaders if they are whips, parliamentary undersecretaries, ministers of state, or members of the cabinet

[3] We were able to obtain this list from the Bundestag administration for the 2005–2009 legislative term. List MPs excuse themselves from 5.2 percent of plenary sessions, whereas district MPs excuse themselves from only 4.5 percent of sessions. A difference of means test reveals no statistical difference in attendance rates between the two types of MP ($t = 1.41$, $p = 0.16$).

or shadow cabinet. In Germany, leaders include whips, spokespersons, party leaders, junior ministers, and cabinet members.[4] For Germany, we also estimate a fixed effect for the electoral tier of the MP to test whether party list MPs or SMD MPs are more active. We specify different random effects. In all models, we allow overall debate activity to vary by MP by introducing random coefficients. Regarding variation over time, we run models with legislative term or with monthly random intercepts. Besides these different model specifications, we also distinguish between two data samples in the United Kingdom and three samples in Germany to check the robustness of the effects. We first consider all MPs ($N = 1{,}474$ for the United Kingdom and $N = 1{,}410$ for Germany). Subsequently, we reduce the sample to those MPs who have switched between backbencher and party leader positions ($N = 535$ for the United Kingdom and $N = 402$ for Germany). Additionally, for Germany, we run an analysis on MPs who switched between electoral tiers during their parliamentary tenure ($N = 160$).

Table 5.2 presents the results of the mixed effects models for the full sample of British MPs. The four models differ in their random effect specification. All models include random intercepts for MPs, thus controlling for idiosyncratic personal factors explaining variation in parliamentary activity not considered in the model. Models 1 and 2 also include time-specific random intercepts (legislative terms or months). Models 3 and 4 additionally allow for random (MP-specific) coefficients for the leader, government, and interaction variables. The results strongly confirm the aggregate analysis. In all models, the leader coefficient – indicating the scenario for opposition MPs – is consistently negative, suggesting that opposition backbencher MPs deliver relatively more speeches per month. Government party leaders, on the other hand, are more likely to give speeches – both the coefficient for government status and for the interaction with leader status are positive, creating a net positive effect of government leaders on speeches. In this case, leaders take on active roles by defending government policy and answering oral parliamentary questions. Next we estimate the same models for those MPs who, at one point, held any type of party

[4] As a robustness check, we run the third model in Tables 5.2 and 5.4 altering the definition of the leader. The results hold and are discussed in more detail in the Appendix.

Table 5.2. ***Models of parliamentary speech in the United Kingdom, 1979–2004 (all MPs)***

	Model 1	Model 2	Model 3	Model 4
Random intercepts: MPs	Yes	Yes	Yes	Yes
Random intercepts: terms	Yes	No	Yes	No
Random intercepts: months	No	Yes	No	Yes
Random coefficients: MPs	No	No	Yes	Yes
Leader	−0.285***	−0.244***	−4.704***	−4.440***
	(0.006)	(0.006)	(0.280)	(0.260)
Government	0.506***	0.369***	3.592***	3.299***
	(0.003)	(0.003)	(0.108)	(0.102)
Leader × government	1.198***	1.170***	5.587***	5.325***
	(0.007)	(0.007)	(0.278)	(0.258)
(Intercept)	1.134***	1.082***	−1.952***	−1.793***
	(0.073)	(0.046)	(0.120)	(0.112)
N	170,636	170,636	170,636	170,636
Deviance	958,128	831,245	784,745	674,073
Groups:				
MPs	1,474	1,474	1,474	1,474
Terms	6	–	6	–
Months	–	262	–	262

Note: Mixed-effect Poisson regressions. All calculations done in R using the lme4 package. $^{***}p \leq 0.01$; $^{**}p \leq 0.05$; $^{*}p \leq 0.1$.

leader position during their tenure. Table 5.3 presents the results for this reduced sample. The results remain robust. As before, opposition leaders give fewer speeches than opposition backbenchers, whereas the opposite is true for government leaders and backbenchers. The results are thus in line with the aggregate party-level analysis. They provide evidence that opposition parties in the United Kingdom allow backbenchers to take the floor.

The effect of party leader status is reversed in Germany. Table 5.4 presents the estimation results for the full sample of MPs. Across the 22-year period, party leaders of opposition parties (the coefficient for leader) are significantly more active on the floor. Government status

Table 5.3. *Models of parliamentary speech in the United Kingdom, 1979–2004 (only MPs switching between backbencher and leader status)*

	Model 5	Model 6	Model 7	Model 8
Random intercepts: MPs	Yes	Yes	Yes	Yes
Random intercepts: terms	Yes	No	Yes	No
Random intercepts: months	No	Yes	No	Yes
Random coefficients: MPs	No	No	Yes	Yes
Leader	−0.317***	−0.272***	−4.655***	−4.375***
	(0.006)	(0.006)	(0.285)	(0.265)
In government	0.404***	0.291***	2.970***	2.707***
	(0.005)	(0.005)	(0.165)	(0.157)
Leader × government	1.277***	1.239***	5.507***	5.243***
	(0.007)	(0.007)	(0.285)	(0.264)
Intercept	1.468***	1.405***	−1.319***	−1.200***
	(0.076)	(0.048)	(0.172)	(0.166)
N	72,250	72,250	72,250	72,250
Deviance	479,065	418,920	374,499	322,692
Groups:				
MPs	535	535	535	535
Terms	6	–	6	–
Months	–	262	–	262

Note: Mixed-effect Poisson regressions. All calculations done in R using the lme4 package. $^{***}p \leq 0.01$; $^{**}p \leq 0.05$; $^{*}p \leq 0.1$.

does not substantially affect the effect of leader status. The effect of the interaction is slightly negative, but the overall net effect of leader status for government parties remains positive. These effects are robust to the random effects specification used. The full model also provides consistent evidence that MPs from the party list tier are more active on the floor, controlling for government participation, leader status, MP-specific, and time effects.

As for the United Kingdom, we consider subsets of the data to determine whether the results hold for those MPs that switch between leader and backbencher positions, in essence isolating the effect of promotion on speech. Table 5.5 presents these results. The results continue to support our theory. Opposition and government leaders alike have positive

Table 5.4. ***Models of parliamentary speech in Germany, 1976–1998 (all MPs)***

	Model 1	Model 2	Model 3	Model 4
Random intercepts: MPs	Yes	Yes	Yes	Yes
Random intercepts: terms	Yes	No	Yes	No
Random intercepts: months	No	Yes	No	Yes
Random coefficients: MPs	No	No	Yes	Yes
Leader	0.454***	0.448***	0.522***	0.519***
	(0.025)	(0.026)	(0.042)	(0.041)
In government	0.029	0.030	−0.029	−0.029
	(0.021)	(0.021)	(0.039)	(0.039)
Leader × government	−0.085***	−0.082**	−0.043	−0.027
	(0.032)	(0.032)	(0.062)	(0.062)
Party list tier	0.153***	0.143***	0.337***	0.324***
	(0.027)	(0.027)	(0.038)	(0.038)
Intercept	−1.647***	−1.795***	−1.787***	−1.920***
	(0.092)	(0.062)	(0.115)	(0.066)
N	126,830	126,830	126,830	126,830
Deviance	101,996	90,498	100,653	89,142
Groups:				
MPs	1,410	1,410	1,410	1,410
Terms	6	–	6	–
Months	–	225	–	225

Note: Mixed-effect Poisson regressions. All calculations done in R using the lme4 package. $^{***}p \leq 0.01$; $^{**}p \leq 0.05$; $^{*}p \leq 0.1$.

leader coefficients, albeit the models predict a slightly smaller effect for government leaders than for opposition leaders (the interaction effect is negative and marginally significant). For these MPs, the party list tier variable also remains positive. In the final robustness test, we reduce the sample to those MPs that managed to get elected in both tiers during their parliamentary tenure. Table 5.6 shows that although the effect of party list remains positive on speech participation, it is no longer significant. Because switching tiers does not happen frequently – only around 10 percent of MPs in the data set have done so – this suggests that the results are driven primarily by the vast majority of MPs

Table 5.5. *Models of parliamentary speech in Germany, 1976–1998 (only MPs switching between backbencher and leader status)*

	Model 5	Model 6	Model 7	Model 8
Random intercepts: MPs	Yes	Yes	Yes	Yes
Random intercepts: terms	Yes	No	Yes	No
Random intercepts: months	No	Yes	No	Yes
Random coefficients: MPs	No	No	Yes	Yes
Leader	0.459***	0.457***	0.470***	0.463***
	(0.027)	(0.027)	(0.045)	(0.044)
In government	0.100***	0.109***	0.003	0.012
	(0.031)	(0.031)	(0.067)	(0.067)
Leader × government	−0.148***	−0.151***	−0.152**	−0.148**
	(0.034)	(0.034)	(0.072)	(0.073)
Party list tier	0.152***	0.145***	0.401***	0.391***
	(0.038)	(0.038)	(0.060)	(0.060)
Intercept	−1.405***	−1.507***	−1.621***	−1.711***
	(0.119)	(0.067)	(0.135)	(0.078)
N	50,763	50,763	50,763	50,763
Deviance	46,764	41,507	45,789	40,523
Groups:				
MPs	402	402	402	402
Terms	6	–	6	–
Months	–	225	–	225

Note: Mixed-effect Poisson regressions. All calculations done in R using the lme4 package. $^{***}p \leq 0.01$; $^{**}p \leq 0.05$; $^{*}p \leq 0.1$.

who are exclusively elected in either the list or district tier of Germany's mixed-member proportional system.

In sum, the longitudinal analysis, covering six legislative terms in both countries and more than 20 years, corroborates the model's predictions with regard to the status and the electoral tier of MPs. A last central component of the model, however, cannot be examined with these data: the effect of ideological disagreement between party leaders and backbenchers. This calls for MP-specific measures of ideology – ideally exogenous to legislative behavior – something we look at in the next section.

Table 5.6. ***Models of parliamentary speech in Germany, 1976–1998 (only MPs switching between electoral tiers)***

	Model 9	Model 10	Model 11	Model 12
Random intercepts: MPs	Yes	Yes	Yes	Yes
Random intercepts: terms	Yes	No	Yes	No
Random intercepts: months	No	Yes	No	Yes
Random coefficients: MPs	No	No	Yes	Yes
Leader	0.631***	0.655***	0.449***	0.473***
	(0.062)	(0.062)	(0.115)	(0.119)
In government	0.032	0.039	0.017	0.022
	(0.044)	(0.044)	(0.078)	(0.079)
Leader × government	−0.104	−0.130*	0.031	0.009
	(0.070)	(0.070)	(0.136)	(0.142)
Party list tier	0.021	0.016	0.042	0.035
	(0.036)	(0.036)	(0.059)	(0.060)
Intercept	−1.667***	−1.808***	−1.711***	−1.846***
	(0.080)	(0.071)	(0.088)	(0.084)
N	21,800	21,800	21,800	21,800
Deviance	17,093	15,688	16,831	15,423
Groups:				
MPs	160	160	160	160
Terms	6	–	6	–
Months	–	225	–	225

Note: Mixed-effect Poisson regressions. All calculations done in R using the lme4 package. $^{***}p \leq 0.01$; $^{**}p \leq 0.05$; $^{*}p \leq 0.1$.

5.3 Ideological disagreement

Ideological disagreement between backbenchers and party leaders is not uncommon. After all, parties are collective actors that must aggregate diverse views and policy stances. The speech delegation model has distinct implications with regard to the effect of ideology on parliamentary debate. For German MPs, our model predicts that the probability of delivering a speech decreases as a backbencher's distance from the party leadership increases. In the United Kingdom, on the other hand, backbenchers with large ideological distances should be more likely to speak.

Ideological disagreement in politics is ubiquitous, but measuring it *within parties* poses a challenge. Parties rarely air internal conflicts publicly, but as collective actors we know that members differ in their view of what policies the party should stand for. We therefore rely on surveys of electoral candidates to estimate the ideological difference between party leadership and backbenchers. To generate ideological distances, we use survey questions regarding candidates' self-placements on a left–right scale from the German Candidate Survey conducted in 2005 (Gschwend et al., 2005; Wüst et al., 2006) and the British Representation Study conducted in 2001 (Norris and Luvenduski, 2001). These candidate surveys provide a measure of MP ideology that is *exogenous* to legislative behavior. Thus, we take this as our best guess for the latent ideological position of MPs. This means that we are restricted to studying the effects for a particular time period and cannot resort to the full data set from the previous section. For causal inference reasons, we use the parliamentary speech counts for the period following the survey. Thus, the dependent variables are the number of parliamentary speeches during the entire 2005–2009 legislative term in Germany and the 2001–2005 term in the United Kingdom.

The two candidate surveys differ with regard to the questions asked about the position of party leadership. The British Representation Study asks each MP to place his or her party's leadership on an 11-point left–right scale. To calculate the position of the party leadership, we take the average response of party members on this question. The German Candidate Survey does not include a question about party leadership. Instead, the survey asked members to place themselves, their party, and all other parties on an 11-point left–right scale. Because MPs rank every party, not just their own, we first apply a rescaling procedure to correct for the fact that every MP might perceive the scales differently (Aldrich and McKelvey, 1977).[5] After rescaling the self-placements, we calculate the leader position for each party as the median of the rescaled self-placements of party leaders. Thus, we define the party leadership position as close to the theoretical idea as possible given the data available for both countries. We then calculate the absolute distance of each MP's left–right position from the party leadership position to arrive at our distance variable.

[5] We use the R package *basicspace* to estimate the location of MPs with the Aldrich/McKelvey algorithm (Poole et al., 2010).

As control variables, we include party dummies and a party leader dummy in both models. The German models also include a dummy indicating whether an MP was elected from a party list (as opposed to from a district) and a variable counting the number of committees on which the MP served. The expectation is that MPs with more assignments are more likely to be experts on policy issues and therefore more likely to be considered for floor time.[6] Finally, in the German case, we control for the fact that MPs from the governing coalition may respond to the constraint imposed by the coalition agreement between the governing parties. To do so, we create a dummy variable indicating whether the MP is located outside the coalition interval defined by the party leadership positions of the CDU/CSU and the SPD. If governing MPs do indeed respond to the coalition agreement, then they should be less likely to speak if they are outside the coalition interval, and the distance variable (which is calculated using the absolute distance from the leadership position) should not explain the variation in speech counts.

We run several negative binomial models predicting the number of speeches delivered by each MP as a function of ideological distance to the party and the control variables.[7] Table 5.7 presents the results for the United Kingdom and Table 5.8 for Germany. As discussed earlier, the United Kingdom and Germany differ with respect to the overall debate activity of their MPs. British MPs gave on average 136 speeches in the 2001–2005 legislative term (median speech count of 101), whereas German MPs delivered 18 speeches on average (median of 15) during the 2005–2009 legislative term.[8] On average, German MPs deliver fewer speeches than their British counterparts. We first run models with all MPs and without the distance variables. These constitute our baseline models.[9]

For the United Kingdom, the party leader variable is positive and significant (model 1). This effect is primarily driven by the governing

6 Because committees play a more significant role in the Bundestag, we consider this variable to be an important control for the recognition likelihood of each MP only in Germany.

7 Likelihood ratio tests for overdispersion are statistically signficant.

8 This difference is slightly deceiving because we were able to remove speeches from the German data set given by MPs in their function as government members, whereas we were not able to do the same for the United Kingdom due to the way speeches are recorded in the parliamentary archives.

9 We only include MPs serving the full term.

Table 5.7. *Modeling the effect of ideological disagreement in the United Kingdom (2001–2005)*

	Model 1	Model 2	Model 3
Distance MP to party leadership			0.118*
			(0.064)
Party leader	0.334**	0.078	0.434
	(0.150)	(0.225)	(0.335)
Party: Conservatives	0.295***		0.379**
	(0.092)		(0.160)
Constant	4.785***	5.100***	4.643***
	(0.052)	(0.066)	(0.171)
Theta	1.105***	1.676***	1.351***
	(0.064)	(0.185)	(0.146)
Log-likelihood	−3056.732	−918.968	−918.180
N	518	152	153

Note: The negative binomial models were estimated using the ZELIG package (Imai, King, and Lau, 2007). Baseline party is the Labour Party, other parties are excluded in the models. Model 1 includes all MPs, model 2 all Conservative MPs, and model 3 all MPs who responded in the candidate survey. *** $p \leq 0.01$; ** $p \leq 0.05$; * $p \leq 0.1$.

Labour Party members, as was suggested by the previous analysis. Once we exclude Labour MPs from the analysis and keep only the opposition Conservative MPs (model 2), the party leader effect disappears. When we include the distance variable, we are able to keep around a third of MPs in the sample. The results confirm our expectation: we find that ideological distance from one's party leadership actually has a slightly positive and significant impact on the likelihood that an MP speaks. Members at odds with their party leadership are not kept off the floor but rather speak more frequently than members closer to their parties' leadership (model 3). This result is robust to the inclusion of a party dummy.

In Germany, our baseline model with all MPs predicts that leaders speak more often, party list MPs are more active, and more committee assignments, that is, higher policy expertise, also lead to higher speech counts on the floor (model 1). These results confirm the aggregate analysis. When we consider ideological distance from the party leadership, we do indeed find a negative effect, as the theoretical model

Table 5.8. ***Modeling the effect of ideological disagreement in Germany (2005–2009)***

	Model 1	Model 2	Model 3	Model 4	Model 5
Distance MP to party leadership		−0.588*	−0.465	−0.571*	−0.829**
		(0.327)	(0.303)	(0.316)	(0.408)
Party leader	0.562***	0.493***	0.242	0.253	0.173
	(0.101)	(0.184)	(0.174)	(0.174)	(0.320)
Party list MP	0.493***	0.615***	0.103	0.102	0.149
	(0.064)	(0.110)	(0.124)	(0.123)	(0.138)
MP position outside coalition interval				0.147	0.190
				(0.133)	(0.149)
Committee assignments	0.108***	0.144***	0.126***	0.129***	0.181***
	(0.020)	(0.036)	(0.033)	(0.033)	(0.044)
Party: CDU/CSU			−0.973***	−1.022***	
			(0.193)	(0.197)	
Party: SPD			−0.892***	−0.979***	0.035
			(0.186)	(0.200)	(0.140)
Party: DIE LINKE			−0.270	−0.279	
			(0.219)	(0.218)	
Party: FDP			−0.094	−0.102	
			(0.195)	(0.194)	
Constant	2.201***	2.107***	3.074***	3.086***	1.917***
	(0.080)	(0.157)	(0.238)	(0.238)	(0.195)
Theta	1.783***	1.979***	2.467***	2.483***	1.996***
	(0.112)	(0.222)	(0.294)	(0.297)	(0.289)
Log-likelihood	−2304.203	−749.818	−731.580	−730.979	−454.915
N	604	197	197	197	132

Note: The negative binomial models were estimated using the ZELIG package (Imai, King, and Lau, 2007). Baseline party are the Greens. Models 1 and 2 include all MPs, model 3 and 4 include all MPs who responded in the candidate survey and for whom a left–right position could be estimated, model 5 includes only government coalition MPs from the SPD and the CDU/CSU who responded to the candidate surveys. $^{***}p \leq 0.01$; $^{**}p \leq 0.05$; $^{*}p \leq 0.1$.

predicts (model 2). This is in stark contrast to the positive effect of distance on speech counts in the United Kingdom. As a German MP's ideological distance from the party leader position on the left–right scale increases, the MP gives fewer speeches. This effect holds when we control for the status of the MP. The findings again confirm the party-level analysis. List MPs tend to give more speeches, as do party leaders. The effects for list/district status and leaders, although always positive, do not remain statistically significant once we include party dummies (models 3–5). This is not surprising as only the large parties, the SPD and CDU/CSU, are successful in winning SMDs. Therefore, party dummies correlate highly with MP status. Lastly, we have included a dummy variable to control for whether MPs from the governing parties (SPD and CDU/CSU) were located inside the interval of the governing coalition (model 4 and 5). This variable allows us to test whether MPs may be expected to follow the coalition, rather than a party, line. However, we find little evidence for this. The ideological distance variable remains statistically significant and the coalition dummy is not. This effect holds both when we consider all MPs (model 4) and only MPs from the governing coalition (model 5). Thus, given the ideological distance for each MP, coalition effects do not explain any additional variation in speech counts.

To understand the substantive magnitude of the effects found in these models, as well as the associated uncertainty, we simulate expected speech counts and corresponding 95 percent confidence intervals for the ideological distance variable on the basis of model 3 (United Kingdom) and model 4 (Germany). The quantities of interest are shown in Figure 5.4. The German model predicts that backbenchers whose left–right position is identical to the party position give around 16 speeches, whereas MPs who maximally disagree with the party leadership deliver only 10 speeches, almost 40 percent *fewer* speeches. The UK model, in contrast, predicts that backbenchers who are ideologically close to the leadership give around 109 speeches, and MPs who disagree the most around 202 speeches, thus almost doubling the number of speeches. The magnitude of the effects of ideological distance is thus substantial.[10]

[10] In addition, we simulate predicted speech counts and 95 percent confidence intervals for different types of German MPs (list vs. district). We report them in the Appendix.

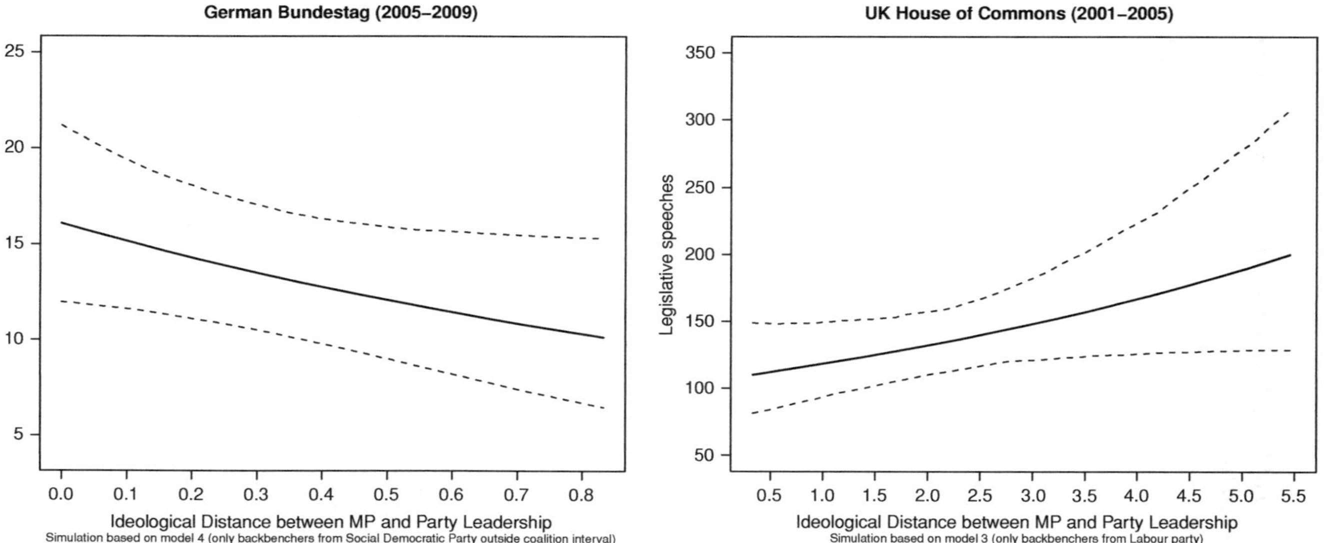

Figure 5.4 Effects of ideological distance between MP and party leadership on legislative speech counts in Germany and the United Kingdom

Note: Expected values and associated 95 percent confidence intervals were simulated using the R package *Zelig* (Imai, King, and Lau, 2007). In the simulations, the party leader dummy was set to zero (to predict the effect for backbencher MPs). Simulations based on model 3 (United Kingdom) and model 4 (Germany).

Table 5.9. ***Probit model of budget speeches in the United Kingdom (2011) and Germany (2010)***

	Germany	United Kingdom
Party leader	0.96***	−0.31**
	(0.19)	(0.12)
Budget committee	2.26***	1.19***
	(0.31)	(0.40)
CDU/CSU	−0.41**	
	(0.20)	
Die Linke	−0.03	
	(0.24)	
FDP	−0.41*	
	(0.24)	
SPD	−0.35*	
	(0.21)	
Labour		0.15
		(0.11)
Liberal democrats		0.19
		(0.19)
(Intercept)	−0.54***	−0.57***
	(0.17)	(0.08)
Log-likelihood	−269.30	−361.91
N	544	616

Note: The dependent variable is coded 1 for any MP who took the floor at any point during the budget debate. The omitted reference categories are the Greens for Germany and the Conservatives for the United Kingdom. In Germany, government ministers are excluded from the analysis. In the United Kingdom, members of government are included – all frontbenchers are coded as party leaders. $^{***}p \leq 0.01$; $^{**}p \leq 0.05$; $^{*}p \leq 0.1$.

The previous analysis does not differentiate between types of speech – a speech on the budget is counted the same as a speech on a private member's bill. It is conceivable, however, that party leaders exert more pressure on their members in highly salient debates than they would when discussing a bill that has little chance of becoming law. To test whether results hold for the most salient debates, we examine the likelihood that members of the House of Commons and the Bundestag gave a speech during budget debates, held in the Bundestag on 14–17 September 2010 and in the House of Commons on 23–24 and 28–29 March 2011. We run a probit model for each country, with participation in the budget debate as the dependent variable and party leadership, budget committee membership, and party dummies as the independent variables. The results are presented in Table 5.4. We find that party leaders were significantly more likely than backbenchers to participate in the budget debate in Germany but significantly less likely to participate in the United Kingdom. In Germany, being a party leader increases one's chance of speaking from approximately 17 to 51 percent, while in the United Kingdom being a party leader decreases the likelihood of speaking from 28 to 19 percent. Thus, our results hold for one of the most important debates of the parliamentary year.

5.4 Summary

The empirical results in this chapter provide support for our theory from two political systems. We are able to test our main hypotheses about who takes the floor as a function of status within the party (leader vs. backbencher) and ideology. Where electoral incentives lead parties to fiercely guard their party label, as is the case in Germany, they are careful about allowing backbenchers, especially those who are unlikely to toe the party line, to take the floor. In systems such as the United Kingdom where rebel floor speeches are less likely to hurt the party as a whole at election time, backbenchers often come to the floor. In fact, dissenters are more likely to give a speech than those members who are more likely to adhere to the party message. Finally, Germany's mixed-member proportional system creates different incentives for different members, depending on whether they were elected from a list or a district. Although MPs elected from districts may wish to take the floor, party leaders have an even greater incentive not to delegate time to them.

6 *Dissent in parliament and the media: Germany and the United Kingdom*

Parliamentary speeches are outlets for legislators to communicate their policy preferences. But there are many other channels MPs can use to voice intraparty dissent. They can cast votes, issue press releases, give interviews to newspapers, appear on television, or create a permanent presence on various Internet platforms. Actions that MPs take outside of parliament may amplify and communicate the actions they take within parliament. In this chapter, we investigate MP behavior across different types of actions: legislative speaking, legislative voting, and statements in the media. When and why do they choose one action over another? We also address the issue of coalition governance in this chapter. Do MPs criticize their own party in speeches and the media, do they criticize their coalition partner, or both? If both, which critique is more prominent?

Back in Chapter 1, we argued that institutions influence which communication outlet MPs use when they disagree with their party leadership. All else equal, MPs are expected to first express dissent in the media. There are few formal constraints in the media on what legislators say. As MPs increasingly disagree with their leadership on policy, they should go on the public record in parliament, first through speeches and, finally, by dissenting in votes. The latter is likely to have the greatest consequences for both the MP and the party. How quickly MPs climb this ladder from taking no action to voting against their party leadership again depends on institutions. Where electoral institutions create an incentive for a personal vote, MPs will more quickly move from doing nothing, to dissenting in the media, and eventually to dissenting in the parliament, as latent disagreement with the party leadership increases.

Examining all dissent across all issues over time even in just one country would be a vast and unfeasible undertaking. Therefore, for comparative purposes, we choose to hold the policy under investigation fixed and compare partisan debates in two countries. The global financial crisis kept parliaments and governments across the advanced industrialized world busy during the late 2000s. Democratic governments initially reacted overwhelmingly with unprecedented spending measures to fight the consequences of the recession that ensued following the crash of a US housing bubble. We focus on the behavior of members of the governing parties in the United Kingdom and Germany. In both instances, governing parties had to address the crisis by changing their existing positions on economic policy. In view of an unprecedented financial – and eventually fiscal – crisis that reverberated around both the United States and Europe, both governments – one single-party, the other a coalition government – proposed fiscal stimulus measures to address the recession and fight unemployment.

Although the nature of the financial crisis varied to some degree from country to country, everywhere it meant that governing parties had to quickly develop policy proposals to handle a crisis they could not have foreseen (or at least did not foresee) at the time of the previous election. The exogenous nature of the financial shock meant that the a priori probability of backbench MP dissent was relatively high – parties could not have weeded out dissenters on the basis of an issue that was nonexistent at the time of the previous election. Therefore, our design allows us to study to what extent backbench MPs went along with the new position of their party leadership on an important and controversial issue. First, we expect some MPs to dissent only in the media, some to express dissent in legislative debates as well, but few, if any, to dissent on votes. Second, given electoral incentives, we expect higher observed cohesion for Germany than for the United Kingdom, and more leadership involvement in debates in Germany than in the United Kingdom.

6.1 Political reaction to the financial crisis, 2008–2009

The UK Labour government reacted to the recession in the fall of 2008 by proposing a fiscal stimulus package, increasing government spending and public investment. It included several components (HM Treasury, 2008, pp. 22, 112): a temporary reduction of the value added tax from 17.5 percent to 15 percent, an additional £3 billion of capital spending that was brought forward from the 2009 and 2010 budgets for housing, education, transport, energy efficiency, and other construction plans, and discretionary action of £16 billion (around 1 percent of GDP) in 2009–2010. The chancellor of the Exchequer, Alistair Darling, announced the fiscal stimulus package in the House of Commons as part of the prebudget report in November 2008:

Every country in the world is facing the impact of this crisis on its own economy, but there is a growing international consensus – although unfortunately not shared in the House – that we must act now to protect people and to help pull our economies out of recession, for there is a choice. One can choose to walk away, let the recession take its course, adopt a sink-or-swim attitude and let families go to the wall. That is no action plan. Or one could decide, as I have decided and as Governments of every shade around the world have decided, to support businesses and to support families by increasing borrowing, which will also reduce the impact and length of the recession.... I will do whatever it takes to support people through these difficult times. That is why my pre-Budget report today represents a substantial fiscal loosening to help the economy now with a £20 billion fiscal stimulus between now and April 2010, around 1 percent of GDP. (*Alistair Darling, Prebudget Debate, 24 November 2008*)

The British finance minister went on to mention the international dimension of the fiscal stimulus, criticizing the Conservative Party for its opposition to the government plans:

Despite what the shadow chancellor said, right across Europe, including on our doorstep, namely France and Germany, Governments have taken action to stimulate their economies. That is important to consider because it is our biggest trading partner. The European Commission has today called for fiscal stimulus. It has called for a reduction in VAT, for capital expenditure and support for small business, as well as for the European Investment Bank to take action – all the things that we are doing in this country. So yet again, that example reveals the isolation of the Conservative party. (*Alistair Darling, Prebudget Debate, 26 November 2008*)

Numerous speeches in the UK House of Commons addressed the fiscal stimulus policy. Figure 6.1 shows the number of speeches in the House that mentioned the term "fiscal stimulus" between 2008 and 2010. It became a prominent topic in late 2008 and early 2009, after the announcement of the package in the prebudget report and prior to debate over the budget. We examine legislative behavior in the two

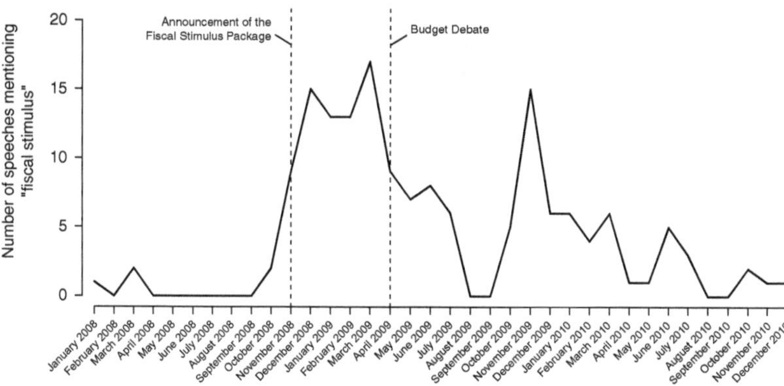

Figure 6.1 Parliamentary speeches in the United Kingdom mentioning "fiscal stimulus," 2008–2010
Source: UK House of Commons Debates, www.theyworkforyou.com.

most important debates: the prebudget debate in November 2008 and the budget debate in April 2009.

In Germany, the government coalition composed of the Christian Democrats and Social Democrats also reacted to the financial crisis by introducing legislation to stabilize financial markets in October 2008, and two fiscal stimulus packages in November 2008 and in January 2009. The first stimulus package (*Konjunkturpaket*) included 15 economic policy measures to protect employment in times of recession, including an investment of 50 billion euros over the course of the subsequent two years (Bundesfinanzministerium, 2008). The measures included temporary abolition of the car tax for new cars, increased opportunities for tax deductions, subsidies for modernizing insulation of buildings, continuing education and job-training programs for elderly and low-skilled employees, increased compensation for workers working reduced hours, and investment in various construction projects.

A couple of months later, in January 2009, the cabinet agreed on a second fiscal stimulus package. The additional measures included, among others, a temporary decrease in the income tax, a temporary decrease in health insurance premiums, additional child allowance, more loans for medium-sized enterprises, investment in broadband Internet, and the German version of the "cash for clunkers" program in which buyers of new cars would get a subsidy for demolishing their

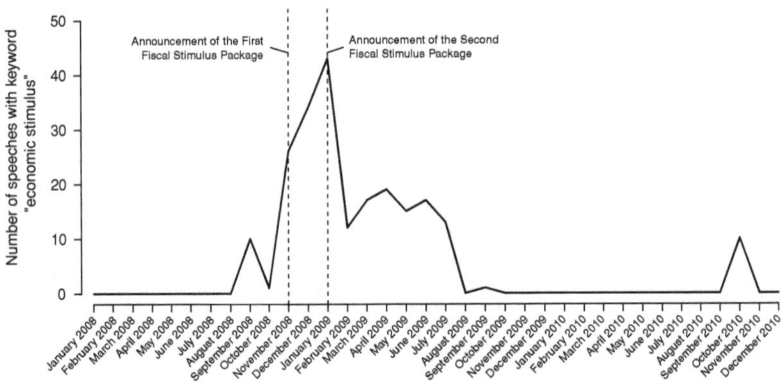

Figure 6.2 Parliamentary speeches in Germany tagged with keyword "economic stimulus," 2008–2010
Source: German Bundestag Documentation System, http://dipbt.bundestag.de.

old car (Bundesfinanzministerium, 2009). Figure 6.2 shows the number of parliamentary speeches tagged as "economic stimulus" speeches. Similar to the United Kingdom, the German parliament debated the stimulus packages at the end of 2008 and early 2009.

As part of her government declaration during the budget debate on 26 November 2008 – the same day that the British finance minister was speaking in parliament – German chancellor Angela Merkel explained the German government's reaction to the financial crisis to parliament:

> Our prosperity is generated in global markets. Therefore, it is clear that we cannot insulate our economy from the consequences of the international financial crisis.... It is true that we cannot predict all of the developments. We know, however, 2009 will be a year full of bad news. We will build a bridge so that it will be better again in 2010 at the latest. This is the approach of the government, and of the majority in this parliament.... The consequence of this financial market crisis is a sharp decline in growth, quite a different decline than we have at the end of a business cycle. This qualitative difference needs to be considered if we want to find the right answers.

Thus, both governments proposed sweeping fiscal stimulus action around the same time that placed a burden on the national budget.

Table 6.1. ***Overview of UK data on legislative action on stimulus package***

Event	Time
Prebudget debate	24 November 2008 26 November 2008
Budget debate	22 April 2009 23 April 2009 27 April 2009 28 April 2009
Media statements	Within two weeks after each legislative debate

We now examine legislators' behavior with regard to the proposed measures.

6.2 Fiscal stimulus debates in the United Kingdom

We first explore intraparty dissent within the governing Labour Party. Our coding strategy is as follows: for each Labour MP, we code whether he or she gave at least one speech during the prebudget and budget debates, and if so, whether the MP criticized the party leadership in that speech.[1] The debates are listed in Table 6.1. Additionally, we searched major newspapers for dissenting statements made by MPs up to two weeks after the respective legislative debates.[2] Additionally, we examined whether there were any recorded votes during the debates and coded the voting behavior of MPs.

6.2.1 Dissent in parliament and the media

To demonstrate how we code dissent, we take two MPs as illustrations. The first example is Labour backbench MP Michael Meacher (Oldham West and Royton), a former minister of state for the environment under Prime Minister Tony Blair. He first criticized the government after the

[1] We coded each speech as supporting the government proposal or disagreeing with it.

[2] The newspapers and news magazines included the *Guardian*, *Weekly Guardian*, *The Times* and *Sunday Times*, the *Telegraph*, the *Independent*, the *Observer*, the *Express, Sunday Express, Sunday Sun*, the *Mirror*, and the *Economist*.

presentation of the fiscal stimulus in the media. The *Independent* captioned a news story on 15 December 2008 with the headline "Labour Backbench Unrest over Fiscal Rescue Package." The story reported increasing intraparty dissent concerning the Labour Party leadership's response:

Frustration is growing among Labour backbenchers over the Government's rescue plan for the economy. Several MPs believe that a VAT cut was the wrong way of spending the bulk of the fiscal stimulus package, and others fear more should have been funded through tax reforms. "Going shopping last week I was offered a little over a pound off a £35 item," the former environment minister Michael Meacher said. "It really isn't doing anything. It seems obvious that at a time when consumers are already being offered much bigger discounts, the VAT cut will have little effect." ... Disquiet on the back benches could expand to wider disapproval if it emerges that the VAT cut has failed to boost trade over Christmas. (*Independent, 15 December 2008*)

In the budget debate that ensued a few months later in April 2009, the MP directed his criticism against the party leadership over the long-term consequences of the budget deficit:

The unrivalled imperturbability and the hallmark coolness of my right hon. Friend the Chancellor meant that he probably made the best fist of the Budget that he could, given all the circumstances, but I wish to set out why it is the wrong Budget and why it could and should be a very different Budget. The reason why the national debt has ballooned out of all historical proportions and why the cost of servicing it this year is thus so enormous is that the Government's response to the credit meltdown has been misconceived. They have been right to pursue the Keynesian strategy of increasing state expenditure to generate demand in order to head off a slump – my right hon. Friend Mr. Clarke spoke powerfully to that end. The Tories have been wrong to advocate letting a brutal self-corrective capitalism play itself out, while keeping a very tight lid on any increase in the national debt incurred by remedial Government action. Having said that, the manner in which the Government have chosen to develop their strategy has been ill-advised. (*Michael Meecher (Labour MP) during the budget debate on 28 April 2009*)

The second example is the Labour MP Frank Field (Birkenhead), also a former minister turned backbencher, who had been an outspoken critic of the Labour Party leadership's response to the financial crisis. He gave dissenting statements in parliamentary speeches and the media. In parliament, he expressed concerns about the costs of the stimulus package and spoke specifically against the abolition of the 10 percent starting income tax rate:

May I express my disappointment that the Government have not yet found the funds fully to compensate those lower-paid taxpayers who lost out with the abolition of the 10p rate? (*Frank Field (Labour MP) during the prebudget debate on 24 November 2008*)

During the budget debates in April 2009, he reinforced his critique:

There was slight disappointment among many of us, if I put it gently, when the Chancellor did not go on to say what he was going to do about the 10p losers. I am sure that the Treasury Front-Bench team will not be too dispirited to know that some of us will return to that issue, to ensure that that red sea is even wider than the Government envisaged in the Budget statement.... My second point is on a similar theme: no crisis, however horrible, should make us waste radical purposes. I have listened to Budget debates in the House for 30 years, yet I have never before felt the excitement, if that is the right word, that I experienced just before 1 o'clock, when the Chancellor announced the public borrowing for this year and next year, £175 billion this year and £173 billion next year. At that very moment, the country's economic future, and much more besides, was cast on the waters of the money markets. If the Government are not successful in raising the record sums of money, we will clearly be in great difficulties.... The Chancellor suggests... that, even after a considerable period of recovery, we will not get revenue to support expenditure – we will not get revenue to reach 38 percent of GDP – by 2013–14. Yet all of us are on the drug of wanting Governments to spend 45 or 50 percent of GDP. I am worried about how the Government will raise the funds, given that a Government who wished to squeeze the rich "until the pips squeak," as Mr. Healey once said, did not get revenue above 37 percent of GDP. Much more than what the Budget outlined today is required. (*Frank Field (Labour MP) during the budget debate on 22 April 2009*)

The MP also used the media to voice and amplify his dissent. Several news outlets reported on Field's "attack on the government's handling of the economy" (*Daily Mail*, 16 April 2009).

On the need to compensate those hit by the abolition of the lower tax rate Field told the *Guardian* yesterday: "The Labour backbenchers will not abandon the poor who have still not been compensated. It is a Rubicon they will not cross, and at a time the government has found £50bn to bail out the bankers, the Treasury can surely find £1bn to ease the resentment of our core voters. . . . We are anxious the government's promise to do all in its power to compensate fully the losers from the abolition of the 10p rate is not only met, but kept clearly separate from other tax reductions the government may announce next Monday. . . . Overwhelmingly these taxpayers are on low earnings. The Institute of Fiscal Studies estimates that the greatest loss of around £112 a year are for taxpayers earning £7,755." (*Guardian, 21 November 2008*)

Frank Field, the former Labour minister, will today launch an extraordinary attack on the Government's handling of the economy, saying it has left Britain as endangered as it was during the Second World War. "It is difficult to overdramatise the danger that is engulfing our country," Mr Field writes in an article for the *Spectator* magazine. "In some ways our position is more precarious than in 1940 when we stood alone against the Nazi tyranny. The danger can be stated easily enough. Far from building up reserves during the latter stages of the boom, the Government went on a borrowing spree amounting to £200 billion or so." The former welfare minister says he believes a spree would result in rising long-term interest rates and a collapse in sterling that would "place a firm grip around the Government's throat." He added: "The Government not only has a moral duty to cut public expenditure, but may be forced to do so by its inability to borrow on the scale necessary." (*Daily Mail, 16 April 2009*)

And the *Independent* reported similarly on 29 April 2009:

And back in Britain Mr Brown was accused by Frank Field, a former Labour minister, of "irresponsible" mismanagement of the public finances after the Budget signalled record borrowing of £175bn this year. (*Independent, 29 April 2009*)

In short, the two examples show how MPs may use both outlets, parliamentary debates and media, to communicate their preferences and criticize the party leadership. Short of voting against the stimulus package, this constitutes the highest level of intraparty dissent an MP can express.

6.2.2 *Dissent in parliament only*

The MP John McFall (Dunbartonshire West) provides an example of someone who dissented in a parliamentary speech but for whom we could find no additional media statements, leading us to code him as having dissented in parliament only.

The Chancellor mentioned the banking and financial sector. That sector will not contribute the same amount to the economy as it has in the past. It will shrink: everyone has acknowledged that, not least the Governor of the Bank of England when he appeared before our Committee. We need to rebalance the economy, and ensure that it functions in all the regions. The banking practices mentioned by the Chancellor generated the highest yields, but they also generated a massive amount of risk, which ultimately led to a global banking crisis and which we are no longer prepared to accept. In the future, our economic growth should not be driven by risky banking practices. At this stage, it is important for us to take a long-term view and to invest in areas that will be drivers for growth, including high-value manufacturing. Our infrastructure will also need investment to support a post-recession economy which, as I pointed out earlier, will be less centred on the City of London.... A fairly wide debate is taking place on the fiscal stimulus and its affordability. Only this week the National Institute of Economic and Social Research, one of the country's leading economic think-tanks, said that the United Kingdom could still afford a fiscal stimulus, and suggested that the Budget should contain a stimulus amounting to 2 percent of GDP – £30 billion.... Given the Government's commitment to helping people and to making this a Budget with a human face, I welcome the initiatives announced today, but are they enough? I fear not. (*John McFall during the budget debate on 22 April 2009*)

Of course, the fact that we failed to uncover dissent in the media does not mean that McFall did not express dissent in the media. He very well could have expressed his disapproval in local media outlets we did not examine. However, we can say with a high degree of confidence he did not seek to air his dissent in the major national print publications immediately after the debate took place.

6.2.3 Patterns of intraparty dissent

Table 6.2 shows the result of our analysis of intraparty dissent in the Labour Party over the reaction to the financial crisis. As expected, the vast majority of Labour MPs did not give a parliamentary speech and made no dissenting statement in the media (approximately 80 percent of MPs). When MPs gave speeches, most were party-line speeches. Around 4 percent of MPs engaged in a low-level dissent activity by making statements to the media. Close to an additional 3 percent communicated medium-level dissent in parliamentary speeches. Around 1 percent of MPs expressed high-level dissent in parliamentary speeches

Table 6.2. *United Kingdom: legislative behavior of Labour MPs in budget debates, 2008–2009*

Type of legislative behavior	MPs	Percent	Dissent intensity
No activity	277	78.7	None (0)
Party-line legislative speech	49	13.9	
Party-line legislative speech; media dissent	1	0.3	Low (1)
Media dissent only	11	3.1	
Legislative speech dissent only	10	2.8	Medium (2)
Dissent in legislative speech and media	4	1.1	High (3)
Voting rebels	0	0	–

Note: The following five recorded votes were considered: (1) prolongation of the emergency debate on the prebudget report on 26 November 2008, (2) corporation tax (charge and main rates for financial year 2010), (3) corporation tax (small companies' rates and fractions for financial year 2009), (4) rates of duty on alcoholic liquor, and (5) fuel duties (rates and rebates from spring 2009), the last four taking place on 28 April 2009. In addition, two recorded votes on the financial crisis management took place on 20 January 2009. The first of these votes acknowledged the EU's framework for action regarding the financial crisis, the European economic recovery plan, and the endorsement of the government to discuss these with European partners. The second vote was a resolution to support the government's promotion of measures to improve the level of assurance given on the Community budget. None of the Labour MPs rebelled in these votes (*Source:* www.publicwhip.org.uk).

and in the media. There were no voting rebels, because all relevant recorded votes were unanimous votes within the Labour Party (see note to Table 6.2). In total, about 7.8 percent of MPs expressed their disagreement with the government. Had those MPs voted against the government proposals, the Labour vote in the House of Commons would have been reduced to a slim majority.

Although this is just one example, it demonstrates that parliamentary speeches can provide better measures of intraparty dissent than recorded votes. In this particular example, votes would actually suggest perfect unity within the party, while the speech and media data reveal that this was clearly not the case. Moreover, pure media dissent is the modal category of dissent, as suggested by the theory. The least costly activity, media dissent offered most MPs the easiest opportunity for dissent. Parliamentary speeches, however, are a close second, reflecting the relatively low institutional constraints on speaking

Table 6.3. ***Ordered probit model of UK MPs' level of dissent***

Variable	Estimate
Party leader	−0.789**
	(0.314)
Margin of victory	0.016**
	(0.007)
Cut 1	1.668***
	(0.201)
Cut 2	1.996***
	(0.216)
Cut 3	2.569***
	(0.273)
Log-likelihood	−112.896
N	352

Note: The dependent variable is the level of intraparty dissent per MP, as coded in Table 6.2. Party leader is a dummy variable indicating whether the MP was a party leader or not. Margin of victory is the difference between the MP's vote share in his or her parliamentary constituency and the runner-up candidate. ** $p < 0.05$; *** $p < 0.01$. Standard errors in parentheses.

activity in the United Kingdom. The data show that the number of MPs dissenting decreases as the intensity of dissent increases, as suggested by the theoretical story in Chapter 1.

We next examine the variation in the level of intraparty dissent expressed by MPs, as shown in the last column in Table 6.2. The two main explanatory variables we consider are the party leadership status of the MP and the MP's margin of victory in the past election. For the United Kingdom, we expect that party leaders are significantly less likely to intervene in debate. We furthermore expect that the margin of victory is a proxy for how strong the MP values constituency interests. MPs from safe districts will be more willing to stand up to the party leadership than MPs who barely got elected and must rely on the support from the party at the next election.

We estimate an ordinal probit model. The results are shown in Table 6.3. For an easier interpretation, Table 6.4 shows the marginal

Table 6.4. *Marginal effects of party leadership status and margin of victory on the level of intraparty dissent in the United Kingdom*

	Changes in predicted probability for			
	No dissent	Low dissent	Medium dissent	High dissent
Leadership status				
Party leader → backbencher	−.07	+.03	+.03	+.01
	(−.12,−.02)	(+.01,+.05)	(+.01,+.05)	(+.00,+.04)
Seat safety: margin of victory				
Minimum → Maximum	−.21	+.07	+.09	+.05
	(−.46,−.02)	(+.01,+.16)	(+.01,+.21)	(+.01,+.13)

Note: First differences for party leader status are calculated holding margin of victory constant at the mean and for margin of victory holding the status constant at backbencher status. The 95 percent uncertainty intervals for the effects are indicated in parentheses. Calculations are based on the model shown in Table 6.3 using 10,000 simulations.

effects of the variables for each outcome category. Being a backbencher, as opposed to a party leader, decreases the probability of no dissent significantly by 7 percentage points. Conversely, it increases the probability of *any* dissent significantly. The results furthermore suggest that seat safety allows MPs to express more independence from the party; they are willing to be critical of the party leadership and voice their disagreement. Changing the margin of victory at the 2005 elections (or by-elections) for a backbench MP from its minimum to its maximum decreases the probability of toeing the party line or remaining silent by 21 percentage points. In contrast, it increases the probability of low dissent by 7 percentage points, for medium dissent that includes parliamentary speech dissent by 9 percentage points and high-level dissent by 5 percentage points. Thus, safe seat backbenchers were particularly likely to express their disagreement with the party leadership.

6.3 Fiscal stimulus debates in Germany

We now turn from the United Kingdom to Germany. Table 6.5 lists the days of the parliamentary debates on the stimulus measures in

Table 6.5. ***Overview of Germany data on legislative action on stimulus package***

Event	Time
Debate on stabilizing Financial markets	15 October 2008 16 October 2008 17 October 2008
Debate on securing Employment and growth	25 November 2008 4 December 2008 5 December 2008 30 January 2009 13 February 2009 20 February 2009
Media statements	Within two weeks after each legislative debate

the German Bundestag. We apply the same procedure as we used for the United Kingdom. First, we identify which MPs participated in these debates. Then, we code whether MPs agreed or disagreed with the party leadership. In addition, we code whether the MPs agreed or disagreed with the coalition partner. Finally, we examine whether there were any voting dissents and whether MPs also made critical statements in the media.[3]

6.3.1 *Intraparty dissent*

First, we examine examples of MPs who dissented in the media but gave a party-line speech. The proportion of such MPs is six times larger in Germany than in the United Kingdom, as expected under the model (1.8% vs. 0.3%). German party leaders exercise much greater control over floor debate than their British counterparts, perhaps making the media the more attractive option for any dissent. Of the eight MPs who dissented in the media but gave a party speech, seven came from the CDU/CSU and one was from the SPD. Of these, two were party leaders. This leaves six backbench MPs who followed this pattern.

[3] The following news media outlets were included in the search: *Die Zeit, Der Spiegel, TAZ, Frankfurter Rundschau, Welt, Welt am Sonntag, Financial Times Deutschland*, and *Handelsblatt*.

Carsten Schneider, a budget policy expert from the SPD, was one of these six. He criticized his party leadership – in particular his own finance minister – in the press but toed the party line in his speeches in parliament. The *Financial Times* in Germany reported the following in October 2008:

Budget politicians from SPD and CDU demand sticking to the goal of a balanced federal budget despite the financial crisis. "A balanced federal budget for 2011 remains our unchanged goal," the budget policy spokesman of the SPD parliamentary group, Carsten Schneider, said yesterday in Berlin. A similar statement came from the CDU budget expert Jens Spahn (CDU).... The budget politicians responded to Chancellor Angela Merkel (CDU) and Finance Minister Peer Steinbrück (SPD), both of which had questioned the consolidation target in view of the financial crisis on Monday. (*Financial Times Deutschland, 15 October 2008, p. 11*)

On two occasions in parliament, Schneider spoke but chose a different tone, praising the finance minister and defending the policy more along the lines of the party position:

I have faith not only in the crisis management of the Finance Minister in the recent days and weeks – I thank him and especially his employees; that was a good thing for our country – but also in the expertise of the Finance Ministry regarding the handling of the procedure, whatever bank the government will have a stake in. As a member of parliament, I do not want to interfere in these matters at all. We must monitor and set guidelines.... We support the fundamental goal of the government bill to partly nationalize the banks. (*Carsten Schneider (SPD MP) during the debate on 15 October 2008*)

I think that the debt brake for public finances is a cornerstone for government action in bad times. This only works if you save money in good times. This has been forgotten in the past.... We are talking today about 16 billion Euros. I'm sure that we can pay off this debt – if not in the next legislative period, then within a reasonable period of time. (*Carsten Schneider (SPD MP) during the debate on 13 February 2009*)

MP Gerd Andres (SPD) provides another good example of the strong incentives to toe the party line within the German parliament. He did not give a speech in parliament during the debates, but he voiced his disagreement in the media. In fact, the daily newspaper *Frankfurter Rundschau* reported on the growing dissatisfaction inside the SPD party group in parliament. Under the headline "SPD Party Group Exits: MPs no longer support coalition discipline out of fear for their mandates," the newspaper reported on several MPs who used the newspaper to state their disagreement with the policy of their party leadership:

It is remarkable when party group members publicly accuse their own leadership of "nonsense." But it is even more remarkable when the deputies scrap two government projects within a few days. In normal times of non-grand coalitions, everyone would talk about a leadership crisis or even a government crisis.... On Tuesday, the SPD parliamentary leader, Peter Struck, noted no less than 30 speeches in the group's internal meeting on the car tax. During the agitated gathering, there was not a single speaker who spoke for the government's plans to make newly purchased cars tax exempt. The right-wing party member Gerd Andres, finally critically remarked that the party group as a whole was asked to unanimously vote for the plans, while no one agreed with them. (*Frankfurter Rundschau, 13 November 2008, p. 4*)

More politicians targeted their critique at the leadership over the reaction to the financial crisis around the same time:

"The SPD must tackle the crisis more resolutely," says a paper available to the *Frankfurter Rundschau* written by members of parliament Klaus Barthel, Hilde Mattheis, Ottmar Schreiner, and the long-standing member of the SPD executive Sigrid Skarpelis-Sperk. Already in August, the four had called, together with many colleagues in and outside of the SPD party group, for a reversal of economic policy.... This time, the four advocate... a bold response to the financial crisis. Under the headline "Regulate financial markets – strengthen the domestic economy," they demand supporting citizens with low incomes and an investment program "with a volume of around one percent of gross domestic product, i.e. about 25 billion Euros a year." The paper includes regulations for financial market rules, which go far beyond the concept of deputy SPD party leader and Finance Minister Peer Steinbrück. (*Frankfurter Rundschau, 4 November 2008, p. 20*)

Intraparty dissent also was evident in the Christian Democrat party group:

It was clear that the last week would turn out to be a bad week for Angela Merkel when Laurenz Meyer publicly spoke up. Meyer is the CDU spokesperson for economic policy of the CDU parliamentary group and he once was Merkel's Secretary General. He usually does not show any disloyalty towards the Chancellor. But on Tuesday, it was too much even for Meyer. For weeks he had advertised in party committees to kick-start the

Table 6.6. ***Germany: party behavior of government MPs (CDU/CSU and SPD) in fiscal stimulus debates, 2008–2009***

Type of party behavior	MPs	Percent	Dissent intensity
No activity	399	89.9	None (0)
Party-line legislative speech	15	3.4	
Party-line legislative speech; media dissent	8	1.8	Low (1)
Media dissent only	21	4.7	
Legislative speech dissent only	0	0	Medium (2)
Dissent in legislative speech and media	1	0.2	High (3)
Voting rebels	0	0	–

Note: The following recorded votes were considered: amendment of the Green Party group on 17 October 2009, final vote on government bill on 17 October 2008, and amendment of Die Linke party group on 13 February 2009. (*Source:* www.bundestag.de.)

economy with public money if necessary. He was personally criticized by budget policy politicians and by the parliamentary group leader himself, Volker Kauder. Still, he had repeatedly raised the issue internally. Because it did not have an impact, he went public. He favors tax cuts as early as next year, he said. Domestic demand should be stimulated. In a patronizing manner, he added that Merkel was "in principle" on the right track. The Chancellor boiled with rage. One should not belittle the economic stimulus package, she railed in front of her confidants. Then it could not be effective as it would create no trust. But it is too late for such warnings. (*Der Spiegel, 1 December 2008, p. 22f.*)

The MP Laurenz Meyer did not participate in the debates in parliament. Thus, this magazine report nicely shows that going public in the media is a particularly attractive strategy for MPs in Germany. We now investigate systematically how all MPs deviated from party policy.

6.3.2 *Patterns of intraparty dissent*

Table 6.6 shows the party behavior of German government MPs for the debates under consideration. First, the overall activity is lower than in the United Kingdom – in Germany just about 10 percent of MPs engaged in some form of behavior (approving or disapproving), whereas more than 20 percent of MPs did so in the United Kingdom (see Table 6.2). What is remarkable and what makes the comparison so interesting is that there were also no voting rebels in Germany. With one exception, all floor speeches followed the party line. Taking into account statements in the media, we see that there are quite a few MPs who disagree with the party. The majority of MPs who made critical statements of party policy in the media did not participate in parliamentary debates. However, when they did, in all but one case they toed the party line. Thus, the example fits our theoretical model that legislative speeches may not measure actual party cohesion. Media statements themselves might not be a good alternative, because there are many MPs who give party-line speeches that will not be reported in the media. Party cohesion is, indeed, latent, and different institutional contexts provide either a coherent arena for debate in parliament (but potentially underestimate party disagreement) or an easier outlet for criticism (media) with a potentially biased filter depending on whom the media wishes to cover, likely overestimating party disagreement.

We create two dependent variables from these data. The first indicates whether an MP spoke at all on the floor of parliament independent of the content of the speech. The second variable is a dummy indicating whether an MP chose to dissent from the party in either legislative debates or the media.[4] Our expectation is that party leaders will have a higher likelihood of participation in debates than backbenchers. Table 6.7 presents our results. The first model uses all MPs from the two governing parties, the CDU/CSU and the SPD. In this model, the party leadership variable is positive and significant, corroborating our expectations. This effect remains robust across two further model specifications. In model 2, we exclude MPs who were ministers or junior ministers because they speak on behalf of the government. In model 3, we only include district MPs. In both models, party leaders are more likely to speak.

As in our previous analyses, we include the electoral status of German MPs who are elected in a mixed proportional representation system. Model 1 suggests that, *ceteris paribus*, during the debates on the economic stimulus, district MPs were actually more likely to

[4] This is possible because our data revealed no case in which an MP dissented in a legislative speech but not in the media, see Table 6.6.

Table 6.7. ***Probit models of German MPs' level of floor activity and dissent***

	Speech (1) (all MPs)	Speech (2) (no ministers)	Speech (3) (no ministers, only district MPs)	Dissent in speech or media (4) (no ministers)	Dissent in speech or media (5) (no ministers, only district MPs)
Party leader	0.679**	0.632**	0.808**	0.492*	0.677**
	(0.275)	(0.293)	(0.324)	(0.292)	(0.324)
Party list MP	−0.435*	−0.392		−0.292	
	(0.242)	(0.247)		(0.220)	
Minister or junior minister	−0.137				
	(0.374)				
Margin of victory in district			0.010		0.010
			(0.011)		(0.011)
(Intercept)	−1.457***	−1.491***	−1.678***	−1.322***	−1.464***
	(0.153)	(0.159)	(0.262)	(0.145)	(0.240)
SPD	−0.245	−0.174	−0.161	−0.328	−0.400
	(0.205)	(0.212)	(0.253)	(0.200)	(0.247)
Log-likelihood	−87.634	−81.267	−61.651	−95.110	−68.533
N	444	403	261	403	261

Note: Standard errors in parentheses. $^{*}p \leq 0.1$; $^{**}p \leq 0.05$; $^{***}p \leq 0.01$. Dependent variable in models 1 through 3 is a dummy indicating whether an MP spoke on the floor of parliament, and in models 4 and 5 a dummy indicating whether an MP chose to dissent from the party in the debate or the media.

participate than list MPs, but this effect is not robust in the more accurate sample in model 2 when we exclude ministers and junior ministers. Thus, the results look similar to our aggregate analysis in the previous chapters, which suggested that district MPs are no more active than list MPs. Of course, we are only looking at one policy debate in the present chapter, and we therefore have more confidence in the aggregate analysis regarding this variable.

As with the United Kingdom, we also investigate whether district MPs respond to competitiveness of the electoral environment. In other words, do safer seats incentivize district MPs to be more active, as in the United Kingdom? Model 3 runs the analysis for the subsample of district MPs using the margin of victory as an independent variable.[5] Although positive, the results do not suggest that German single-member district MPs respond to the same pressure from the district. This seems to imply that there are indeed qualitative differences between constituency MP behavior in pure first-past-the-post and mixed-member systems. Our next analysis examines which types of MPs are likely to voice dissent in speeches or the media. Model 4 and model 5 show that the only significant predictor is party leader status. However, the effect is positive, meaning party leaders are more likely to dissent in both debates and in the media. Because media dissent is so much more frequent in our data set than speech dissent, internal party divisions were voiced in the media by fairly high-ranking party members.

6.3.3 *Coalition dissent*

The analysis of a coalition government raises the question to what extent speeches and media statements also reflect dissatisfaction with the potential coalition compromise. In other words, it could be that the same members of parliament use legislative debates to attack the coalition partner to clearly highlight their own party's contribution to the government. Our elite survey has revealed that parties in government face a conflict over the communication of policy, torn between sticking to the coalition compromise and touting the party policy (Figure 4.10). We therefore code whether MPs make dissenting statements with

[5] As before, the margin of victory is the difference between the winner's vote share in the district and the vote share of the runner-up candidate.

Table 6.8. ***Germany: coalition behavior of government MPs (CDU/CSU and SPD) in fiscal stimulus debates, 2008–2009***

Type of coalition behavior	MPs	Percent	Coalition dissent intensity
No activity	430	96.8	None
Coalition dissent in media	10	2.3	Low
Coalition dissent in speech	1	0.2	Medium
Coalition dissent in media and speech	3	0.7	High
Voting rebels	0	0	–

regard to the coalition. For example, Philipp Mißfelder (CDU) mentioned in his legislative speech that he was looking forward to the upcoming elections because it would give the Christian Democrats the opportunity to form a coalition with the opposition FDP:

With your interjections today, Mr. Brüderle and Mr. Wissing [members of the FDP], you have made your anticipation of September of next year very clear, a time when, so I hope, you will form the government with us. I would like to share this anticipation. (*Philipp Mißfelder (CDU MP) during the legislative debate on 4 December 2008*)

Within the SPD, some criticized the course of action of the coalition partner:

When I picture . . . what the CSU chairman Seehofer, but also others in the CDU and CSU, have said in recent days, I notice that for some the goal of a balanced budget no longer seems to mean very much. It is astonishing – and I must say that as a member of the coalition government quite clearly – how quickly the former credo "no tax cuts on credit" is being given up, especially in Bavaria. For the subsequent generation, such a message is indeed not reassuring. . . . The uncertainty about tax policy within the ranks of our coalition partners confuses people and amplifies the downturn. That is why I'm asking that this issue be clarified. (*Joachim Poß (SPD MP) during the legislative debate on 25 November 2008*)

We code all such dissenting coalition statements made both during the debates and in the media. Table 6.8 shows the summary. First, the vast majority of MPs do not engage in such behavior. Almost 97 percent of them remain silent. Thus, coalition dissent happens less

Table 6.9. ***Germany: relationship between intraparty and coalition dissent on activities of government MPs (CDU/CSU and SPD) in fiscal stimulus debates, 2008–2009***

	Coalition dissent			
	No coalition dissent	Media	Speech	Speech and media
No speech	394	5	0	0
Party-line speech	13	1	0	1
Party dissent in media	19	2	0	0
Party-line speech, media dissent	3	2	1	2
Party dissent in speech and media	1	0	0	0

Note: Cell entries are the number of MPs (rows for intraparty dissent, columns for coalition dissent).

Table 6.10. ***Germany: legislative behavior of government MPs (CDU/CSU and SPD) in fiscal stimulus debates, 2008–2009 (ministers and junior ministers excluded)***

		Coalition dissent	
		Yes	No
Party dissent	Yes	6 (1.5%)	21 (5.2%)
	No	7 (1.7%)	369 (91.6%)

Note: Cell entries are the number of MPs.

frequently than intraparty dissent (3 percent of MPs compared with 7 percent of MPs dissenting from the party, see Table 6.6). When MPs do express dissatisfaction with the coalition partner, they typically do so in media outlets.

This raises questions about the relationship between coalition dissent and intraparty dissent. Because we have coded these two types of behavior for each MP, we can investigate the relationship between these activities. Tables 6.9 and 6.10 cross-tabulate the various patterns of legislative behavior during legislative debates and in the media. They

Table 6.11. *Probit models of German MPs' coalition dissent*

	(1) (all MPs)	(2) (only district MPs)
Party leader	0.637*	0.676
	(0.337)	(0.419)
Party list MP	0.244	
	(0.253)	
Margin of victory in district		0.007
		(0.015)
SPD	−0.246	−0.380
	(0.255)	(0.365)
(Intercept)	−1.923***	−1.993***
	(0.203)	(0.344)
Log-likelihood	−55.139	−30.253
N	403	261

Note: Standard errors in parentheses. $^{*}p \leq 0.1$; $^{**}p \leq 0.05$; $^{***}p \leq 0.01$. The dependent variable is a dummy indicating if an MP made a negative statement about the coalition partner either in the legislative speech or the media.

show that there are some MPs who are critical of their party as well as of their coalition and voice this in the media. This happens in 1.5 percent of the cases. The next most frequent dissenting behavior is coalition dissent, but party-line behavior, occurring in around 1.7 percent of cases. The most frequent instances of dissent are statements against the party, with no specific references to the coalition partner (see Table 6.10, ministers and junior ministers are excluded). Therefore, while delineating oneself from the coalition, intraparty dynamics seem to be more relevant for driving legislative behavior and media behavior of MPs in the case examined here.

In our final examination, we explore who is responsible for negative statements about the coalition partner. Table 6.11 shows the results from probit models. The dependent variable is coded 1 if an MP made a negative statement about the coalition partner either in the legislative speech or the media. Again, party leaders seem to be responsible for this. In the full model 1, the variable is positive and significant. None of the other variables – electoral status of the MP and seat safety measured by the margin of victory for single-member district MPs – achieve standard levels of statistical significance. Thus, it appears that party leaders in a coalition government wish to communicate what their party contributes to the government while distinguishing their party's position from that of their coalition partner.

6.4 Summary

The financial crisis in 2008 marked a new challenge for European governments and the beginning of what later would become a severe fiscal crisis. Governments needed to respond swiftly to an impending recession in both Germany and the United Kingdom. As a result, government party leaders needed to adjust official party policy. Fiscal consolidation was replaced by temporary, but extensive, public spending to stimulate the economy and dampen the effects of the crisis on unemployment. This led to political controversy as the handling of the crisis generated a substantial amount of intraparty disagreement in both countries. The conventional way to estimate such disagreements – voting dissent – revealed that governing parties in both countries were actually *perfectly cohesive*. In contrast, parliamentary speeches offered MPs opportunities to dissent from the party, but more so in the United Kingdom than in Germany. This result is in line with our theoretical expectations. Moreover, this chapter demonstrates that media dissent remains an important possibility for backbench MPs. In Germany, however, a higher proportion of MPs dissented in the media, but then decided to toe the party line in parliamentary speeches. Again, this shows the different constraints for debate on legislators in these political systems.

7 *Candidate selection and debate participation: a European perspective*

In the previous two chapters, we used the speech delegation model to explain variation in debate participation in two parliamentary systems with different electoral systems. In this chapter, we take another cross-national look at the institutional incentives for debate participation, but we focus on the effects of a specific electoral system variable – candidate selection. The European Parliament (EP) provides us with a unique opportunity to isolate the effects of candidate selection rules while holding many other factors constant. All members of the EP (MEPs) are elected under proportional rules in national campaigns and are members of both national parties and, with a few exceptions, European political groups. The formal parliamentary rules governing debate participation are the same for all MEPs, and all debate takes place within the same strategic environment. The rules governing how candidates are nominated for their respective national party lists, however, differ across countries, with parties in some countries employing more control than in others. This institutional variation across EU member states allows us to examine the effects of candidate selection on the debate participation rates of party leaders and MEPs while controlling for the parliamentary context.

MEPs are members of national parties, but once elected, they join European political groups in parliament. These groups control access to many offices in the EP, as well as access to the floor. As a result, and in contrast to MPs in national parliaments, MEPs must speak to the concerns of both national and European parties. At the same time, they are less focused on the concerns of the general public, due to the second-order nature of EP elections (Reif and Schmitt, 1980; Hix and Marsh, 2007). We argue that the speech delegation model can capture the variation in speech participation in the EP because different candidate selection rules affect which audience – the national party or the European political group – the MEPs choose to address when they take the floor.

Using a survey of European political groups, analogous to the survey of national parties presented in Chapter 4, we first examine how European political groups structure debates and the variables they consider important when allocating floor time to members. Second, we conduct an empirical analysis of the debate participation of MEPs. We find that, unlike in closed-list parliamentary systems, rebels – those MEPs who vote against their political group – often take the floor to explain their dissent, usually in terms of their support for their national party. As the speech delegation perspective suggests, MEPs are more likely to go on the floor if national parties have greater central control of the candidate selection process.

7.1 Party debate rules in the European Parliament

To understand the process of speaking-time allocation in the EP, we conducted a survey in which we queried the European political group secretariats in Brussels. Similar to the survey of parties in national parliaments, we asked the senior group administrators responsible for the administrative details of speaking time allocation to complete a brief questionnaire.[1] First, we asked each European political group to describe the process by which speaking time is allocated internally. Second, we asked the European group secretariats to indicate which factors are most important when deciding on the allocation of available speaking time.

Table 7.1 shows that European political groups do not follow a uniform procedure in the allocation of speaking time among their MEPs. In all instances, MEPs send their requests for speaking time to the political group secretariat. Following these requests, a proposal on the allocation is made by the group secretariat (for instance, by the secretary-general). The final decision is then taken either by the group leadership (European People's Party–European Democrats (EPP-ED), Union for Europe of the Nations (UEN)), the national party representatives (European United Left–Nordic Green Left), or the MEPs themselves (Alliance of Liberals and Democrats for Europe). Overall, this means that group leaders do not necessarily have a final say

[1] Thus, there was one response from an administrative staff member per political group. The responses were collected in 2007 and 2008. No response was obtained from the Independence/Democracy group, the Greens, and the nonattached members.

Table 7.1. *European Parliament: process of allocating speaking time*

European political group	Proposal made by	Decision taken by
ALDE	Secretary-general	Full group
EPP-ED	Permanent working groups	Vice chairman for parliamentary work
GUE-NGL	Deputy secretary-general responsible for plenary sessions	Political secretariat (composed of one member per national party)
PES	Coordinator of relevant committee or party vice-president when multiple committees are involved	Coordinator of relevant committee together with secretariat
UEN	Group secretariat	Two co-presidents of group

over the speaker list. In addition, we asked political group secretariats about their group's priorities when allocating speaking time. For several items, we asked each group to indicate whether each item was always (4), frequently (3), rarely (2), or never important (1) when making a decision. Table 7.2 presents the results. The answers in the table are sorted with the most important item listed at the top, measured by the mean response across groups. The most important considerations in the allocation process are formal criteria, such as membership in a responsible committee, group leadership position, issue expertise, and the contributions in committee meetings. National issue relevance as well as the tenure of a national delegation within each group are less important, as is the seniority of the MEP requesting speaking time. Characteristics such as speaker quality, MEP contribution in party meetings, attendance record, or whether the MEP speaks in one of the working languages of the EU hardly have any significance for the allocation of speaking time.

Most interestingly, an MEP's loyalty to his or her political group does not seem to play a role in allocating speaking time according to the political group secretariats. In other words, MEPs do not appear to get "rewarded" with extra speaking time for voting with the majority, nor are rebels punished. Only the Socialist group suggests that

Table 7.2. ***European Parliament: political group priorities in allocating speaking time***

Item	ALDE	EPP-ED	UEN	GUE-NGL	PES	Average
Committee membership	4	3	4	4	4	3.8
Expertise	4	4	3	3	4	3.6
EP group leader	3	4	3	4	3	3.4
MEP request	4	3	3	4	3	3.4
MEP contribution in committees	4	4	3	2	4	3.4
National issue relevance	2	3	3	3	3	2.8
National party tenure within group	2	3	1	1	2	1.8
Loyalty to political group	2	2	1	1	3	1.8
MEP contribution in party meetings	2	2	1	1	3	1.8
Seniority of MEP	2	2	1	1	2	1.6
Good attendance record in plenary	2	2	1	1	2	1.6
Speaker quality	1	3	1	1	1	1.4
Major language (EN, DE, FR)	1	2	1	1	1	1.2
Equal allocation among MEPs	1	1	1	2	1	1.2

Note: 4 = always important, 3 = frequently important, 2 = rarely important, 1 = never important. EN, English; DE, German; FR, French.

group loyalty is frequently important in allocating time, but the group qualifies this, stating that "depending on the subject, minority views of special countries [are] taken into consideration." Even in the political group most concerned with loyalty, rebels may be allocated time to express national opinions on sensitive matters. Given the electoral incentives in the EP, this is precisely what we would expect – European political groups have little need to protect a party label. The survey results therefore suggest that groups do not keep rebels off the floor. We now move on to examine actual speech participation rates in the EP.

7.2 Votes, rebels, and speaking time

We expect that MEPs who, for electoral reasons, vote with their national party on roll calls but against their European political group are more likely to put their opposition on the speech record. When an MEP's national party and European political group disagree on how to instruct their MEPs to vote, MEPs tend to vote with their national party majority to avoid punishment at election time. The national party could punish them by moving them down the party list or even by kicking them off the list entirely (Hix, 2004). These "national rebel" MEPs may make public statements in the EP, offering a national explanation for their rebellious behavior, to minimize possible punishments by their EP group leadership. In addition, by making a speech they bolster their public record of support for the national party, which may prove especially important to MEPs from member states where national parties use centralized means of candidate selection. Because there is such a weak electoral connection between European political groups and citizens, dissident floor speech does little to sully the political group's brand. Unlike in Germany but similar to the United Kingdom, there is little incentive for EP group leaders to keep rebels off the floor. Thus, we expect that MEPs who defect from their EP group to vote with their national party delegation (national rebels) are more likely to speak than those who do not defect. We derive the following hypothesis for MEPs:

Hypothesis 1: *National rebel MEPs – members who vote against the majority of their political group to vote with the majority of their national party – are more likely to go on the public record than those MEPs who do not defect. This effect is stronger for MEPs from parties using centralized candidate selection rules.*

Although our dependent variable – debate participation – is the same as for the analysis of the British and German parliaments in the previous chapters, some of the independent variables differ. First, rather than using a self-reported measure of ideology from candidate surveys, we use an observational measure that allows us to distinguish between the two principals (national party and political group). We take voting defection from the majority of an MEP's European political group as an indicator that the member was ideologically at odds with the group leadership. One may object to the use of voting records as a measure of ideological distance on the grounds that voting is strategic behavior. Although true, voting records offer us two significant advantages. First, we are able to link speeches to votes. In other words, rather than simply looking at aggregate speech counts, we can examine whether members were more or less likely to speak on issues where it is known they were opposed to the majority of their political group. Second, voting records are not subject to the same nonresponse problems that candidate surveys, such as those used in the Germany and UK analysis, are. We have voting records for every member of the EP. We are also able to examine some hypotheses in the EP we are unable to explore in Germany and the United Kingdom. Because levels of partisan control differ across EU countries, we can explore the interactive effects of candidate selection and electoral systems on MEP behavior.

To systematically evaluate speech participation in the EP, we rely on two data sources. The first data source is a sample of roll-call votes and their associated speech records from the first 18 months of the Sixth European Parliament (2004–2005). These data allow us to directly test whether an MEP's probability of going on the record is higher when he or she is a national rebel – an MEP who votes with the national party majority against the majority of the EP group. The potential drawback of such an analysis is the fact that we can only study the record related to roll-call votes and must exclude all other forms of debate because many votes are not recorded. Yet MEPs might have an incentive to put a statement on the record even if votes are not recorded, in particular when the legislative proposal under debate is significant. Therefore, to complement our analysis, we have collected aggregate data for the entire Fifth European Parliament (1999–2004) on the total number of speeches given by each MEP, as well as the proportion of (recorded) votes on which each MEP was a national rebel. This data set allows us to study debate participation for an entire legislative term and covers tens of thousands of speeches on numerous topics. In the following, we demonstrate that the logic of the model holds consistently across these analyses.

The first task is to link MEPs' decisions to defect from their EP group to whether or not they gave a speech regarding the vote. Ideally, parliamentary debates would be clearly linked to subsequent votes, and all voting decisions would be recorded. Yet it is well known that only a small number of votes in the EP are recorded. At the same time, the only speeches that the EP database consistently links to votes are those given during the "explanation of votes" period. Before the start of the Sixth Parliament, linking roll-call votes to speeches was practically impossible because speeches may refer to more than one bill, whereas a roll-call vote is often held only on a specific amendment to a bill. But beginning with the Sixth Parliament, the EP created a separate website category containing all speeches and statements that directly relate to legislation voted on earlier the same day. Moreover, speeches are organized according to the bill to which they refer. We were able to link debates to roll-call voting decisions for the first 18 months of the Sixth Parliament using roll-call voting data collected by Hix and Noury (2009). We focus our analysis on the MEPs from the EU-15 member states to clearly investigate the link between candidate selection, voting decision, and speech participation. MEPs from the new member states that joined the EU in 2004 were much less likely to speak during the first two years in the EP than MEPs from the "old" member states – MEPs from EU-15 states were approximately six times more likely to give a speech than MEPs from new member states. We therefore have reason to suspect that MEPs from new member states were in a "learning period" (Hix and Noury, 2009, p. 173; Lindstädt, Slapin, and Vander Wielen, 2012), and exclude them from our sample.

Using these data, we were able to link 144 roll-call votes to 710 MEP statements, for an average of 4.9 speeches per vote.[2] For each vote, we determined whether an MEP was a national rebel and whether he or she gave a speech. Our unit of analysis is therefore vote-speech, making our dependent variable binary – did the MEP give a speech on a particular roll-call vote? We present results from two sample tests of proportions, with one sample being the national rebels and the other one the MEPs who were not national rebels. We focus on two independent variables – whether an MEP rebelled from his or her EP group to vote with the national party and the nature of the mechanism used to select candidates to the EP in the MEP's member state. As hypothesis 1 states, we suspect that rebels are more likely to speak than those MEPs who do not rebel against their EP group. We also believe that this effect should interact with the candidate selection mechanism used in the

[2] The term "speeches" here is used rather loosely to encompass both speeches given on the floor of parliament as well as brief written statements that may be appended to the debate record. Because such statements are included in the public record, we include them in our analysis as well.

MEP's member state. Where the candidate selection process is centralized and controlled by the MEP's national party, we expect that rebels are even more likely to speak. When national parties are stronger in terms of their power to control the reelection chances of MEPs, MEPs should try even harder to highlight when they stand up for the national party over the EP group. The candidate selection variable was coded by Hix (2004) and is based on a survey of national parties conducted by Raunio (2000). The variable equals 1 for MEPs from member states where all parties have centralized candidate selection mechanisms and zero where one or more of the major parties do not have a centralized candidate selection mechanism.[3]

The data show that just slightly over 1 percent of MEPs who are loyal to their political group are expected to speak, while the proportion of national rebels who give a speech is 2.5 times higher (approximately 2.8%). When national parties have centralized control over candidate selection this effect should be amplified. When candidate selection is centralized, MEPs have an even greater incentive to send signals back to the national party that they support the national delegation's position. To examine this effect, Table 7.3 presents the proportions of MEPs who make statements both by their voting decisions as well as whether parties in their member state use centralized candidate selection mechanisms. National rebels are more likely to give speeches regardless of the candidate selection mechanism employed in their member state. However, MEPs are more likely overall to give a speech if they come from a member state where all major parties use centralized candidate selection mechanisms. In addition, the effect of the national rebel variable is even more pronounced in these countries. In member states where at least some parties have decentralized selection mechanisms, rebelling against the EP group roughly doubles the likelihood that an MEP gives a speech. In centralized member states, however, rebelling

[3] Countries coded as having centralized candidate selection mechanisms are Austria, Belgium, Denmark, Spain, France, Greece, Luxembourg, the Netherlands, Portugal, and Sweden. Of course, ideally, this variable would be measured at the level of national party rather than member state. However, the original Raunio survey was unable to obtain responses from approximately 45 percent of national parties represented in the EP, meaning that a party-level variable would contain a substantial number of missing values. Although a crude measure, this simple dummy is easier to measure and preserves more data. Hix (2004) has demonstrated that it does predict MEP behavior.

Table 7.3. ***Proportion of MEPs giving a speech as a function of voting and candidate selection mechanisms (vote-speech sample from Sixth European Parliament, 2004–2005)***

		Candidate selection	
		Decentralized	Centralized
National rebel voting decision	No	0.74% (192 of 25,982)	1.60% (459 of 28,609)
	Yes	1.41% (17 of 1,208)	4.52% (42 of 930)

Note: Cells display proportion of MEPs falling within each category who give a speech. For coding of the variables, please refer to the text.

almost triples the likelihood of giving a speech.[4] This provides additional evidence that MEPs use speeches not only as an opportunity to explain their votes to the EP group but also to highlight their loyalty to their national party.

The individual roll-call vote-speech analysis solves an ecological inference problem that plagues aggregate-level tests of individual-level theories. However, only an aggregate analysis of the Fifth EP allows us to study legislative speech participation for an entire parliamentary term and to consider the speaking-time allocation mechanism during debates. Moreover, the aggregate analysis allows us to consider debates on issues not subject to roll-call votes. It may be the case that MEPs likely to rebel against their EP group take the floor on important issues not subject to roll-call votes. We have collected a complete data set on speaking time for the Fifth EP (1999–2004) to complement our vote-level analysis. The dependent variable is the total number of speeches given by each MEP. We calculate this variable using the available data from the speech archive of the EP. The speeches include all part-sessions in Strasbourg and Brussels during this period.

[4] The results reported here consider only "yes" and "no" votes, but the results do not change when abstentions are included. This is true regardless of whether abstentions are counted as votes in favor of or against the legislation. We also ran a multilevel logit model with member state random effects. Our national rebel variable is highly statistically significant and positive, as expected. Our candidate selection variable is positive but not statistically significant.

Our main independent variable captures the degree to which an MEP is a national rebel, measured as the proportion of votes on which the MEP defected from his or her EP political group majority to vote with the national party majority.[5] We expect that MEPs who defect more often from the EP group to support the national party should also speak more frequently.

As a control, we also examine defection from the national party majority to the EP group. We would expect these defectors to speak no more than average. They should not want to draw their national party's attention to their vote and they have nothing to explain to their EP group. In addition, we include a dummy variable that takes on a value of one for MEPs from member states where parties use centralized candidate selection mechanisms and zero otherwise, as in the individual-level analysis. We interact this variable with our national rebel variable. We would expect that the national rebels who are most likely to benefit electorally from taking a national stand are even more likely to speak. They stand to gain the most from highlighting their defection.[6]

We control for other variables likely to affect how often MEPs speak. First, we include the length of parliamentary tenure of each MEP in the analysis. More senior MEPs may be more influential and get to speak on the floor more frequently than junior MEPs. We control for an MEP's presence in the chamber by counting the number of roll-call votes each MEP missed (voting absence). Members who miss

[5] We exclude MEPs who belong to a national delegation with fewer than three members because it would be impossible to know the national party majority. We also drop MEPs who do not belong to an EP group (nonattached MEPs). This leaves us with a sample size of 563 MEPs. As with the analysis of the Sixth EP, we calculate the defection variable by dropping abstentions. However, we have also run all models recoding abstentions as "yes" votes as well as "no" votes. In both instances, the results are similar to those we report here, and their substantive interpretation is the same.

[6] Carrubba et al. (2006) argue that unrepresentative EP roll calls are likely to significantly underestimate the degree of dissent within the political groups. Specifically, they suggest that members of the EP most likely to dissent from their political group are least likely to vote on roll calls. If this is true, it would suggest that when regressing the number of speeches given by MEPs on our measure of roll-call dissent, the coefficients of the defection variables should be negatively biased. If we find a null result, or a positive coefficient on our dissent variable, we can be confident that parties do not punish dissenters by limiting their speaking time. In fact, the finding would support our research strategy of complementing the individual-level analysis with an aggregate analysis.

votes may make fewer speeches either because the party punishes them for missing votes or simply because they have fewer opportunities to give a speech.[7] The survey responses received from the EP group secretariats seem to suggest that the latter is more likely. None of the EP groups suggested that attendance record was an important factor when allocating speaking time. Accounting for attendance at votes thus helps control for MEPs' demand for speaking time. We also include the number of rapporteurships held by each MEP, using available data from the EP website. Rapporteurs are guaranteed speaking time, so MEPs who held more rapporteurships will speak more often. We include dummy variables to capture whether the MEP was a political group or EP leader as these leaders give speeches more frequently. We control for the number of committee assignments per MEP as well as the number of committee chairmanships. Finally, because larger political groups are allotted more time for their MEPs, we include the size of the MEP's political group in the analysis, as well as the share of each national party delegation within each political group.

As in the Germany and UK analysis in Chapter 5, we estimate a negative binomial model. We estimate one model without EP group and member-state dummies and one model including those dummies. The estimation results are presented in Table 7.4. The coefficients on our variable of interest "national rebel defection score" are positive, meaning that MEPs with higher voting defection scores participate more in debates. The interaction between the national rebel score and candidate selection is also positive. This suggests that centralized selection mechanisms do indeed yield higher speech counts. The defection score variable is significant in the first model without group and country dummies and the interaction is not, whereas the interaction becomes significant when we introduce the dummies. This is not surprising, however, because the fixed effects are highly collinear with the country dummy variable for candidate selection. The substantive effect, however, remains the same: national rebels give more speeches than

[7] It is more important to control for these variables in the EP than in Germany and the United Kingdom for several reasons. Controlling for seniority is important because members are much more likely to leave (or join) the parliament midterm than a German or British MP would their national parliament. In addition, because MEPs must travel so frequently between their home country, Brussels, and Strasbourg, absences are a much greater problem compared with most national parliaments. The results we present are robust to the exclusion of these control variables.

Table 7.4. ***Explaining parliamentary speeches in the European Parliament (1999–2004)***

Variable	(1)	(2)
National rebel defection score	2.8591	0.1343
(Votes with NP & against EP group)	(0.7470)***	(1.1105)
European group defection score	−3.0777	−3.0238
(Votes with EP group & against NP)	(1.3567)**	(1.3585)**
Centralized candidate selection	0.1030	0.2595
	(0.1013)	(0.2883)
National rebel score × candidate selection	1.4744	3.2620
	(1.1773)	(1.3783)**
Tenure	0.0001	0.0001
	(0.0000)***	(0.0000)***
Voting absences	−0.0005	−0.0005
	(0.0001)***	(0.0001)***
Rapporteurships (number)	0.0618	0.0668
	(0.0108)***	(0.0103)***
EP group leader	0.3676	0.5019
	(0.1260)***	(0.1210)***
EP leadership	0.0501	0.0747
	(0.1139)	(0.1076)
Committee assignments	0.1236	0.1255
	(0.0343)***	(0.0327)***
Committee chairs	−0.0370	−0.0090
	(0.0707)	(0.0664)
EP political group size	−0.0040	
	(0.0005)***	
National party relative size	−1.7851	−0.9040
	(0.5064)***	(0.7977)
(Intercept)	4.4045	4.1110
	(0.1803)***	(0.4984)***
Theta	1.441***	1.676***
	(0.086)	(0.103)
Observations	563	563
Log-likelihood	−2747.6	−2704.9
EP political group dummies	No	Yes
Country dummies	No	Yes

Note: Standard errors in parentheses. $^{*}p \leq 0.1$; $^{**}p \leq 0.05$; $^{***}p \leq 0.01$. The dependent variable is the number of speeches given by each MEP during the Fifth European Parliament (1999–2004).

other MEPs. The fixed effects model indicates that this is especially true when candidate selection mechanisms are centralized. We have also run models without the candidate selection variables and interaction (both with and without fixed effects), and we have run the same models with robust standard errors. We consistently find a strong, statistically significant, and positive effect for our national rebel variable on speech counts. As expected, the opposite defection score (defection from the national party majority) does not have a positive effect, in fact the coefficient is negative and significant.

The coefficient signs on the control variables are in the expected direction. The number of rapporteurships is significant and positively correlated with speaking time, but this was expected given that rapporteurs have speaking time ex officio. MEPs who are absent more often from roll-call votes speak less. Independent of tenure in the EP, political group leaders are more likely to take the floor than lower-ranking MEPs. EP leadership positions, however, do not have any effect on the number of speeches. As far as committee assignments and chairmanships are concerned, the assignments variable has the expected positive sign and is significant in all models, as the survey of EP political groups suggested it should be. Committee leadership positions (chairman or vice-chairman) has a negative effect, but it is not statistically significant. The coefficients for political group and national party delegation size are negative. The rules for allocating speaking time among EP groups is not exactly proportional because a first share of debating time is allocated equally among groups and then in proportion to the seat share. Thus, smaller groups are slightly favored when speaking on the floor.

Interpreting the effects of the variables is facilitated using simulated expected values of speech counts. Such simulations also properly take into account the interaction effects between variables and allow us to examine whether there are truly significant and substantive differences between centralized and decentralized selection countries and national rebels and nonrebels. Table 7.5 is similar to Table 7.3, except that the cells now report simulated expected speech counts per MEP instead of the proportion of MEPs giving a speech. They show what we can expect if we set the independent variables to values of substantive interest while holding all other variables constant. We choose the 10th and 90th percentiles of the national rebel voting defection variable as low and high values respectively. The results show a substantial

Table 7.5. ***Predicted speech counts in the Fifth European Parliament (1999–2004): substantive effects of national rebel defection and candidate selection***

		Candidate selection	
		Decentralized	Centralized
National rebel Defection score	Low	32 (28,37)	36 (32,41)
	High	44 (38,52)	59 (50,70)

Note: Cells display the simulated expected speech counts from a negative binomial model, and their 95 percent confidence intervals are indicated in parentheses. The simulations are based on model 1 and were performed in R using the Zelig package (Imai, King, and Lau, 2007). A low national rebel voting defection score is the 10th percentile of this variable (0.01), and a high national rebel voting defection score the 90th percentile (0.12). All other variables are held constant at their mean, except for the rapporteur and committee controls (median) and the dummy control variables (leadership).

interaction effect between defection and candidate selection mechanisms on speech counts. MEPs with low national rebel defection scores from decentralized candidate selection systems speak less, whereas those from centralized candidate selection systems speak slightly more. Yet this difference is not significantly different because the simulated confidence intervals overlap. However, MEPs with high national rebel defection scores from centralized systems give about 34 percent more speeches than those from decentralized systems (59 instead of 44), and the confidence intervals barely overlap. The substantive effects of defection on speech counts found in the aggregate data are similar to those found in the individual-level data from the Sixth EP, suggesting that the ecological inference problem is not too severe in these data.

7.3 Summary

This chapter has demonstrated that the same theoretical model that explains who takes the floor in parliamentary democracies also explains speech participation in the EP. However, given the different institutional arrangements and electoral incentives in the EP, the allocation of floor time is somewhat different from what we find in other national parliaments. Political groups have little incentive to keep rebels off the floor as the groups do not run elections. Rather, rebels have an incentive to explain, and reinforce, their national positions for electoral reasons. Thus, MEPs who rebel from their groups for national reasons are the most likely to give speeches on the floor.

8 *Changing institutions: New Zealand*

In this final empirical chapter, we alter our identification strategy. Rather than comparing MP behavior across countries, we examine whether a set of MPs change their behavior over time following a change in electoral rules. Specifically, do the same MPs (and their parties) drastically change their behavior in parliament over time as a result of a shift from a plurality electoral system to proportional representation? We take advantage of the 1996 electoral law change in New Zealand to examine whether the introduction of a party-centered proportional electoral system affects the ways in which parties exert pressure on their backbenchers, and how backbenchers take the floor to connect with the electorate. We do so by tracing the participation of MPs in budget debates in the period before the referendum on electoral reform, the period between the referendum and the first election under the new rules, and the period after the new rules took effect. Our analysis shows that the same rebel backbenchers are less likely to participate in debates after the electoral system change to proportional representation.

8.1 Electoral system change

As discussed in Chapter 3, in a 1993 binding referendum, New Zealand voters opted to change their electoral laws, abandoning their first-past-the-post, single-member district system in favor of a mixed-member proportional system, similar to the German electoral system. The first elections under the new law were held in October 1996, and they substantially changed New Zealand's political landscape. Before 1993, only two parties – the Labour Party and the National Party – regularly received votes and seats in parliament, and, as a result, single-party majority governments were the rule. Although the 1993 elections saw two smaller parties pick up a substantial number of votes – the Alliance with 18.2 percent and the New Zealand First Party with 8.4 percent –

these parties gained only two parliamentary seats each. In contrast, the 1996 elections saw five parties receive more than 5 percent of the vote, and six parties win seats in parliament. For the first time, no party won a majority of seats, and the National Party and the New Zealand First Party formed a minimum winning coalition with a bare majority of seats – 61 of the 120-seat Parliament.[1]

Even before the first MMP election, parties and their MPs anticipated the effects of the electoral system change for legislative organization. As briefly discussed in Chapter 3, the parliament revised its standing orders and created a powerful business committee where party whips gained control over many important decisions, including the allocation of speaking time among parties. Individual MPs anticipated the changes as well. Many MPs decided not to run again in the 1996 elections and took the rules change as an opportunity to retire from electoral politics. Others split from their parties to form new parties (Barker et al., 2001).

8.2 Rules change in parliament

On the surface, parliamentary debate in New Zealand did not change much with reform. Parliamentary debate culture is still confrontational – more similar to the UK House of Commons than the German Bundestag – and the House has retained many of its Westminster traditions. The Speaker still calls on members, who still rise to catch the Speaker's eye, and new members are still entitled to a maiden speech. Although the traditions continue to resemble those of a Westminster parliament, the rules governing both debate and parliamentary practice no longer do. For example, the Standing Orders of the House specifically state how the Speaker must prioritize speakers. According to Standing Order 102, which was added to the rules as part of the 1995 overhaul, the Speaker must "[take] account of the following factors: a) if possible, a member of each party should be able to speak in each debate; b) overall participation in a debate should be approximately proportional to party membership in the House; c) priority should be given to party spokespersons in order of size of party membership in the House; d) the seniority of members and the interests and

[1] For a history of the referendum, see Denemark (2001) and Nagel (2004), and for a description of its effects, see Boston et al. (1996), Barker et al. (2001), and Vowles, Banducci, and Karp (2006).

expertise of individual members who wish to speak." The rules now grant some MPs, in particular party leaders, an explicit speaking priority. Moreover, the Business Committee, that is, the party whips, divide speaking time proportionally among parties and draft speaker lists, which they present to the Speaker. Although the Speaker retains discretion to deviate from the list, party leaders clearly possess more formal control than they did before 1995.[2]

Specifically, the Speaker has recognized the rights of parties to draft their speaker lists. In a 2002 Speaker's Ruling, in which the Speaker applies and interprets the parliamentary Standing Orders, the Speaker asserted that "how a party utilises its speaking and question rights is an internal matter for that party to determine" (New Zealand Parliament, 2012, p. 25). Party whips inform the Speaker which of their members will be seeking calls, thus if MPs wish to give a speech, they first liaise with their whips. Alternatively, whips may contact MPs directly about giving a speech. Party leaders may get directly involved in these decisions but tend to delegate them to the whips.[3]

Following the election of a new parliament, the parties present the Business Committee with an "order of calls" for debates on the first, second, and third readings of government bills. All debates consist of 12 ten-minute speeches. For instance, in the 49th Parliament (2008–2011), debates consisted of five National Party speeches, four Labour Party speeches, and one each from the Green, ACT, and Maori parties.[4] However, in some instances, a member may still make a speech even if his or her party has exhausted its allocated number of speeches. If no other MP requests speaking time by rising to catch the Speaker's eye, the Speaker may recognize a standing member from a party whose allocation has been exhausted. This may occur because the total number of speeches is stipulated by the standing orders, although the order is not.[5] In short, although traditionally New Zealand's House remains

[2] Before 1995, the Speaker did not receive speaker lists from the parties, however government and opposition whips did coordinate with members regarding debate participation.

[3] Personal communication with senior parliamentary staff, 2011.

[4] The Progressive Party and United Future Party each had one seat in the 49th Parliament and could request speaking time through the major party with which they were allied – Labour in the case of the Progressive Party, and the National Party in the case of United Future.

[5] The House may also establish a committee of the whole House between second and third readings, presided over by the Deputy Speaker. In this committee,

a debate parliament, the rules give party leaders significant control over who has access to the floor.

8.3 Behavioral change: budget debate participation

The changes in electoral rules and partisan control have had a significant impact on both how MPs view parties and how MPs act in parliament. Using the New Zealand Candidate Survey (Karp, 2002; Vowles et al., 2002), we first examine the changing attitudes of candidates competing for political office during the electoral reform period. Candidates in New Zealand consider acts of support for the party leadership and giving speeches in parliament activities of increasing importance over time, while representing the electorate becomes less important following electoral system reform.

Figure 8.1 shows the mean responses of candidates for the House of Representatives to the survey question asking about the importance of various aspects of an MP's job. We show the three activities most relevant to our study. Representing the electorate is the most important activity, followed by party leader support and speaking in parliament. Over time, though, the importance of representing the electorate has declined. By 2002, this activity was only slightly more important than supporting the party leader and speaking in parliament. The latter two activities have increased in average importance over time. Thus, within six years after the first MMP election, political candidates in New Zealand considered speaking an important part of their job, and they considered offering support to the party leadership as important as representing the electorate and delivering speeches.

Responses from candidate surveys cannot tell us whether MPs who consider speaking an important part of their job are persuaded that they must toe the party line when delivering their speeches, in particular after the electoral system change. To empirically examine the effects of the electoral rules change on debate participation, we analyze which MPs spoke in budget debates between 1991 and 1999, focusing on a set of 43 MPs from the Labour and National parties who served in all

speaking-time allocations are somewhat looser, and, with some restrictions, debate may continue until no more calls are sought. However, the government may seek a closure motion to cut off debate, which must be agreed to by the chairperson (Deputy Speaker).

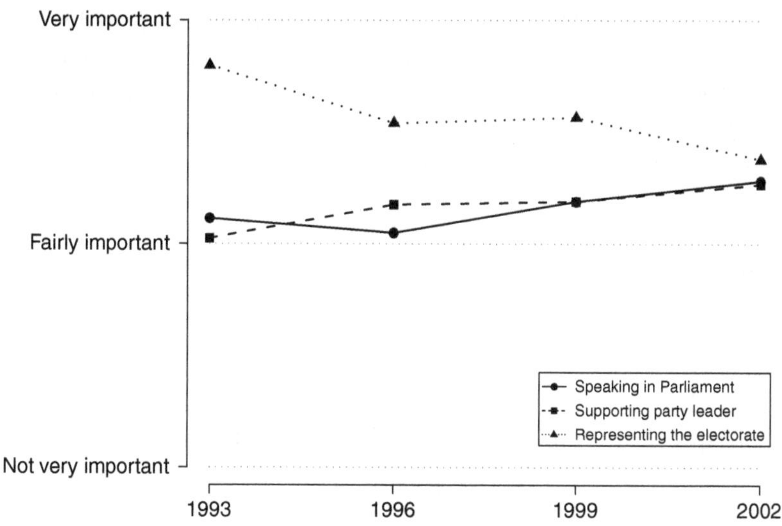

Figure 8.1 Importance of representational activities in New Zealand (responses from candidate surveys)
Note: The plot shows response means from each respective candidate survey. Category "not important at all" not shown for presentational purposes.
Source: New Zealand candidate surveys (Karp, 2002; Vowles et al., 2002)

three parliaments during this time period (and did not switch parties). Thus, this research design allows us to trace MPs' history of debate participation before, during, and after electoral reform. In particular, we are interested in determining whether rebel MPs were more likely to take the floor in the prereform era and less likely in the post-reform era. We focus on budget debates for two reasons. First, they constitute important annual events for both government and opposition parties. Government parties can defend proposed policies and budget changes, whereas opposition parties have the opportunity to present policy alternatives. Second, unlike in the other parliaments we examine, New Zealand's online parliamentary database is not searchable by MP name, preventing us from gathering information about all debate participation. Instead, we code debate participation from the New Zealand Hansard for budget debates in each year. The Appendix includes more information on the data and coding process.

To determine the ideological agreement of each MP with his or her party, we calculate roll-call vote agreement rates from the

1991–1993 period.[6] After removing all abstentions and paired votes, we then examine the percentage of roll-call votes on which each MP voted with his or her party majority. Of course, in an ideal world, we would be able to construct an exogenous measure of ideological disagreement using candidate surveys, as we have done for the United Kingdom and Germany in previous chapters. Unfortunately, as was also the case in the EP, the information in the New Zealand candidate survey does not provide sufficient information to construct such a measure. In using roll calls, we make two assumptions; first, we assume that higher rates of agreement on roll calls in the early period under single-member district plurality are indicative of MPs who are more ideologically similar to their party, and second, ideology (or, more specifically, the latent degree of agreement between the MPs and their party) remains constant over the entire period of investigation.[7] Moreover, as our theoretical model suggests, defections on votes represent a severe form of defection, and they should be relatively rare. Thus, our measure should underestimate the degree to which MPs differ from their leadership. In the empirical analysis, our results will be biased toward a null finding, meaning our findings are actually likely stronger than we report.

As expected, overall roll-call agreement is high, with the mean MP in our data set voting with the party majority 98.55 percent of the time. However, there is variation, with MPs ranging in their voting agreement scores from 95.75 to 100 percent. We normalize (z-transform) these agreement scores within parties so that MPs who vote with their party majority more than average receive positive scores, and those who vote with their party less than average receive negative scores. Additionally, we code each MP's backbencher or parliamentary leader status during each parliamentary term.

According to our theoretical model, backbench MPs who are more willing to defect from the party in the 1991–1993 period should take the floor more often in the early period under SMD plurality rules but

[6] Data were originally collected by Chris Kam and we take them from John Carey's legislative vote data (Carey, 2009). They are available at www.dartmouth.edu/~jcarey/Legislative_Voting_Data_files/lvdatatable.htm.

[7] This is a strong assumption but one that is primarily due to data availability. We cannot examine dissent on votes in later periods as the new standing orders, introduced in 1995 in anticipation of the MMP elections, introduced party bloc voting and roll-call votes became exceedingly rare.

less often once the electoral change takes effect in 1996. We expect the interim period to represent a transitional phase in which speech participation of rebellious MPs ought to lie somewhere in between the earlier and later periods. Moreover, in comparison to rebellious backbenchers, we expect party leaders to be less active in debates in the prereform period and more active in postreform period. We can summarize these expectations in two hypotheses here.

Hypothesis 1: *Rebellious MPs are more likely to speak during budget debates in the prereform period but less likely to speak in the post-reform period.*

Hypothesis 2: *Party leaders are less likely to speak during budget debates in the prereform period but more likely to speak postreform period.*

We test these hypotheses using a logit model in which our dependent variable is coded 1 for MPs who speak during the budget debate and 0 for those who do not. The unit of analysis is the MP-debate year. As independent variables, we include the transformed agreement score calculated from roll-call votes between 1991 and 1993, dummies for the parliamentary term (transitional period 1994–1996 and post-reform 1997–2000 with prereform as the omitted category), a party leader dummy, a dummy controlling for party affiliation (National Party dummy), and interactions between the parliamentary terms and the agreement score, and between term and party leader. We expect the agreement score to be negatively related to taking the floor in the early years, but positively related in the later years. We have also run a model including the size of parties' parliamentary caucuses because a larger parliamentary caucus may translate into fewer opportunities for any single MP to take the floor.[8] We find that the seat share variable is not statistically significant, has no substantive effect, and no effect on the other variables included in the model, so we opt not to include it here.[9]

8 Together with the term dummies, this variable also controls for the fact that the parliament expanded from 99 to 120 seats in 1996 at the time of the electoral law change.

9 We have also run a model with random effects for MPs, and we find that results are similar. For ease of interpretation, we present the simpler model here.

Table 8.1. ***Budget debate participation in New Zealand (logit)***

Transformed MP voting agreement with party	−0.511**
	(0.243)
Postreform period (Dummy)	−1.319***
	(0.439)
Transitional period (Dummy)	−0.176
	(0.455)
Party leader (Dummy)	−0.477
	(0.415)
National party (Dummy)	−1.143***
	(0.267)
MP voting agreement × postreform	0.596*
	(0.318)
MP voting agreement × transitional	0.404
	(0.317)
Postreform × party leader	0.920
	(0.561)
Transitional × party leader	0.529
	(0.578)
(Intercept)	1.775***
	(0.362)
Log-likelihood	−233.590
N	382

Note: The unit of analysis is the MP-debate year. Standard errors in parentheses. * $p \leq 0.1$; ** $p \leq 0.05$; *** $p \leq 0.01$.

The results of the logit model are displayed in Table 8.1. We find support for our hypotheses. Backbenchers who agree with their parties are less likely to take the floor before 1993, just as was the case in the United Kingdom. Following the electoral law change, those exact same MPs were more likely to participate in budget debates. Under the single-member district (SMD) plurality system, there was less need for those who agreed with the party to take the floor, so they did not. Once parties established greater control over access to the floor, those members who were least likely to defect from the party platform were precisely the members the party leaders wanted to hear on the floor.

These effects are easier to visualize by plotting predicted probabilities. We do so in Figure 8.2. This plot shows the predicted probability

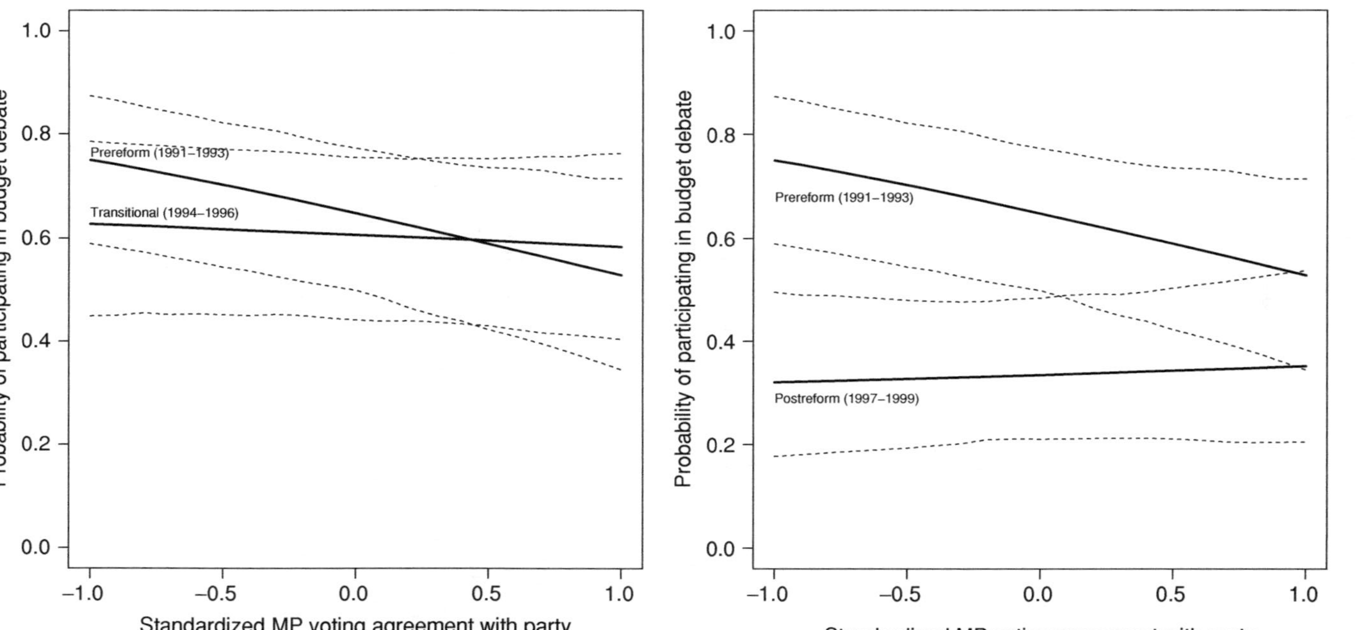

Figure 8.2 Predicted probability of budget debate participation in New Zealand
Note: The left panel shows the predicted probabilities as a function of voting agreement with the party during the prerefom period (1991–1993) and the transitional period (1994–1996). The right panel shows these probabilities during the prereform period (1991–1993) and the postreform period (1997–2000). The 95 percent confidence intervals are shown. Simulations based on logit model.

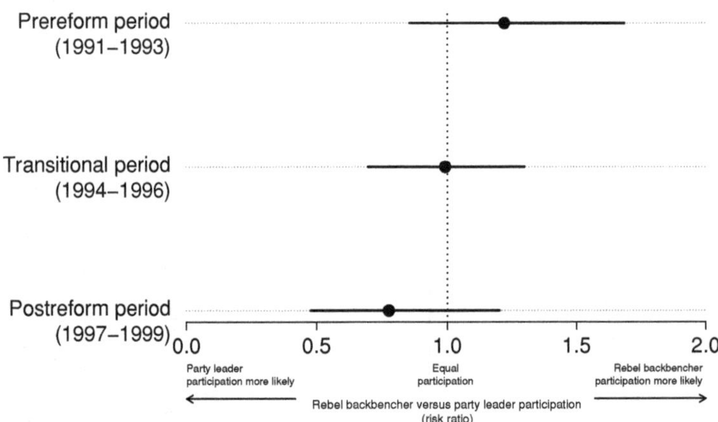

Figure 8.3 Comparison of debate participation of rebel backbenchers and party leaders in New Zealand
Note: The points show the risk ratios of debate participation for rebel backbenchers and party leaders (Pr(Y = 1|Rebel Backbencher)/Pr(Y = 1|Party Leader)) and corresponding 95 percent confidence intervals. Simulations based on logit model.

of budget debate participation for backbenchers as agreement scores vary from one standard deviation below the party mean to one standard deviation above. The lefthand plot shows the prereform period compared with the transitional period, and the righthand plot compares the prereform period with the postreform period. In the prereform period, the relationship between the probability of taking the floor and agreement with the party is clearly negative. In the transitional period, the relationship effectively disappears, but this period is not statistically different from the prereform period. In the postreform period, the relationship between the probability of speaking and agreement is clearly positive and statistically different from the prereform period for members with low agreement scores.

Next we analyze patterns of leader speeches. Using our model, we calculate risk ratios – the probability that a backbencher gives a speech relative to the probability that a party leader does. A risk ratio of 1 implies that backbenchers and party leaders are equally likely to participate in debate. A ratio greater than 1 implies that backbenchers are more likely to participate, and a ratio less than 1 implies that leaders are more likely to participate. Although the results are not statistically significant at the 95 percent level because of the low number of MPs in the analysis, the substantive effects, plotted in Figure 8.3, are clearly in the direction predicted by our model. We simulate three scenarios. In each period (prereform, transitional, and postreform), we examine the risk ratio of rebel backbencher participation relative to leader participation. Here a rebel backbencher is an MP with a party agreement score one standard deviation below the mean, and the party leader is assumed to have an agreement score one standard deviation above the mean. In the prereform period, the expected risk ratio is 1.22, meaning the probability that rebel backbencher speaks is 22 percent greater than the probability that the leader speaks. In the postreform period, this pattern is reversed, with a risk ratio of 0.77. In the transitional period, both rebel backbencher and leader are equally likely to take the floor. In sum, the results are in the line with the expectations of our model.

8.4 Summary

The electoral law change in New Zealand has presented us with a unique opportunity to examine how individual members change their participation in debates following institutional change. The organization of the New Zealand Parliament changed dramatically and rapidly following the introduction of the MMP electoral system. Importantly for our argument, parties developed new tools to provide leaders with more control over backbenchers. These tools include the introduction of party bloc votes and new rules emphasizing party control over speaker lists. The changing attitudes of candidates running for office, as evidenced by the candidate survey, and changing MP behavior, as evidenced in debate participation, reflect the impact of these electoral rules changes. The exact same MPs who were least likely to speak under the old electoral rules – those members who closely toed the party line on roll-call votes – were much more likely to take the floor under the new rules, which gave parties more control. Interestingly, given the introduction of party bloc votes, debate participation represents the best way to examine empirically the changing relationship between the party leadership and their backbenchers, and in particular those backbenchers most likely to rebel.

Conclusion

Studies of legislative behavior and party politics have long overlooked a key element of democracy – parliamentary debate – focusing instead on MP actions directly related to policy-making (e.g. roll-call voting and committee behavior). In our view, parliamentary speech provides key insights into how parties manage internal dissent among their MPs and communicate positions to their electorate. How parties and their members use debate is a function of institutions and the electoral incentives they generate. Parliamentary speech rarely has persuasive effects on in policy-making. MPs do not normally take the floor with the intention of actually convincing their colleagues of the virtue of their position, nor do they expect their speech to alert fellow members to new policy options. In many parliaments, they are not even looking to engage in fruitful policy debate. Deliberation over policy issues is much more likely to occur in committees, government offices, or in closed-door party meetings. The nature and content of floor speeches are, instead, best viewed as the result of strategic party competition. Members of parliamentary parties use speeches to send and reinforce messages about their policy positions to voters. In most systems, MPs have the electorate in mind as the intended receiver of this message. Even in parliaments where the public is not listening, such as the European Parliament, MPs behave strategically to communicate their loyalty to parties that control important electoral resources. In political systems where institutions provide parties with a greater incentive to protect the party label, party leaders exercise greater control over who has access to the floor. In systems where it is more important for individual members to create a name for themselves, party leaders allow backbenchers greater access. In this Conclusion, we examine the implications of our findings for other literature on party competition, democratic representation and electoral systems, and the use of political texts as data. Lastly, we discuss directions for future research.

Party competition and intraparty politics

Comparative literature on political parties and party competition has tended to treat parties as unitary actors. When estimating ideological congruence between voters and parties, studies typically use point estimates for party positions obtained through a variety of methodologies – hand-coding manifestos, computer-coding manifestos, or asking experts. The goal is generally to use party position estimates to explain law production (e.g. Tsebelis, 1999), government formation (Martin and Stevenson, 2001), or some other aspect of the political system. Rarely do researchers care about the distribution of positions within parties. The party-as-a-unitary-actor assumption has been justified on the grounds that parties are cohesive, and backbench dissent on roll-call votes is relatively rare. Of course, even on votes, this assumption is not always justified (Carey, 2009; Kam, 2009). Our argument suggests that, to understand important aspects of parliamentary behavior, a theoretical model must approach parliamentary politics at the level of the individual MP. Only by considering strategic dissent within parties are we able to understand and provide a logic for parliamentary speech and understand what it can tell us about internal party politics. Examining parliamentary speech provides us with insights into the degree of party cohesion and helps us explore how parties handle intraparty dissent while trying to maximize their electoral competitiveness.

Parties care about policy, office, and votes (Müller and Strøm, 1999). We have presented a model in which individual legislators have a preference for publicly expressing their policy preferences while retaining public office. Party leaders, meanwhile, care about the perception of the party policy in the electorate and the implications for maximizing party votes. Thus, our model embeds a strategic intraparty delegation game into the broader literature on what parties do. The intraparty speech delegation game is only one of many strategic interactions that go on in parliamentary politics. Thus, a possible extension of our framework might be to consider our game as nested in other strategic political settings (Tsebelis, 1990). An interaction that comes to mind is the coalition governance game that has been alluded to throughout this book (see also Martin and Vanberg, 2008, 2011). When MPs navigate among their own interests, party interests, and coalition policy – all while worrying about their own career prospects – they have multiple opportunities to trade off these interests in parliament and in the media. Examining in detail which strategies bring the greatest reward electorally for MPs is a question that deserves careful attention. Other extensions of our work could investigate intraparty dynamics and the interactions between committees and the full chamber.

Electoral systems, representation, and the ideological congruence debate

A large body of work in comparative politics is concerned with how political systems represent voters. Numerous studies have been undertaken to study the effect of electoral rules by investigating the ideological congruence between the preferences of voters, MPs, parties, and governments (e.g. Huber and Powell, 1994; Powell, 2000; McDonald and Budge, 2005; Blais and Bodet, 2006; Budge and McDonald, 2007; Powell, 2009; Ezrow, 2010; Golder and Stramski, 2010; Hug and Martin, 2012). Because of differences in conceptualization and measurement, these studies disagree about the extent to which proportional representation systems promote ideological congruence. Some scholars have suggested that proportional systems are better at covering the position of the median voter (Huber and Powell, 1994; Powell, 2000), but others remain more skeptical of this link (Blais and Bodet, 2006; Golder and Stramski, 2010), or argue that single-member districts create a connection between MPs and constituents (Cain, Ferejohn, and Fiorina, 1987). To the degree that both of these features of electoral systems are normatively desirable, some have proposed that mixed-member systems offer the best of both worlds. Such systems retain the advantages of a proportional system while creating a connection between members and their constituents (Shugart and Wattenberg, 2003).[1]

Rather than adding yet another study to this "ideological congruence controversy" (Powell, 2009), this book sheds light on how electoral *and* parliamentary institutions affect the intraparty dynamics of position-taking. The findings suggest that electoral systems that encourage personal vote seeking allow a greater number of MPs to

[1] The authors, though, do suggest that mixed-member majoritarian systems may be better at achieving a balance between the goals of proportional representation and SMD plurality than mixed-member proportional systems (Shugart and Wattenberg, 2003, p. 592).

take the floor of parliament and to express a wider range of opinions. Such parliamentary activity can help MPs create a permanent record of their positions, communicate with their constituents, and highlight the ways in which they are standing up for the concerns of their district. In this sense, our findings challenge perspectives that claim that ideological congruence is necessarily low in majoritarian systems. Although aggregate deviations between median voters and parties may be larger, the distribution of preferences *within* parties may be more accurately reflected in parliamentary speeches.

Our findings furthermore suggest that the introduction of a mixed-member system, at least the proportional variant, will not generate the same behavior in its single-member district members as pure plurality systems do. Because party leaders need to maximize the party vote to increase seat share in parliament, they have an incentive to keep an extra close watch on members with the greatest incentive to deviate from the party line – those MPs elected out of single-member districts. It is precisely because these MPs wish to represent the interests of small constituencies that party leaders need to exercise greater control. Thus, as a result of the electoral law change in New Zealand, we see parties develop mechanisms to exercise more control over their MPs' actions on the floor. Likewise, we see much stricter party control in Germany compared with the United Kingdom, even over members elected out of single-member districts.

Finally, we have shown that party leaders are active in proportional representation systems, monitoring and intervening in parliamentary debates when ideological disagreement within parties increases. This finding challenges the notion that proportional representation systems are superior to majoritarian systems in representing preferences. Voters may have greater choice at the polls when choosing parties with a policy platform close to their own. But at the same time, institutional incentives limit rhetorical representation. Because parties carefully delegate speaking time and members moderate their positions, the diversity of views expressed by MPs is smaller. In this sense, our study may also provide a partial explanation for the mixed findings in the literature studying electoral institutions and satisfaction with democracy referred to in the Introduction. Despite the fact that proportional systems offer voters more choice at election time, citizens may well enjoy more satisfaction with democratic institutions in majoritarian systems than proportional systems if the range of intraparty preferences is better represented in debates in the former than the latter.

Political speech as data: understanding the data-generating process

Our findings indicate when legislative speech data are best able to provide insights into intra- and interparty politics. Parliaments spend tremendous resources to carefully store the speech record of their MPs. These records hold great potential to provide data that researchers can use to uncover information about the flexibility of party positions and other features of party systems (e.g. Laver, Benoit, and Garry, 2003; Proksch and Slapin, 2010; Quinn et al., 2010). But few have actually looked into the constraints on speakers and the strategic nature of parliamentary speech. This book argues that party strategy affects the data-generating mechanism of political speech. Not all speeches are created equally. Some speakers are significantly more active than others, and the identity of these speakers depends on political institutions as well as latent intraparty heterogeneity. To draw conclusions about both internal party cohesion and party positioning from speech data, we therefore need to be aware of the data-generating mechanism. Our speech delegation model presents one stylized mechanism that can serve as a guide to scholars interested in estimating intraparty cohesion. First, we find that speech provides more information about intraparty dissent than roll-call votes. Rebels are more likely to express disapproval with the party in a speech than they are to vote against the party. Scholars, including ourselves, have claimed that legislative speech may indeed be a more useful source for studying intraparty politics than votes. However, rebel speech will be a better indicator of true latent party dissent in systems that create incentives for cultivating a personal vote. In systems where party labels matter more, party leaders will try to suppress dissent from coming to the floor to the best of their ability. Of course, even in these systems, party leaders are more likely to allow dissenting floor speeches than dissenting votes.

Taken together, this means that researchers need, at the very least, to be careful when using parliamentary speeches as data. The estimation of positions or cohesion should follow from a data-generating mechanism inspired by theory. Whether one applies the logic of our delegation model or considers an alternative model is certainly up for debate. But we believe that comparative institutional analysis can be a useful source of inspiration when creating new ways to estimate ideological positions and cohesion.

Directions for future research

In discussing how the findings from our book fit into and build on the existing literature, we have already hinted at avenues for future research. For example, future studies ought to carefully consider institutions when using speech as data to estimate ideology or other concepts, such as intraparty cohesion. We also see two additional paths for future work following from the results we have presented in this book. First, we have only just begun to scratch the surface of the different types of institutional arrangements within legislatures that can govern parliamentary speech. Moreover, there may be significant variation within a single legislature. In some instances, governments may be able to allot more time to debate, or shorten debate. The nature of debate on government and private member bills may vary. Parties likely use these different types of debate in a variety of ways and may give more leeway to members to deviate from the party message in some parliamentary settings than in others. Researchers must look into why such rules exist, the purpose they serve for parties and members, and their effects on how parties and MPs communicate their message to voters.

Second, with the advent of MPs' personal websites and the increasing importance of social media in politics, there is an ever-increasing number of outlets for intraparty dissent beyond parliament. Our findings suggest that parties may view dissent in the media as less costly than dissent in parliament, and such dissent does appear to be somewhat more prevalent both in Germany and the United Kingdom – the cases we have examined here. Future research ought to examine the effects of extra-parliamentary dissent on parties and electoral outcomes. In addition, researchers may examine the tools that parties use to rein it in or even coordinate and control it. There are many more sources of data for examining intrapolitics today than roll-call votes in parliaments, and scholars need to take full advantage of them to increase our understanding of intraparty politics.

Delivering a political message is the daily business of democratic politics. Democratic accountability calls for the communication of policies. Parliamentary debates serve this purpose. But voters rarely think about which MPs receive priority on the floor. We have shown that one can learn more about representation by closely linking political institutions and intraparty politics. In doing so, this book has offered a new theoretical account for a previously understudied aspect of parliamentary behavior. We hope to have shed greater light on both intra- and interparty competition in comparative context. Parliamentary debate is not a fruitless activity; rather, it provides parties and their MPs with a forum for effectively communicating positions.

Appendix

Proof of speech delegation game

When delegated floor time, party member M's utility is $U_M = -\lambda_M(x_S - x_M)^2 - (1-\lambda_M)x_S^2$. Rearranging leads to $U_M = -\lambda_M x_S^2 + 2\lambda_M x_S x_M - \lambda_M x_M^2 - x_S^2 + \lambda_M x_S^2$. The party member maximizes his or her utility by setting the policy content of the speech x_S. Formally, $x_S^* = \arg\max_{x_S} U_M$. The first-order condition is: $\frac{\partial U_M}{\partial x_S} = -2\lambda_M x_S + 2\lambda_M x_M - 2x_S + 2\lambda_M x_S = 0$. This leads to the optimal position of the member's speech: $x_S^* = \lambda_M x_M$.

The party leader delegates if the expected utility of delegation exceeds the utility of delivering the speech himself: $-\pi_L(x_S^M)^2 - c_L + 1(c_L + (1-\pi_L)e_L) \geq -\pi_L(x_S^L)^2 - c_L$. When delegating, the leader knows that the party member will express the position x_S^*. When the leader does not delegate, he or she will deliver a speech at his or her own ideal point $x_L = 0$. Substituting into the utility function of the leader, this leads to $-\pi_L(\lambda_M x_M)^2 + (1-\pi_L)e_L \geq -c_L$. Rearranging leads to the threshold condition: $x_M \leq \sqrt{\frac{e_L(1-\pi_L)+c_L}{\pi_L\lambda_M^2}}$. The condition holds for $x_M > 0$, $\pi_L > 0$ and $\lambda_M > 0$ (true by assumption).

Collection of parliamentary speech data

Collecting parliamentary speeches for the full set of MPs and over a long time period used to be an arduous task. University libraries around the world still hold numerous printed volumes of parliamentary debates for parliaments. With the digital revolution, most parliaments have established their own electronic databases for storing the activities of members of parliament. The data we examine make use of these publicly available databases. This Appendix serves as a detailed description of how we collected the data and what coding decisions we made along the way. The rapid technological changes that come with the digital age, enabling us to conduct a quantitative analysis of this scale, also mean that databases can change. Our descriptions that follow demonstrate the different steps that were involved in collecting the data in the years 2010 and 2011.

United Kingdom

We first assembled a data set of all MPs in the House of Commons between 1979 and 2005, coding the monthly backbencher status or leader positions the MPs held (sources used include Butler and Butler 2005, and Gay, 2009) and assigning each MP a unique identifying number. The electronic archive "Historic Hansard" is sponsored by the House of Commons (but not officially part of the parliament website) and available at http://hansard.millbanksystems.com. The archive is generated from digitized versions of Hansard, the official report of debates in the House of Commons. The next step was to match the MPs in the status data set with those in the electronic archive. Using an R script, we used regular expression pattern matching to match the MP names and extract the MPs' page on the Historic Hansard site. In case of no match or multiple matches, we manually extracted and assigned the correct MP page.

Using the data set with MPs' unique URLs for the Historic Hansard site, we wrote a Perl script that accessed the site and automatically pulled out the number of speeches given in each month. We excluded MPs' written questions in this count. We then merged the two data sets and reshaped the final data into MP–month observations. In this step, we assigned zero speech counts to MP–months, as nonoccurrence of speech is not listed in the Historic Hansard. We also coded for each MP–month the government status of the MP's party, the legislative term, removed speeches from the Speaker of the House (as they are procedural), and created a dummy variable indicating whether MPs had switched between backbencher and leader status during their tenure. Finally, we removed those months from the data set during which no MP gave any speech as parliament was out of session. The final data set includes 170,636 MP–month observations.

Germany

The procedure to assemble the German data set was similar to the British data set. First, data on the backbencher and leader status of MPs were obtained from a Bundestag publication listing all MPs (Bundestag, 1998). Using the parliamentary archive available at http://dip.bundestag.de, we searched for all parliamentary speeches in a given legislative period. After a personal communication with a member of the Bundestag administration, we used the following search parameters for the database: information type: *Parlamentarische Vorgänge*, Person (Urheber): *redner'o'protok.rede*, and Dokument: *bt'u'plpr'n'nein*. We then counted the number of monthly speeches for each MP and merged the resulting data set with the leader dataset using unique MP identifiers. Finally, we added information about the electoral tier the MP was elected in (single-member district or party list) to the data set.

European Parliament

All debates are publicly available on the EP's website at www.europarl.europa.eu. From a list of identifiers unique to each member of the EP, we counted the number of speeches using an automated Perl script. The data analysis was conducted before the major redesign of the EP website in 2011.

New Zealand

Data on New Zealand budget debate participation were gathered from the website www.vdig.net. First, a Perl script was written to scrape all days on which appropriations bills were debated. Then appropriation debates on those days were manually read and individual MP debate participation was coded. Party leadership data were taken from Chris Kam's data on New Zealand roll-call votes, available at John Carey's legislative votes database www.dartmouth.edu/~jcarey/Legislative_Voting_Data_files/lvdatatable.htm. Leadership data from 1996 was culled from information on New Zealand parliament's online biographies of current and former MPs www.parliament.nz/en-NZ/MPP/MPs, the Official Yearbooks www.stats.govt.nz/yearbooks, and supplemented with information from the parliamentary library's information service. Leadership roles include government ministers, shadow ministers, whips, junior whips, party leaders, and deputy leaders. Committee chairs and other members with no official party role are coded as backbenchers.

Chapter 5 robustness checks

As additional robustness checks of the MP-level longitudinal count models, we have rerun Model 3 in both Tables 5.2 and 5.4 using different definitions of party leader. In the United Kingdom, we ran one model counting only whips as party leaders and a second model in which leaders were defined solely as ministers of state plus members of cabinet (or shadow cabinet for the opposition). These redefinitions of leader did not affect our findings. In Germany, we ran an additional model in which we did not code government ministers as party leaders. Again, the results remained substantively unchanged.

Table A.1. *Chapter 5 simulated predicted speech counts (with 95 percent confidence intervals) for different types of German MPs*

Type	Elected from	Ideological distance	Inside coalition interval	Committee assignments	Predicted speeches	95% Lower	95% Upper
Backbencher	List	Average	Yes	Average	12.45	9.61	16.23
Backbencher	List	Average	No	Average	14.46	11.27	18.45
Backbencher	District	Average	No	Average	13.04	10.37	16.36
Leader	List	Average	Yes	Average	16.45	10.62	24.46
Backbencher	List	Min in coal int.	Yes	Average	9.92	6.66	14.55
Backbencher	List	Max in coal int.	No	Average	11.48	8.09	15.67
Backbencher	List	Average	No	1st quartile	12.53	9.76	16.05
Backbencher	List	Average	No	3rd quartile	16.05	12.38	20.13
Backbencher	List	Maximum	No	Average	10.11	6.35	15.62
Backbencher	List	Minimum	No	Average	16.09	12.07	21.01

Note: Mean ideological distance between MP and party leader = 0.18, minimum = 0, maximum inside the coalition interval = 0.60, maximum = 0.83. Committee assignments: mean = 3.2, first quartile = 2, third quartile = 4. Simulated effects were calculated using the *R* package *Zelig* and based on model 4 in Table 5.8. coal int., coalition interval.

Bibliography

Aarts, Kees, and Jacques Thomassen. 2008. "Satisfaction with Democracy: Do Institutions Matter?" *Electoral Studies* 27(1): 5–18.

Aldrich, John H. 1995. *Why Parties? The Origin and Transformation of Political Parties in America*. University of Chicago Press.

Aldrich, John H., and Richard D. McKelvey. 1977. "A Method of Scaling with Applications to the 1968 and 1972 Presidential Elections." *American Political Science Review* 71(1): 111–130.

Alivizatos, Nikos. 1990. "The Difficulties of 'Rationalization' in a Polarized Political System: The Greek Chamber of Deputies." In *Parliament and Democratic Consolidation in Southern Europe: Greece, Italy, Portugal, Spain, and Turkey*, ed. Ulrike Liebert, and Maurizio Cotta. Pinter, 131–153.

Ames, Barry. 1995. "Electoral Strategy under Open-List Proportional Representation." *American Journal of Political Science* 39(2): 406–433.

2001. *The Deadlock of Democracy in Brazil*. University of Michigan Press.

Anderson, Christopher J., and Christine A. Guillory. 1997. "Political Institutions and Satisfaction with Democracy: A Cross-National Analysis of Consensus and Majoritarian Systems." *American Political Science Review* 91(1): 66–81.

Austen-Smith, David. 1990. "Information Transmission in Debate." *American Journal of Political Science* 34(1): 124–152.

Austen-Smith, David, and Timothy Feddersen. 2006. "Deliberation, Preference Uncertainty and Voting Rules." *American Political Science Review* 100(2): 209–217.

Bächtiger, André, and Dominik Hangartner. 2010. "When Deliberative Theory Meets Empirical Political Science: Theoretical and Methodological Challenges in Political Deliberation." *Political Studies* 58(4): 609–629.

Barker, Fiona, Jonathan Boston, Stephen Levine, Elizabeth McLeay, and Nigel S. Roberts. 2001. "An Initial Assessment of the Consequences of MPP in New Zealand." In *Mixed-Member Electoral Systems: The Best of Both Worlds?*, ed. Matthew Shugart and Martin Wattenberg. Oxford University Press, pp. 297–322.

Bawn, Kathleen, and Michael F. Thies. 2003. "A Comparative Theory of Electoral Incentives: Representing the Unorganized under PR, Plurality, and Mixed-Member Electoral Systems." *Journal of Theoretical Politics* 15(1): 5–32.

BBC. 2009. "MP Suspended after Mace Protest (15 January 2009)." http://news.bbc.co.uk/2/hi/uk_news/politics/7830937.stm.

Benoit, Kenneth, Michael Laver, and Slava Mikhaylov. 2009. "Treating Words as Data with Error: Uncertainty in Text Statements of Policy Positions." *American Journal of Political Science* 53(2): 495–513.

Bernauer, Julian, and Thomas Bräuninger. 2009. "Intra-Party Preference Heterogeneity and Faction Membership in the 15th German Bundestag: A Computational Text Analysis of Parliamentary Speeches." *German Politics* 18(3): 385–402.

Blais, André, and Marc André Bodet. 2006. "Does Proportional Representation Foster Closer Congruence between Citizens and Policy Makers?" *Comparative Political Studies* 39(10): 1243–1262.

Boston, Jonathan, Stephen Levine, Elizabeth McLeay, and Nigel S. Roberts. 1996. *New Zealand under MMP: A New Politics?* Auckland University Press.

Bowler, Shaun. 2000. "Parties in Legislatures: Two Competing Explanations." In *Parties without Partisans: Political Change in Advanced Industrial Democracies*, ed. R.J. Dalton and M.P. Wattenberg. Oxford University Press, pp. 157–179.

Budge, Ian, and Michael D. McDonald. 2007. "Election and Party System Effects on Policy Representation: Bringing Time into a Comparative Perspective." *Electoral Studies* 26(1): 168–179.

Bundesfinanzministerium. 2008. "Schutzschirm für Arbeitsplätze. Die Bundesregierung stärkt mit 15 Maßnahmen die Wirtschaft, sichert Arbeitsplätze und entlastet private Haushalte (5 November 2008)." www.bundesfinanzministerium.de/nn_69120/DE/Buergerinnen_und_Buerger/Gesellschaft_und_Zukunft/themenschwerpunkt_konjunkturpakete/073_Schutzschirm_arbeitsplaetze.html?_nnn=true.

2009. "Das zweite Konjunkturpaket. Deutschland in Bewegung halten (14 January 2009)." www.bundesfinanzministerium.de/nn_69120/DE/Buergerinnen_und_Buerger/Gesellschaft_und_Zukunft/themenschwerpunkt_konjunkturpakete/Stellschrauben-des-Konjunkturpakets-2/075_in_Bewegung_halten.html?_nnn=true.

Bundestag. 1998. "Die Mitglieder des Deutschen Bundestages 1.-13. Wahlperiode." *Materialien des Wissenschaftlichen Dienstes des Deutschen Bundestages* 127.

Butler, David, and Gareth Butler. 2005. *British Political Facts since 1979*. Palgrave Macmillan.

Cain, Bruce, John Ferejohn, and Morris Fiorina. 1987. *The Personal Vote: Constituency Service and Electoral Independence*. Harvard University Press.

Carey, John M. 2007. "Competing Principals: Political Institutions and Party Unity in Legislative Voting." *American Journal of Political Science* 51(1): 92–107.

2009. *Legislative Voting and Accountability*. Cambridge University Press.

Carey, John, and Matthew Shugart. 1995. "Incentives to Cultivate a Personal Vote: A Rank Ordering of Electoral Formulas." *Electoral Studies* 14(4): 417–439.

Carrubba, Clifford J., Matthew J. Gabel, and Simon Hug. 2008. "Legislative Voting Behavior, Seen and Unseen: A Theory of Roll-Call Vote Selection." *Legislative Studies Quarterly* 23(4): 543–572.

Carrubba, Clifford J., Matthew J. Gabel, Lacey Murrah, Ryan Clough, Elizabeth Montgomery, and Rebecca Schambach. 2006. "Off the Record: Unrecorded Legislative Votes, Selection Bias and Roll-Call Vote Analysis." *British Journal of Political Science* 36(4): 691–704.

CDU/CSU. 2005. "Arbeitsordnung der CDU/CSU Bundestagsfraktion der 16. Wahlperiode (28 November 2005)." www.cducsu.de.

Chang, Eric C.C., and Miriam A. Golden. 2007. "Electoral Systems, District Magnitude and Corruption." *British Journal of Political Science* 37(1): 115–137.

Clinton, Joshua, Simon Jackman, and Douglas Rivers. 2004. "The Statistical Analysis of Roll Call Data." *American Political Science Review* 98(2): 355–370.

Corbett, Richard, Francis Jacobs, and Michael Shackleton. 2007. *The European Parliament*. 7th ed. John Harper.

Cox, Gary. 2006. "The Organization of Democratic Legislatures." In *The Oxford Handbook of Political Economy*, ed. Barry Weingast, and Donald Wittman. Oxford: Oxford University Press, pp. 141–161.

Cox, Gary, and Mathew D. McCubbins. 1993. *The Legislative Leviathan*. University of California Press.

2005. *Setting the Agenda: Responsible Party Government in the US House of Representatives*. Cambridge University Press.

Cox, Gary W., and Michael F. Thies. 1998. "The Cost of Intraparty Competition: The Single, Nontrasferable Vote and Money Politics in Japan." *Comparative Political Studies* 31(3): 267–291.

Cox, Karen E., and Leonard J. Schoppa. 2002. "Interaction Effects in Mixed-Member Electoral Systems: Theory and Evidence from Germany, Japan, and Italy." *Comparative Political Studies* 35(9): 1027–1053.

Crisp, Brian, Maria Escobar-Lemmon, Bradford Jones, Mark Jones, and Michelle Taylor-Robinson. 2004. "Vote-Seeking Incentives and

Legislative Representation in Six Presidential Democracies." *Journal of Politics* 66(3): 823–846.

Cronbach, Lee J. 1951. "Coefficient Alpha and the Internal Structure of Tests." *Psychometrika* 16(3): 297–334.

Dalton, Russell J., David M. Farrell, and Ian McAllister. 2011. *Political Parties and Democratic Linkage: How Parties Organize Democracy*. Oxford University Press.

Denemark, David. 2001. "Choosing MMP in New Zealand: Explaining the 1993 Electoral Reform." In *Mixed-Member Electoral Systems: The Best of Both Worlds?*, ed. Matthew Shugart and Martin Wattenberg. Oxford: Oxford University Press, pp. 70–95.

Deutscher Bundestag. 2011*a*. "130. Sitzung des Deutschen Bundestages am Donnerstag, 29 September 2011. Endgültiges Ergebnis der Namentlichen Abstimmung Nr. 1." www.bundestag.de/bundestag/plenum/abstimmung/20110929_euro.pdf.

2011b. "Stenografischer Bericht. 130. Sitzung (17/130). 29 September 2011." http://dipbt.bundestag.de/dip21/btp/17/17130.pdf.

Dewan, Torun, and David P. Myatt. 2008. "The Qualities of Leadership: Direction, Communication, and Obfuscation." *American Political Science Review* 102(3): 351–368.

Die Welt. 2011. "'Für mich war klar, Berlin muss Hauptstadt sein' (Interview with Wolfgang Schäuble, 19 June 2011)." www.welt.de/politik/deutschland/article13438037/Fuer-mich-war-klar-Berlin-muss-Hauptstadt-sein.html.

Diermeier, Daniel, and Timothy Feddersen. 1998. "Cohesion in Legislatures and the Vote of Confidence Procedure." *American Political Science Review* 92(3): 611–621.

Diermeier, Daniel, Jean-François Godbout, Bei Yu, and Stefan Kaufmann. 2012. "Language and Ideology in Congress." *British Journal of Political Science* 42(1): 31–55.

Döring, Herbert. 1995. "Time as a Scarce Resource: Government Control of the Agenda." In *Parliaments and Majority Rule in Western Europe*, ed. Herbert Döring. Campus Verlag, pp. 223–246.

Downs, Anthony. 1957. *An Economic Theory of Democracy*. Harper.

Eurogroup. 2010. "Terms of Reference of the Eurogroup: European Financial Stability Facility (7 June 2010)." www.consilium.europa.eu/uedocs/cms_Data/docs/pressdata/en/misc/114977.pdf.

Ezrow, Lawrence. 2010. *Linking Citizens and Parties: How Electoral Systems Matter for Political Representation*. Oxford University Press.

Farrell, David. 2011. *Electoral Systems: A Comparative Introduction*. 2nd ed. Palgrave Macmillan.

FDP. 2005. "Geschäftsordnung der FDP Fraktion im Deutschen Bundestag beschlossen am 12.11.1991 zuletzt geändert am 13.12.2005." www.fdp-fraktion.de.

Ferrara, Federico, and Erik S. Herron. 2005. "Going It Alone? Strategic Entry under Mixed Electoral Rules." *American Journal of Political Science* 49(1): 16–31.

Follesdal, Andreas, and Simon Hix. 2006. "Why There Is a Democratic Deficit in the EU: A Response to Majone and Moravcsik." *Journal of Common Market Studies* 44(3): 533–562.

Gallagher, Michael, and Michael Marsh, eds. 1988. *Candidate Selection in Comparative Perspective: The Secret Garden of Politics*. Sage.

Gallagher, Michael, and Paul Mitchell, eds. 2005. *The Politics of Electoral Systems*. Oxford University Press.

Gallagher, Michael, Michael Laver, and Peter Mair. 2006. *Representative Government in Modern Europe*. McGraw-Hill.

Gay, Oonagh. 2009. "Members since 1979." *House of Commons Library Research Paper* 09/31.

Giannetti, Daniela, and Michael Laver. 2005. "Policy Positions and Jobs in the Government." *European Journal of Political Research* 44(1): 91–120.

Golder, Matthew, and Jacek Stramski. 2010. "Ideological Congruence and Electoral Institutions." *American Journal of Political Science* 54(1): 90–106.

Greens. 2007. "Geschäftsordnung der Fraktion Bündnis 90/Die Grünen im Bundestag, beschlossen am 27.9.2005, geändert mit Beschluss vom 5.9.2007." *GRÜNE Bundestagsfraktion*.

Gschwend, Thomas, Hermann Schmitt, Andreas Wüst, and Thomas Zittel. 2005. *German Candidate Survey, Bundestag Election 2005 (ZA4923 data set)*. Mannheim Center for European Social Research (MZES) and GESIS Cologne.

Guardian. 2009. "Labour Survives Vote on Heathrow Expansion but 28 MPs Join Revolt (29 January 2009)." www.guardian.co.uk/politics/2009/jan/28/labour-survives-heathrow-expansion-vote.

Habermas, Jürgen. 1985. *The Theory of Communicative Action*. Vols. 1 & 2. Beacon Press.

Hall, Richard L. 1998. *Participation in Congress*. Yale University Press.

Harris, Douglas B. 2005. "Orchestrating Party Talk: A Party-Based View of One-Minute Speeches." *Legislative Studies Quarterly* 30(1): 127–141.

Hazan, Reuven Y., and Gideon Rahat. 2006. "The Influence of Candidate Selection Methods on Legislatures and Legislators: Theoretical Propositions, Methodological Suggestions and Empirical Evidence." *The Journal of Legislative Studies* 12(3): 366–385.

Herron, Erik S. 2002. "Electoral Influences on Legislative Behavior in Mixed-Member Systems: Evidence from Ukraine's Verkhovna Rada." *Legislative Studies Quarterly* 27(3): 361–382.

Hix, Simon. 2002. "Parliamentary Behavior with Two Principals: Preferences, Parties, and Voting in the European Parliament." *American Journal of Political Science* 46(3): 688–698.

2004. "Electoral Institutions and Legislative Behavior: Explaining Voting Defection in the European Parliament." *World Politics* 56(1): 194–223.

Hix, Simon, and Michael Marsh. 2007. "Punishment or Protest? Understanding European Parliament Elections." *Journal of Politics* 69(2): 495–510.

Hix, Simon, and Abdul Noury. 2009. "After Enlargement: Voting Patterns in the Sixth European Parliament." *Legislative Studies Quarterly* 34(2): 159–174.

Hix, Simon, Abdul Noury, and Gerard Roland. 2007. *Democratic Politics in the European Parliament.* Cambridge University Press.

HM Treasury. 2008. *Pre-Budget Report. Facing Global challenges: Supporting People through Difficult Times.* The Stationery Office (CM 7484).

Hopkins, Daniel J., and Gary King. 2010. "A Method of Automated Nonparametric Content Analysis for Social Science." *American Journal of Political Science* 54(1): 229–247.

Huber, John D. 1996. "The Vote of Confidence in Parliamentary Democracies." *American Political Science Review* 90(2): 269–282.

Huber, John D., and G. Bingham Powell. 1994. "Congruence between Citizens and Policymakers in Two Visions of Liberal Democracy." *World Politics* 46(3): 291–326.

Hug, Simon. 2010. "Selection Effects in Roll Call Votes." *British Journal of Political Science* 40(1): 225–235.

Hug, Simon, and Danielle Martin. 2012. "How Electoral Systems Affect MPs' Positions." *Electoral Studies* 38:192–200.

Imai, Kosuke, Gary King, and Olivia Lau. 2007. "negbin: Negative Binomial Regression for Event Count Dependent Variables." In *Zelig: Everyone's Statistical Software*. http://gking.harvard.edu/zelig.

Jensen, Christian B., Sven-Oliver Proksch, and Jonathan B. Slapin. 2013. "Parliamentary Questions, Oversight, and National Opposition Status in the European Parliament." *Legislative Studies Quarterly* 38(2): 259–282.

Kam, Christopher J. 2009. *Party Discipline and Parliamentary Politics.* Cambridge University Press.

Karp, Jeffrey. 2002. "Members of Parliament and Representation." In *Proportional Representation on Trial: The 1999 New Zealand General Election and the Fate of MMP*, ed. Jack Vowles, Peter Aimer, Jeffrey

Karp, Susan Banducci, Raymond Miller, and Ann Sullivan. Auckland University Press, pp. 130–145.

2009. "Candidate Effects and Spill-Over in Mixed Systems: Evidence from New Zealand." *Electoral Studies* 28(1): 41–50.

Katz, Richard S. 1986. "Intraparty Preference Voting." In *Electoral Laws and Their Political Consequences*, ed. Bernard Grofman and Arend Lijphart. Agathon Press, pp. 85–103.

Kiewiet, D. Roderick, and Mathew D. McCubbins. 1991. *The Logic of Delegation: Congressional Parties and the Appropriations Process*. University of Chicago Press.

Klingemann, Hans-Dieter. 1999. "Mapping Political Support in the 1990s: A Global Analysis." In *Critical Citizens: Global Support for Democratic Government*, ed. Pippa Norris. Oxford University Press, pp. 31–56.

Klingemann, Hans-Dieter, Andrea Volkens, Judith Bara, Ian Budge, and Michael McDonald. 2006. *Mapping Policy Preferences II: Estimates for Parties, Electors and Governments in Central and Eastern Europe, European Union and OECD 1990–2003*. Oxford University Press.

Koger, Gregory. 2010. *Filibustering: A Political History of Obstruction in the House and Senate*. University of Chicago Press.

Kreppel, Amie. 2002. *The European Parliament and Supranational Party System*. Cambridge University Press.

Laver, Michael, and Kenneth Benoit. 2002. "Locating TDs in Policy Spaces: Wordscoring Daíl Speeches." *Irish Political Studies* 17(1): 59–73.

Laver, Michael, Kenneth Benoit, and John Garry. 2003. "Extracting Policy Positions from Political Texts Using Words as Data." *American Political Science Review* 97(2): 311–332.

Lijphart, Arend. 1999. *Patterns of Democracy: Government Forms and Performance in Thirty-Six Countries*. Yale University Press.

Lindstädt, René, Jonathan B. Slapin, and Ryan J. Vander Wielen. 2011. "Balancing Competing Demands: Position Taking and Election Proximity in the European Parliament." *Legislative Studies Quarterly* 36(1): 37–70.

2012. "Adaptive Behaviour in the European Parliament: Learning to Balance Competing Demands." *European Union Politics* 13(4).

Londregan, John. 2002. "Appointment, Reelection, and Autonomy in the Senate of Chile." In *Legislative Politics in Latin America*, ed. Scott Morgenstern and Benito Nacif. Cambridge University Press, pp. 341–376.

Maltzman, Forrest, and Lee Sigelman. 1996. "The Politics of Talk: Unconstrained Floor Time in the US House of Representatives." *The Journal of Politics* 58(3): 819–830.

Marsh, Michael. 1998. "Testing the Second-Order Election Model after Four European Elections." *British Journal of Political Science* 28(4): 591–607.

2000. "Candidate Centred by Party Wrapped: Campaigning in Ireland under STV." In *Elections in Australia, Ireland and Malta under the Single Transferable Vote*, ed. Shaun Bowler and Bernard Grofman. University of Michigan Press, pp. 114–130.

Martin, Andrew D., and Kevin M. Quinn. 2006. "Applied Bayesian Inference in R Using MCMCpack." *R News* 6(1): 2–7.

Martin, Andrew D., Kevin M. Quinn, and Jong Hee Park. 2011. "MCMCpack: Markov Chain Monte Carlo in R." *Journal of Statistical Software* 42(9): 1–21.

Martin, John E. 2006. "A Shifting Balance: Parliament, the Executive and the Evolution of Politics in New Zealand." *Australasian Parliamentary Review* 21(2): 113–131.

Martin, Lanny W., and Randolph T. Stevenson. 2001. "Government Formation in Parliamentary Democracies." *American Journal of Political Science* 45(1): 33–50.

Martin, Lanny W., and Georg Vanberg. 2008. "Coalition Government and Political Communication." *Political Research Quarterly* 61: 502–516.

2011. *Parliaments and Coalitions: The Role of Legislative Institutions in Multiparty Governance*. Oxford University Press.

Martin, Shane. 2010. "Electoral Rewards for Personal Vote Cultivation under PR-STV." *West European Politics* 33(2): 369–380.

2011. "Using Parliamentary Questions to Measure Constituency Focus: An Application to the Irish Case." *Political Studies* 59(2): 472–488.

Mayhew, David R. 1974. *Congress: The Electoral Connection*. Yale University Press.

McDonald, Michael D., and Ian Budge. 2005. *Elections, Parties, Democracy: Conferring the Median Mandate*. Oxford University Press.

McKay, William, ed. 2004. *Erskine May's Treatise on The Law, Privileges, Proceedings and Usage of Parliament*. 23rd ed. Lexis Nexis Butterworths.

Mill, John Stuart. 1991. *Considerations on Representative Government*. Promethus Books (originally published in 1861).

Monroe, Burt L., Michael Colaresi, and Kevin M. Quinn. 2008. "Fightin' Words: Lexical Feature Selection and Evaluation for Identifying the Content of Political Conflict." *Political Analysis* 16(4): 372–403.

Monroe, Burt L., and Ko Maeda. 2004. "Talk's Cheap: Text-Based Estimation of Rhetorical Ideal-Points." 21st Meeting, Society for Political Methodology, July 29–31.

Morgenstern, Scott. 2004. *Patterns of Legislative Politics: Roll Call Voting in the United States and Latin America's Southern Cone*. Cambridge University Press.

Morris, Jonathan S. 2001. "Reexamining the Politics of Talk: Partisan Rhetoric in the 104th House." *Legislative Studies Quarterly* 26(1): 101–121.

Müller, Wolfgang C., and Kaare Strøm, eds. 1999. *Policy, Office or Votes? How Political Parties in Western Europe Make Hard Decisions*. Cambridge University Press.

Nagel, Jack H. 2004. "New Zealand: Reform by (Nearly) Immaculate Design." In *Handbook of Electoral System Choice*, ed. Josep M. Colomer. Palgrave Macmillan, pp. 530–543.

Neblo, Michael A., Kevin M. Esterling, Ryan P. Kennedy, David M.J. Lazer, and Anand E. Sokhey. 2010. "Who Wants to Deliberate – and Why?" *American Political Science Review* 104(3): 566–583.

New Zealand Parliament. 2012. "Speakers' Rulings. 1876 to 2011 Inclusive." Office of the Clerk of the House of Representatives, New Zealand Parliament.

Norris, Pippa. 1999. "Institutional Explanations for Political Support." In *Critical Citizens: Global Support for Democratic Government*, ed. Pippa Norris. Oxford University Press, pp. 217–235.

2004. *Electoral Engineering: Voting Rules and Political Behavior*. Cambridge University Press.

2011. *Democratic Deficit: Critical Citizens Revisited*. Cambridge University Press.

Norris, Pippa, and Joni Luvenduski. 2001. "The British Representation Study, 2001." Available at www.hks.harvard.edu/fs/pnorris/datafiles/BRS2001.zip.

Page, Benjamin. 1996. *Who Deliberates? Mass Media in Modern Democracy*. University of Chicago Press.

Poole, Keith, and Howard Rosenthal. 1985. "A Spatial Model for Legislative Roll Call Analysis." *American Journal of Political Science* 29(2): 357–384.

Poole, Keith, Howard Rosenthal, Jeffrey Lewis, James Lo, and Royce Carroll. 2010. "basicspace: A Package to Recover a Basic Space from Issue Scales." *Ver. 0.01*.

Powell, G. Bingham. 2000. *Elections as Instruments of Democracy: Majoritarian and Proportional Visions*. Yale University Press.

2004. "Political Representation in Comparative Politics." *Annual Review of Political Science* 7: 273–296.

2009. "The Ideological Congruence Controversy." *Comparative Political Studies* 42(12): 1475–1497.

Proksch, Sven-Oliver, and Jonathan B. Slapin. 2010. "Position Taking in European Parliament Speeches." *British Journal of Political Science* 40(3): 587–611.

2011. "Parliamentary Questions and Oversight in the European Union." *European Journal of Political Research* 50(1): 53–79.

2012. "Institutional Foundations of Legislative Speech." *American Journal of Political Science* 56(3): 520–537.

Quinn, Kevin M., Burt L. Monroe, Michael Colaresi, Michael H. Crespin, and Dragomir Radev. 2010. "How to Analyze Political Attention with Minimal Assumptions and Costs." *American Journal of Political Science* 54(1): 209–228.

Rahat, Gideon, and Reuven Y. Hazan. 2001. "Candidate Selection Methods: An Analytical Framework." *Party Politics* 7(3): 297–322.

Rahat, G., R.Y. Hazan, and R.S. Katz. 2008. "Democracy and Political Parties: On the Uneasy Relationships between Participation, Competition and Representation." *Party Politics* 14(6): 663.

Rasch, Bjørn Erik. 2000. "Parliamentary Floor Voting Procedures and Agenda Setting in Europe." *Legislative Studies Quarterly* 25(1): 3–23.

Rasch, Bjørn Erik, and George Tsebelis, eds. 2011. *The Role of Governments in Legislative Agenda Setting*. Routledge/ECPR Studies in European Political Science.

Raunio, Tapio. 2000. "Losing Independence or Finally Gaining Recognition? Contacts between MEPs and National Parties." *Party Politics* 6(2): 211–223.

Reif, Karlheinz. 1984. "National Election Cycles and European Elections, 1979 and 1984." *Electoral Studies* 3(3): 244–255.

Reif, Karlheinz, and Hermann Schmitt. 1980. "Nine Second-Order National Elections: A Conceptual Framework for the Analysis of European Election Results." *European Journal of Political Research* 8(1): 3–45.

Roberts, Jason M. 2007. "The Statistical Analysis of Roll-Call Data: A Cautionary Tale." *Legislative Studies Quarterly* 32(3): 341–360.

Ryckewaert, Laura. 2013. "Tory Backbenchers Voice Support for a House Committee to Better Protect MPs' Freedom, Powers in Commons." *The Hill Times Weekly* 22 April.

Salmond, Robert C. 2007. *Parliamentary Question Times: How Legislative Accountability Mechanisms Affect Citizens and Politics*. PhD thesis, University of California, Los Angeles.

Scarrow, Susan. 1997. "Political Career Paths and Their Consequences in the European Parliament." *Legislative Studies Quarterly* 22(2): 253–263.

Schonhardt-Bailey, Cheryl. 2005. "Measuring Ideas More Effectively: An Analysis of Bush and Kerry's National Security Speeches." *PS: Political Science and Politics* 38(4): 701–711.

Schonhardt-Bailey, Cheryl. 2008. "The Constitutional Debate on Partial-Birth Abortion: Constitutional Gravitas and Moral Passion." *British Journal of Political Science* 38(3): 383–410.

Schreiner, Hermann J. 2005. "Die Berliner Stunde – Funktionsweise und Erfahrungen: Zur Redeordnung des Deutschen Bundestages." *Zeitschrift für Parlamentsfragen* 36(3): 573–588.

Shepsle, Kenneth A., and Barry R. Weingast. 1987. "The Institutional Foundations of Committee Power." *The American Political Science Review* 81(1): 85–104.

Shugart, Matthew S. 2003. "Extreme Electoral Systems and the Appeal of the Mixed-Member Alternative." In *Mixed-Member Electoral Systems: The Best of Both Worlds?*, ed. Matthew S. Shugart and Martin P. Wattenberg. Oxford University Press, pp. 25–54.

Shugart, M.S., M.E. Valdini, and K. Suominen. 2005. "Looking for Locals: Voter Information Demands and Personal Vote-Earning Attributes of Legislators under Proportional Representation." *American Journal of Political Science* 49(2): 437–449.

Shugart, Matthew S., and Martin P. Wattenberg, eds. 2003. *Mixed-Member Electoral Systems: The Best of Both Worlds?* Oxford University Press.

Slapin, Jonathan B., and Sven-Oliver Proksch. 2008. "A Scaling Model for Estimating Time-Series Party Positions from Texts." *American Journal of Political Science* 52(3): 705–722.

Smith, Steven. 1989. *Call to Order: Floor Politics in the House and Senate.* The Brookings Institution.

SPD. 2004. "Beschluss zum Selbstverständnis der Fraktion vom 23.6.1981 in der Fassung vom 19.5.1992." In *Das Regierungssystem der Bundesrepublik Deutschland*, ed. Joachim J. Hesse and Thomas Ellwein. De Gruyter, p. 466.

Spiegel Online. 2011. "Euro Abweichler erzürnen die Parteigranden (29 September 2011)." www.spiegel.de/politik/deutschland/0,1518,789100,00.html.

Steiner, Jürg, André Bächtiger, Markus Spörndli, and Marco R. Steenbergen. 2004. *Deliberative Politics in Action: Analysing Parliamentary Discourse.* Cambridge University Press.

Stern. 2011. "Zoff um Redezeit für Rebellen (29 September 2011)." www.stern.de/politik/deutschland/euro-abstimmung-im-bundestag-zoff-um-redezeit-fuer-rebellen-1733571.html.

Stewart, John. 2010. "Victory against All the Odds: The Story of How the Campaign to Stop a Third Runway at Heathrow Was Won." http://hacan.org.uk/resources/reports/victory.pdf.

Stone, Walter J., and Elizabeth N. Simas. 2010. "Candidate Valence and Ideological Positions in the U.S. House Elections." *American Journal of Political Science* 54(2): 371–388.

Strøm, Kaare, Wolfgang C. Müller, and Torbjörn Bergman, eds. 2003. *Delegation and Accountability in Parliamentary Democracies*. Oxford University Press.

Stuttgarter Zeitung. 2011. "'Auch Minderheiten haben Rechte' (Interview with Norbert Lammert, 5 October 2011)." www.stuttgarter-zeitung.de/inhalt.interview-mit-norbert-lammert-auch-minderheiten-haben-rechte.1136cfc4-1de3-482e-ab5a-7f6424777e58.html.

Süddeutsche Zeitung. 2011. "Abstimmung über Euro-Rettungsschirm – Rotkäppchen unter Fraktionszwang (28 September 2011)." www.sueddeutsche.de/politik/abstimmung-ueber-euro-rettungsschirm-rotkaeppchen-unter-fraktionszwang-1.1151514.

Thames, Frank, and Martin Edwards. 2006. "Differentiating Mixed-Member Electoral Systems: Mixed-Member Majoritartian and Mixed-Member Proportional Systems and Government Expenditures." *Comparative Political Studies* 39(7): 905–927.

Thomas, Matt, Bo Pang, and Lillian Lee. 2006. "Get Out the Vote: Determining Support or Opposition from Congressional Floor-Debate Transcripts." *Proceedings of Empirical Methods in Natural Language Processing Conference*, pp. 327–335.

Thompson, Dennis F. 2008. "Deliberative Democratic Theory and Empirical Political Science." *Annual Review of Political Science* 11: 497–520.

Tsebelis, George. 1990. *Nested Games: Rational Choice in Comparative Politics*. University of California Press.

1999. "Veto Players and Law Production in Parliamentary Democracies: An Empirical Analysis." *American Political Science Review* 93(3): 591–608.

2002. *Veto Players: How Political Institutions Work*. Russell Sage/Princeton University Press.

UK Hansard. 2009. "Daily Hansard – Debate on 15 January 2009, column 367." www.parliament.uk/business/publications/hansard.

Vowles, Jack, Peter Aimer, Helena Catt, Jim Lamare, and Raymond Miller. 1995. *Towards Consensus? The 1993 General Election and Referendum in New Zealand and the Transition to Proportional Representation*. Auckland University Press.

Vowles, Jack, Peter Aimer, Jeffrey Karp, Susan Banducci, Raymond Miller, and Ann Sullivan, eds. 2002. *Proportional Representation on Trial: The 1999 New Zealand General Election and the Fate of MMP*. Auckland University Press.

Vowles, Jack, Susan A. Banducci, and Jeffrey A. Karp. 2006. "Forecasting and Evaluating the Consequences of Electoral Change in New Zealand." *Acta Politica* 41(3): 267–284.

Welt Online. 2011. "Heftiges Nachspiel nach Rederecht für Euro-Rebellen (29 September 2011)." www.welt.de/politik/deutschland/article 13633653/Heftiges-Nachspiel-nach-Rederecht-fuer-Euro-Rebellen.html.

Wüst, Andreas M., Hermann Schmitt, Thomas Gschwend, and Thomas Zittel. 2006. "Candidates in the 2005 Bundestag Election: Mode of Candidacy, Campaigning and Issues." *German Politics* 15(4): 420–438.

Index

Aarts, Kees, 5
ACT Party (NZ), 165
Alivizatos, Nikos, 62
Alliance Party (NZ), 163
alternative vote electoral system, 44, 80
Anderson, Christopher, 4
Andres, Gerd, 138–139
Argentina, 48
Austen-Smith, David, 19
Australia, 44, 46
Austria, 93

Bächtiger, André, 8
backbenchers
- closed-list proportional systems, 48
- debate participation, United Kingdom vs. Germany, 100–101, 104–114, 129–132, 135–137, 140–141
- disagreement with leaders, 70–72
- dissent by, 25–27, 125, 129–132, 135–137, 140–141
- ideological disagreement within parties, 115–123
- majoritarian systems, 44–46
- MMM systems, 51
- MMP systems, 50
- New Zealand, 169–173
- overview, 11–12
- utility function of, 36–37

ballot structures, 24, 44, 48, 80–81
Beck, Volker, 33
Blair, Tony, 129
Brazil, 48
budget debate participation (NZ), 166–173
Bundestag, *see* Germany

cabinet, 17, 103, *see also* Westminster system
Cameron, David, 30
Canada, 44, 62, 83–84
candidate selection (European Parliament)
- dissent and, 152–162
- empirical implications, 51–52
- overview, 12–13, 148–149, 161
- rules of parliamentary debate and, 149–151

capital relocation debate (Germany), 17
Carey, John, 47
Carruba, Clifford J., 157
case studies
- cultural effects, 61
- electoral systems, 61–62
- European Parliament, 66–69
- Germany, 63–64
- institutional effects, 61
- New Zealand, 69–70
- rules of parliamentary debate, 62–63
- United Kingdom, 64–65

Chile, 48
Christian Democratic Union (CDU/CSU) (Germany)
- allocation of speaking time, 63–64
- capital relocation debate, 17
- euro crisis debate, 31–34, 55
- fiscal stimulus debate, 127, 137, 139–140, 144–145
- ideological disagreement within, 120

closed-list proportional electoral systems, 11, 25, 37, 48–49
coalition governments
- dissent in, 143–147
- Germany, 31, 117, 120, 127–128, 143–147
- impact on intra-party dynamics, 175
- New Zealand, 69, 164

coalition governments (*cont.*)
parliamentary debate in, 6, 97–99
United Kingdom, 30
cohesion within parties, 25–27, 56, 86–99, *see also* dissent; party leaders
ideological congruence, 4, 91–93, 176–178
Comparative Study of Electoral Systems (CSES), 5
competition among political parties, 174–175
Congress, US, *see* United States
congruence, ideological, 4, 176–178, *see also* cohesion within parties; dissent
consensus systems, *see* proportional systems
Conservative Party (Canada), 83
Conservative Party (UK), 104, 118, 126
control variables, 93–94, 157–158
Costa Rica, 48
country-level variables, 44–49
Cox, Gary, 5–6, 27
Cronbach, Lee, 90
cross-national comparison, 61
cultural effects, case studies and, 61–63

Darling, Alistair, 126
data, parliamentary speech as, 23–24, 178–179
debate agenda, access to, 27
defections, *see* dissent
delegation model of parliamentary debate, *see also* participation in parliamentary debate
comparative statics, 40–41
elements of, 35
empirical implications of, 43–55
equilibria of, 39–40
European Parliament perspective, 148–149
Germany, illustrations from, 31–34, 41, 50
incentives in, 34–35, 36–39
opposition's role in, 102, 103–104
overview, 8–10, 17–18, 41–42, 175–176
research design of, 56–73
United Kingdom, illustrations from, 28–30, 41
utility functions of backbenchers and party leaders in, 36–39
deliberative democracy, 8
Democratic Party (US), 45
discipline, party, 7, 46, *see also* cohesion within parties; party leaders
discourse quality index, 8
dissent
backbenchers, 25–27, 125, 129–132, 135–137, 140–141
euro crisis debate, 31–34
European Parliament, 152–162
fiscal stimulus debate, 129–147
Germany, 11–12, 31–34, 136–147
incentives, 124
latent disagreement and observed dissent, 26–27
media and parliaments in United Kingdom, 129–132
New Zealand, 166–173
overview, 6–7, 11–13, 124–125, 147
party leaders' monitoring of, 86–89, 136
probit models for levels of, 135–136, 141, 142, 146
roll-call votes, 25–27
sanctions for, 87–88
United Kingdom, 11–12, 28–30, 129–136
websites, 179

Ecuador, 48
electoral systems, *see also* mixed-member electoral systems; proportional systems
alternative vote system, 44, 80
closed-list systems, 11, 25, 37, 48–51
first-past-the-post system, 28–30, 143, 163
majoritarian systems, 4, 44–46, 61–62, 163–166, 176–178
open-list system, 46–48
single nontransferable vote systems, 47
single transferable vote systems, 47

euro crisis debate (Germany), 31–34, 55
Eurobarometer survey, 4
European Financial Stability Facility, 31, 32, 33
European Parliament
  allocation of speaking time in, 149–151
  candidate selection, 12–13, 148–162
  case study, 66–69
  dissent in, 152–162
  division of parliamentary debate in, 68–69
  elections in, 66–68
  empirical strategy, 58
  incentives in, 151, 152, 155, 162
  latent concepts, measurement of, 71–72
  participation in parliamentary debate, 152–162
  political groups in, 148
  research design, 10, 72
  rules of parliamentary debate in, 149–151
  theoretical implications in, 10, 52

FDP (Free Democratic Party) (Germany), 31–34, 55, 63–64
Field, Frank, 130–132
filibusters, 6, 79
financial crisis of 2008, 147, *see also* fiscal stimulus debate
first-past-the-post electoral system, 28–30, 143, 163
fiscal crisis of 2008, 125–129
fiscal stimulus debate (Germany and United Kingdom)
  CDU/CSU, 127, 137, 139–140, 144–145
  coalition governments, 143–147
  dissent in, 129–136, 140–143, 145–147
  Labour Party, 125, 129–132, 133–134
  legislative behavior, 134, 140, 145
  media's role in United Kingdom, 129–132
  overview, 125–129
  SPD, 127, 137–139, 141, 144–145
floor time, allocation of, 62–70, 78–79, 81, 84–85, 149–151
France, 44, 46
Free Democratic Party (FDP) (Germany), 31–34, 55, 63–64

game-theoretic model of floor speeches, 10, 35–41, 175–176
Germany, *see also* Christian Democratic Union (CDU/CSU); fiscal stimulus debate; Social Democratic Party
  backbencher debate participation, 100–101, 104, 114, 137, 141
  Berliner Stunde, 63
  budget speeches, probit model of, 122–123
  Candidate Survey, 116
  capital relocation debate, 17
  case study, 63–64
  coalition governments, 31, 117, 120, 127–128, 143–147
  delegation model of parliamentary debate, 31–34, 41, 50
  dissent in, 11–12, 31–34, 136–147
  division of parliamentary debate in, 63–64
  empirical strategy, 56–58
  euro crisis debate, 31–34, 55
  FDP, 31–34, 55, 63–64
  Green Party, 31, 33, 63–64
  ideological disagreement, intra-party, 115–123
  latent concepts, measurement of, 71–72
  Left Party, 33, 63
  MMP system in, 63, 93, 107–109, 113–114, 123, 141–143
  models of parliamentary speech in, 111–114
  New Zealand compared to, 69
  parliamentary activities and debate investment, 21
  parliamentary speeches overview, 101–103
  party leaders' debate participation, 107, 109, 111–114, 118–120
  research design, 11, 72
  SMD elections in, 101
  speaking time allocation in, 63–64
Greece, 62

Green Party (Germany), 31, 33, 63–64
Green Party (NZ), 165
Gregor Gysi, 33
Guillory, Christine, 4

Habermas, Jürgen, 18
Hall, Richard, 44
Harris, Douglas, 45
Heathrow expansion debate (UK), 28–30, 54–55
Hix, Simon, 154–155
Hoey, Kate, 29–30
Hoon, Geoffrey, 29
House of Commons, *see* United Kingdom
House of Representatives (NZ), *see* New Zealand
House of Representatives (US), *see* United States
Hungary, 51
hybrid electoral systems, *see* mixed-member electoral systems

ideological congruence, 91–93, *see also* cohesion within parties; dissent, 176–178
ideological disagreement within parties, 115–123
incentives
  allocation of speaking time, 81
  delegation model, 34–35, 36–39
  dissent, 124
  European Parliament, 151, 152, 155, 162
  majoritarian systems, 44–46
  MMM systems, 51
  MMP systems, 50, 177
  participation in parliamentary debate, effect on, 27, 100–101, 123
  personal vote seeking, for, 79–83
  proportional systems, 46–49
  rules of parliamentary debate, 79–83, 91–97, 99
Ireland, 47, 62
Italy, 51

Japan, empirical implications of delegation model in, 47, 51

Kam, Christopher, 25
Kauder, Volker, 33

Labour Party (NZ), 163, 165, 167
Labour Party (UK)
  fiscal stimulus debate, 125, 129–132
  Heathrow expansion debate, 28–30
  ideological disagreement within, 117–118
  participation in parliamentary debate, 104
Lammert, Norbert, 32–34, 55
latent concepts, measurement of, 70–72
leaders, party, *see* party leaders
Left Party (Germany), 33, 63
Lijphart, Arend, 4
Lithuania, 51

majoritarian electoral systems
  backbenchers in, 44–46
  case studies, 61–62
  delegation theory, 44–46
  ideological congruence, 176–178
  incentives, 44–46
  MMM system, 49–51, 176
  New Zealand's shift from, 163–166
  party leaders, 44–46
  satisfaction with democracy, 4–5
Maltzman, Forrest, 44–45
Maori Party (NZ), 165
Martin, Lanny, 6, 98
McDonnell, John, 28–30, 54–55
McFall, John, 132–133
Meacher, Michael, 129–130
media
  amplification of dissent role, 129–132
  fiscal stimulus debate, 137
  monitoring of speech by party leaders in, 88–89
  reporting on dissent in Germany, 22, 138–140
  websites, dissent on, 179
members/MPs, *see* backbenchers; party leaders; specific country
MEPs, *see* European Parliament
Merkel, Angela, 31, 128
Meyer, Laurenz, 139–140
Mißfelder Philipp, 144

Mill, John Stuart, 8
mixed-member electoral systems, *see also* European Parliament; mixed-member proportional electoral systems; mixed-member majoritarian systems
  democratic satisfaction level, 5
  electoral tiers in, 49–51
  impact on parliamentary speech, 43
  incentives for vote seeking, 81
  MMM system, 176
  preferences for, 176–177
mixed-member majoritarian (MMM) electoral systems, 49–51, 176
mixed-member proportional (MMP) electoral systems
  backbenchers in, 50–51
  electoral tiers in, 49–51
  Germany, 63, 93, 113–114, 123, 141–143
  ideological congruence, 176
  incentives, 50–51, 177
  New Zealand, 13, 69, 93, 163
  participation in parliamentary debate, 54, 107–109
  personal vote seeking, 93
MMM systems, *see* mixed-member majoritarian (MMM) electoral systems
MMP systems, *see* mixed-member proportional (MMP) electoral systems
monitoring of speech by party leaders
  analysis of, 91–99
  control variables, 93–94
  dissent and, 86–89, 136
  extraparliamentary activities, 88–89
  hypotheses regarding, 91
  intraparty cohesion, 91–93, 96–97
  linear regression models, 94–97
  media's role, 88–89
  party leadership monitoring scale, 85, 89–91
  personal vote seeking, 93, 96–97

National Party (NZ), 163, 165, 167
national rebel defection score, 158, 160–161
national rebel voting decision, 155–157
Netherlands, 93
New Zealand
  ACT Party, 165
  Alliance Party, 163
  backbencher debate participation, 169–173
  budget debate, 166–173
  Business Committee, 70, 165
  Candidate Survey, 166
  case study, 69–70
  dissent in, 166–173
  empirical implications of delegation model in, 50
  empirical strategy, 58
  Germany compared to, 69
  Green Party, 165
  Hansard, 167
  importance of representational activities in, 166
  Labour Party, 163, 165, 167
  latent concepts, measurement of, 71–72
  Maori Party, 165
  MMP system in, 69, 93, 163
  National Party, 163, 165, 167
  New Zealand First Party, 163
  overview, 13, 163
  party leader debate participation, 172–173
  Progressive Party, 165
  research design, 11, 72–73
  roll-call votes, 167–168
  rules of parliamentary debate, 164–166
  SMD elections, 69, 168
  Standing Order 102, 164
  United Kingdom compared with, 13, 69–70
  United Future Party, 165
New Zealand First Party (NZ), 163
normative political theory, 18
Norris, Pippa, 4–5
Norway, 93
Noury, Abdul, 154

open-list proportional electoral system, 46–48
opposition, debate role of parties in
  coalition governments, 97
  critical policy influence role, 6

opposition, debate role (*cont.*)
delegation theory testing, 102, 103–104, 107, 111, 112, 118
importance of speech-making for, 62, 63
incentives for unity vs. dissent, 46
party leaders' monitoring, 94–96
satisfaction with democracy, 4

parliamentary debate, 20–24, *see also* delegation model of parliamentary debate; rules of parliamentary debate
participation in parliamentary debate, *see also* dissent
backbenchers, 100–101, 104, 114, 129–132, 135–137, 140–141, 169–173
European Parliament, 152–162
ideological disagreement, 115–123
incentives, effects of, 52–55, 100–101, 123
member-level analysis, 109–114
MMP systems, 54, 107–109
overview, 11–13, 100, 123
party leaders, 100–114, 172–173
party-level analysis, 103–109
party leaders, *see also* monitoring of speech by party leaders
closed-list systems, 48–49
disagreement with backbenchers, 70–72
dissent, effect of status on, 136
exogenous nature of, 78n
majoritarian systems, 44–46
MMM systems, 51
MMP systems, 50–51
participation in parliamentary debate, 100–114, 172–173
proportional systems, 177–178
rules of parliamentary debate, 79–81
utility function of, 37–39
party whips, 26, 35, 67, 164, 165
personal vote seeking
incentives for, 79–83
low-level, 48–49
MMP systems, 93
moderate-level, 46–48
monitoring of speech by party leaders, 93, 96–97
strong-level, 44–46
Peru, 48
plenary time, 5–6, 27
Poß, Joachim, 144
policy, parliamentary debate's role in, 6–7, 20–21
position-taking, 7–9, 17–18, 20–21, 176
positivism, parliamentary debate and, 18–19
presidential systems, 44–45, 47–48
proportional electoral systems
case studies, 61–62
delegation model, 46–49
European Parliament, 148–149
ideological congruence, 176–178
incentives in, 25
party leaders in, 177–178
political parties in, 25
satisfaction with democracy, 4–5
proportional systems, *see* mixed-member proportional (MMP) electoral systems; New Zealand

Quinn, Kevin, 45

rapporteurs, 160
Raunio, Tapio, 155
rebellions, *see* dissent
research design
case studies, 61–70
cross-national comparison, 58–61
empirical strategy, 56–58
latent concepts, measurement of, 70–72
overview, 10–11, 56, 72–73
party survey, 59–61
roll-call votes, 25–27, 152–155, 167–168
rules of parliamentary debate, *see also* monitoring of speech by party leaders
access to floor, 78–79
allocation of speaking time, 78–79
candidate selection, 149–151
case studies, 62–63
coalition governments, 97–99
coming to floor, 78–79
demand for speaking time, 84–85

European Parliament, 149–151
filibusters, 79
incentives, 79–83, 91–97, 99
New Zealand, 164–166
overview, 11, 77, 99
party leaders, 79–81
political party rules, 83–99
speaker lists, 78–79, 85–88
Russia, 51

sanctions for dissent, 87–88
satisfaction with democracy, 2–5
Schäffler, Frank, 32–33, 55
Schäuble, Wolfgang, 17
Schneider, Carsten, 138
Senate, *see* United States
Sigelman, Lee, 44–45
single-member district (SMD) elections
Germany, 101, 107–109
implications of delegation model in, 44, 47, 49–51, 54
New Zealand, 168
SMD elections, *see* single-member district (SMD) elections
Smith, Steven, 20
Social Democratic Party (SPD) (Germany)
allocation of speaking time, 63–64
euro crisis debate, 31
fiscal stimulus debate, 127, 137–139, 141, 144–145
ideological disagreement within, 120
sovereign debt crisis, EU, 31–34, 55
Spörndli, Markus, 8
speaker lists vs. Speaker recognition, 32, 34, 62, 65, 78–79, 85–88
speaking time, allocation and access, 62–70, 78–79, 81, 84–85, 149–151
speech delegation model, *see* delegation model of parliamentary debate
speech, parliamentary, *see* parliamentary debate
Steenbergen, Marco, 8
Steiner, Jörg, 8
Stewart, John, 30
supermajority requirements, 5–6
Sweden, 93

Thomassen, Jacques, 5
unitary actors, political parties as, 174–175
United Future Party (NZ), 165
United Kingdom, *see also* Labour Party (UK)
backbencher debate participation, 129–132, 135–136
British Representation Study, 21, 116
budget speeches, probit model of, 122–123
case study, 64–65
Conservative Party, 104, 118, 126
delegation model of parliamentary debate, 41, 44, 46
dissent in, 11–12, 28–30, 129–136
division of parliamentary debate in, 64–65
empirical strategy, 56–58
fiscal stimulus debate, 129–136
Heathrow expansion debate, 28–30, 54–55
ideological disagreement, intra-party, 115–123
latent concepts, measurement of, 71–72
models of parliamentary speech in, 109–111
New Zealand compared to, 13, 69–70
parliamentary activities and debate investment, 21
parliamentary speeches overview, 101–103
party leaders' debate participation, 104–107, 109–111, 117–118
research design, 11, 72
Standing Order 23, 65
United States
delegation model empirical implications, 44–45, 48
Democratic Party, 45
filibusters in, 6, 79
financial crisis of 2008, 125
utility functions of backbenchers and party leaders, 36–39

Vanberg, Georg, 6, 98
votes, *see* electoral systems; personal vote seeking; roll-call votes
voting agenda, access to, 27

Westminster system
  Canada, 83–84
  floor time access, 62–63, 78–79
  New Zealand, 13, 58, 164
  parliamentary activity break-down, 21
  presidential systems comparison to, 48
  UK, 56, 62–63, 64–65
whips, party, 26, 35, 67, 164, 165
Willsch, Klaus-Peter, 32–33, 55
World Values Survey, 4

Lightning Source UK Ltd.
Milton Keynes UK
UKHW02f1014181117
312905UK00008B/111/P

9 781107 421073